Clinton's Legacy?

Also by Alex Waddan

THE POLITICS OF SOCIAL WELFARE

Clinton's Legacy?

A New Democrat in Governance

Alex Waddan
Lecturer in Politics
University of Sunderland

First published 2002 by
PALGRAVE
Houndmills, Basingstoke, Hampshire RG21 6XS and
175 Fifth Avenue, New York, N.Y. 10010
Companies and representatives throughout the world

PALGRAVE is the new global academic imprint of
St. Martin's Press LLC Scholarly and Reference Division and
Palgrave Publishers Ltd (formerly Macmillan Press Ltd).

ISBN 0–333–73575–7

This book is printed on paper suitable for recycling and
made from fully managed and sustained forest sources.

A catalogue record for this book is available
from the British Library.

Library of Congress Cataloging-in-Publication Data

Waddan, Alex, 1964–
    Clinton's legacy? : a new democrat in governance / Alex Waddan.
        p. cm.
    Includes bibliographical references and index.
    ISBN 0-333-73575-7 (cloth)
        1. Clinton, Bill, 1946—Influence. 2. United States—Politics and
government—1993–2001. 3. Political culture—United States—
History—20th century. 4. Political leadership—United States—
History—20th century. 5. Democratic Party (U.S.)—History—
20th century. I. Title.

E885 .W33 2001
973.931—dc21   2001046009

10   9   8   7   6   5   4   3   2   1
11   10   09   08   07   06   05   04   03   02

Printed and bound in Great Britain by
Antony Rowe Ltd, Chippenham, Wiltshire

To My Father

Contents

List of Abbreviations

AFDC	Aid to Families with Dependent Children
CBC	Congressional Black Caucus
CBO	Congressional Budget Office
CDM	Coalition for a Democratic Majority
CEA	Council of Economic Advisers
CETA	Comprehensive Employment and Training Act
DLC	Democratic Leadership Council
EITC	Earned Income Tax Credit
FSA	Family Support Act
GATT	General Agreement on Tariffs and Trade
GOP	Grand Old Party
HSA	Health Security Act
NAFTA	North American Free Trade Agreement
OMB	Office of Management and Budget
PPI	Progressive Policy Institute
PRWORA	Personal Responsibility and Work Opportunity Reconciliation Act
RJA	Racial Justice Act
SFC	Senate Finance Committee
STW	School-to-Work
TAA	Trade Adjustment Assistance
WRA	Work and Responsibility Act
WTO	World Trade Organization

Acknowledgements

A number of family and friends have given generous support and shown patience and understanding while I worked on this book. I should also thank hard-pressed colleagues at the University of Sunderland who did not complain too much when I became distracted from other duties. Thanks are also due to those at Palgrave who have helped with the production of this book, particularly Alison Howson and Linda Auld.

I would also like to express gratitude to those who have allowed me to bounce ideas off them without being too rude about the content of those ideas. In particular Mike Kenny helped give direction to sometimes confused trains of thought and Daniel Beland was an animated source of theories and information about US politics. In addition members of the American Politics Group consistently offered constructive advice. Financial support, which was crucial to the completion of the necessary research, was provided by a grant from the Nuffield Foundation.

Most of all, however, I would like to thank Cheryl for her serenity as I constantly deferred our rendezvous times.

1
Introduction: The Problem of Defining Clintonism

When Clinton took office in January 1993 few would have predicted that he would be leaving the White House eight years later with the country's fortunes apparently so changed for the better. In particular, as the campaign to elect Clinton's successor heated up it did so against a very different economic and fiscal backdrop to that of the 1992 presidential election campaign. In 1992 the story of the US economy appeared to be an unhappy one and candidate Clinton was able to attack the Bush administration's record on employment, wage growth and the climbing budget deficit. Two terms of Clinton government later the economic indicators showed the lowest unemployment rates in over a quarter century, no significant inflation, and a debate in Washington circles about what to do with a budget surplus. If anyone had foreseen these developments in 1992 then they would also have surely predicted Clinton's elevation to a position alongside the most respected of American presidents. This latter scenario, however, appears even more unlikely to unfold than sustained economic revitalisation and fiscal harmony seemed in 1992.

Much of the disaffection with Clinton of course stems from his personal failures. Dogged by scandal throughout his presidency, the Monica Lewinsky saga eventually left even those closest to him, both personally and politically, feeling betrayed. The central concern of this book, though, is not to pass comment on Clinton's morality, but is to ask whether beneath the surface scandalization there was something of political substance. In other words, is it possible to identify something which was Clintonism which in turn left a substantive Clintonian legacy upon which to build? In particular, did his presidency help the Democratic Party find a new equilibrium after the traumas it suffered during the 1970s and 1980s in presidential politics?

Prior to Clinton's triumph, Jimmy Carter's four years as President at the end of the 1970s had been the only period of Democratic occupancy of the White House since Lyndon Johnson left office in January 1969. This left the party with a record of five defeats in six presidential elections – a sequence which was difficult to put down to bad luck. Not only Republican strategists but also academic analysts of elections had begun to talk of the GOP having a 'lock' on the White House (Wattenberg, 1991). Democratic candidates had not only lost, but at times they had barely been combative. In 1972 Nixon won with 60.7 percent of the vote. In a three way race in 1980 incumbent President Carter received only 41 percent of the vote. Reagan was re-elected in 1984 with 58.7 percent of the vote and in 1988, although the Democrat nominee, Michael Dukakis, briefly looked threatening through the spring, his Republican opponent George Bush won comfortably enough in November by a margin of 54 to 46 percent. In this context Clinton's victory was a relief to all Democrats if only because it at least proved that they could be competitive in presidential level elections. On the other hand, for the Clinton story to be one of lasting significance for his party and the nation, it was imperative that he do more than simply win and then occupy office. He had to lead government in a manner which illustrated the importance of his ideas and political direction. He had to demonstrate that his brand of Democratic politics made a worthwhile difference.

This need was particularly pressing in light of the fact that Clinton came to office professing his attachment to a *new* type of Democratic politics. The promise of the 'New Democracy' was that it would address America's problems in a deliberative and constructive fashion rather than relying on established partisan dogmas. Thus, although Clinton was a steadfast Democrat, he was not committed to a range of established party aphorisms. Instead he declared himself to be part of a New Democrat movement and central to this was a sense that although many of the aims traditionally associated with the Democratic Party had a continuing resonance others did not; and, furthermore, even some of the enduring principles were past their sell by date inasmuch as they needed to be realigned with the new economic, social and political realities which had engulfed America since the New Deal era and which along the way ate up and spat out the tortured administration of Jimmy Carter. The task which the New Democrats set themselves then was to define for the party a public philosophy combining progressive values with an approach to government based on finding out what worked in the real world.

The question then is whether the Clinton presidency, through its actions in key policy areas, accomplished this assignment to establish a genuine, what might be termed, 'space of ideas', which in turn set out identifiable patterns which will have a lasting value beyond January 2001.

The New Democrats

The post-1968 election results provided ample evidence that at presidential level the Democrats had a problem. Not too surprisingly the different ideological groups of the party had alternative explanations and solutions to this dilemma, but an increasingly strident voice after the 1988 reverse came from the faction parading themselves as the New Democrats who essentially asserted that the party had leaned too far to the liberal-left and had thus alienated much of the electorate.

These were an increasingly self-assertive and well organized group co-ordinated by a body called the Democratic Leadership Council, with its think tank arm, the Progressive Policy Institute. The DLC was founded in the wake of Walter Mondale's unsuccessful presidential run in 1984. Initially it was composed mostly of southern and western congressional conservative and moderate Democrats, but was itself, at this stage, relatively temperate in its public approach and largely avoided too much criticism of fellow Democrats. Following Dukakis's defeat in 1988, however, the organization took on a more aggressive stance and began to draw more clear-cut lines in the sand separating New Democrat style centrism from the party's liberal wing (Hale, 1995). As Byron Shafer points out, the original objective of restoring the party's majority status, without too many details of how this should be done, raised relatively few heckles. Once, however, specific means had to be ascribed to this rather general end, it 'was bound to be highly conflictual' (Shafer, 2000, p.11). That is, in order to become distinct, New Democrats had explicitly to distinguish themselves from old ones and explain why theirs was the right path and the alternative the wrong one.

The rationale and rise of the New Democrat movement and Clinton's place in it will be more fully explored in the next chapter but essentially there was nothing too unusual about the DLC's assessment of what had gone wrong for the Democratic Party. Defeat, they maintained, was due to the party's movement away from the political centre. In particular New Democrats railed against what they saw as the 'liberal fundamentalism' of too many of the party's activists which was alienating traditional Democrat voters by its emphasis on (unpopular) cultural attitudes rather than on pocketbook issues (Galston and Kamarck, 1989). By the late 1980s, they also argued that the nature of pocketbook issues had changed and that the New Deal philosophy, which had served the party well for the decades following the 1930s, needed revision. They concluded that the answer lay in re-establishing the party's credibility by converging with majority sentiment on cultural values and redesigning socio-economic policy in the light of the post-New Deal environment. In short, it was imperative to drag the party out of the 1960s liberal time warp in which many of its ideas were stuck.

Their take-over seemed complete both within the party and then the nation when Clinton, who was a self-identified member of the camp and indeed previous chairman of the DLC, was first nominated and then elected in 1992.[1] Clearly then, the DLC had developed from its beginnings as a talk shop into a dominant player in internal Democratic Party politics by the early 1990s. Before moving on, however, to look at the Clinton presidency as a test of the New Democrat program, it is important to place this in the context of the American political and party system. US political parties are much more ramshackle in their organization than most of those in Western European democracies, particularly their British counterparts. This is significant because there is an obvious comparison to be made between the New Democrats in the US and New Labour in the UK.[2] While, however, there is indeed much that is similar about the aims and objectives of the two sets of 'New' leaders, and while there has been considerable interaction between them, it is critical to note the different institutional constraints at work in the two countries. These have significantly affected the respective capacities of the Clinton administration and the Blair government to implement their 'New' agendas and need to be taken into account when measuring the two experiences; and, as is usually the case when American parties and governing institutions are discussed in a comparative context, trying to fathom the US case is the more complicated.

In the British instance it is clear how New Labour fought to establish its hold over both the Labour Party's machinery and its ideology. This control is, of course, not complete but in a series of landmark battles, both organizational and symbolic (notably the removal of Clause IV of the original party constitution), New Labour leaders asserted their authority. The same cannot be said of the New Democrats in the US. The DLC did make a conscious decision in the late 1980s to organize at local as well as elite level, which did extend its influence in the party's internal affairs, but American party structures simply do not allow for the type of control exercised by Blair and company in the UK. Moreover, it is not just party structures which need to be taken into consideration but the wider institutional environment as well. If Prime Minister Blair proposes legislation in the guise of New Labour then, however much old Labour may dislike the idea, it is still almost certain to become law even if many Labour MPs are kicking and screaming as they vote for it. However, as was demonstrated on several significant occasions, President Clinton had no such equivalent power over Democrat members of Congress.

A further complicating feature is that while in the UK the actions of the Blair government define 'New Labour' to the extent that whatever the government does is thus New Labour policy, the same is not entirely true in the US. Clinton was pretty well identified with the New Democrat cause, but he was not necessarily a personification of it. That is, because the *DLC* was seen as the original and authentic voice of the New Democrat movement it was possible for there to be divergence between the DLC's vision of the New Democracy and the political expression of Clintonism and, as will be seen, there was at times such divergence – perhaps most emphatically over health care reform which, in turn, was perhaps the most ambitious project of the presidency.

These are issues which will persistently complicate the discussion through the rest of this book in its effort to determine whether Clinton's tenure as President produced a legacy of substance and gave meaning to the discourse of the New Democracy. For all these qualifications and intricacies, however, during his campaign for the presidency, candidate Clinton was keen to get across the message that he was a 'a different type of Democrat' and more particularly a New Democrat. This, of course, still leaves us to define quite what Clinton and fellow New Democrats meant by 'new' and 'different' as these terms do not in themselves have much descriptive value. Obviously there was an important political message in the very act of rebranding; presumably if there is a need to be new and different this reflects a perceived need to get away from the old and traditional, though again, of course, this does not in itself define what was old and traditional. What was and is meant by these terms will be fleshed out in more detail in the next chapter but here is a brief explanation.

First, who were the old Democrats that had to be replaced? Unfortunately this is not a straightforward story. The New Democrats are often portrayed as wishing to leave behind the party's 'liberal' tag. In general terms this is true, but it is important not to oversimplify the narrative.

By the end of the 1980s there were in fact two types of liberal Democrat politics and policy which the New Democrats wished to change. One was perhaps to be half-retired and half-repaired (or, more accurately, updated), the other to be cast out. The first, the old Democracy of the New Deal, was seen as being of an honourable tradition, the other, the New Politics liberalism which emerged at the end of the 1960s and the early 1970s, less so. The New Deal version of the old Democracy lasted from 1933 to somewhere in the mid-to-late 1960s and in these three decades it was the dominant shaping force of twentieth-century America (Leuchtenburg, 1963). It was during the New Deal era that federal government established itself as having the ultimate responsibility for the nation's socio-economic well-being. This period also saw the Democrats emerge as the undisputed majority party in American political life. By the late 1980s, however, the New Democrats, while recognising the continuing emotional resonance of the New Deal and particularly its appeal to blue-collar America, deemed it to be of diminishing practical and policy relevance as they maintained that the old economic conditions no longer applied. In particular 'tax and spend liberal' became a term of abuse. The dominant ideological message was that the days of expansive and expensive Big Government were over. The Reagan and Bush administrations in fact had a mixed record in their efforts to cut taxes and spending and, for all the talk about good financial housekeeping, the federal budget deficit simply grew and grew. It was difficult, however, for Democrats, more popularly associated with taxing and spending, properly to exploit Republican hypocrisy in this area, and the accelerating deficit and debt left little scope for the government to take on new responsibilities.

The second strand of liberalism, which, according to the DLC, had usurped the first version and led the party down an intellectually elitist and politically redundant track, was the cultural 'New Politics' Democracy personified by Senators Eugene McCarthy and then George McGovern in their presidential bids in 1968 and 1972. To the New Democrats this type of liberal Democracy constituted a kind of 'liberal fundamentalism' which was qualitatively different from the inclusive and non-judgmental attitude of the New Deal. According to the New Democrat analysis, it was the high mindedness of the New Politics which alienated voters and explained many of the woes of Democratic presidential candidates through the 1970s and 1980s, culminating in the 'L-word' election of 1988 when Republican candidate George Bush, hardly a rags-to-riches politician and not someone with the personal appeal of Reagan, was able to persuade enough voters that

Michael Dukakis was an intellectual snob who was divorced from their values and everyday concerns.

Second, having decided what was wrong, what was the positive message which the New Democrats wished to send out in order to reverse the decline of the party's electoral fortunes? Electorally speaking, the key for Clinton in 1992 was to win back the so-called 'Reagan Democrats', a group given real-life form in the residents of Macomb County, Michigan (Greenberg, 1995). Clinton wooed these by his constant talk of the middle-class and telling them how he understood the financial pain they had endured through the recession of 1991 and 1992. The not so subtle message was that here was a Democratic candidate who once again realized who the party's core supporters were; and that this candidate would make sure that their interests were not secondary to those of the poor and minorities. Clinton's overarching theme was the need for a 'New Covenant' whereby those who played by the rules would be rewarded for their efforts. In the early days of his formal candidacy in October 1991 he explained his intent of 'forging a New Covenant of change that will honor middle-class values, restore the public trust, create a new sense of community, and make America work again' (quoted in Greenberg, 1995, p.214).

The challenge and limits of office:
Clinton as a pre-emptive leader

Not surprisingly, the New Democrats were keen to celebrate Clinton's 1992 triumph as evidence that the country wanted to move in their direction and, early in Clinton's presidency, the President of the DLC, Alvin From, reflected that while Clinton 'cannot be expected to enact all of the DLC-New Democrat agenda overnight...the challenges he faces in the months ahead offer many opportunities to apply the New Democrat philosophy' (1993a, p.2). Being faced with issues, however, and being able to provide decisive responses to them are quite different matters; and the situation Clinton found himself in when he took office was not particularly conducive to dynamic leadership – even if this was what his campaign had promised to provide. The extent to which any President can set the agenda both rhetorically and in practice is defined as much by the circumstances in which they operate as by their predilections. That is, all Presidents come to office in an environment which offers both opportunities and inhibitions. Looking back at Clinton's position in 1992 it is easier to see the latter rather than the former.

One problem in terms of implementing a bold new agenda was that although Clinton's victory was a direct rebuke to President Bush's regime and its failure to tackle the US's economic problems of the early 1990s, it was not a resounding victory for anything in particular in the way of Clintonism as a new progressive force. He won in 1992 with only 43 percent of the vote – a smaller share than Dukakis had received in 1988. In a three way race Ross Perot, someone with no previous political experience, received 19 percent of votes cast. Thus the tendency after Clinton's victory to describe it as a watershed election ignored important evidence both from the vote itself and the various exit polls asking about voters' opinions (Barnes, 1992). There certainly was some good news for the Democrats. Clinton had won and challenged in several southern and western states which had appeared to have become Republican strongholds at presidential level. There were nine states, including the big prize of California, which he was the first Democrat since Johnson in 1964 to win. In addition 1992 was the first time since 1936 that a Democrat had carried Illinois, Michigan and Ohio in the same election. There were, however, also indications that some of the deep-rooted problems had not gone away. In the much analysed quintessential home of Reagan Democrats, Macomb County, Clinton still lost by four points to Bush, 42 percent to 38 percent (Cook, 1992a, p.3810). Exit polls also showed that he won only the same percent of white and male votes as Dukakis. In a race with a significant third horse, doing as well as usual proved to be good enough, but as one commentator reflected, 'The candidate who frequently said that he represented a new kind of Democrat won the same old Democratic vote and not much more' (Barnes, 1992, p.2537).

All this could hardly be construed as a positive endorsement for Clinton or indeed the political process. In other words, while the 1992 election clearly expressed the dissatisfaction of much of the electorate, it hardly constituted a positive mandate for the new President. Furthermore, the Democrats had been on the backfoot in American politics since at least the late 1970s inasmuch as the Republicans had been the party of ideas and intellectual dynamism. Whatever the dissatisfaction with the Bush administration, this did not reflect a wider anger with the Reaganite conservative legacy of the 1980s. Clinton was not elected to revoke the 1980s and, while he was quite prepared to use rhetoric which blamed the Reagan and Bush administrations for the economic problems of the early 1990s, he did not repudiate all aspects of the 1980s. The message was that he and the Democratic Party had heard what the voters had been saying through the 1980s and the implication was that they accepted the legitimacy of much of what had happened in that decade. A particularly helpful way of understanding the implications of this is to look at the typology of presidential leadership developed by Stephen Skowronek which suggests that Clinton's room for maneuver was always likely to be limited.

Skowronek identifies four principal types of presidential leadership, but the options available to each occupant of the White House are determined according to the political environment in which they are elected (1997). That is, some Presidents are elected in circumstances which offer them the opportunity to transform the political landscape, to a greater or lesser degree, but most are given much more limited room for maneuver. Those Presidents deemed the most important and successful are those elected with a behest to engage in 'reconstructive' politics. That is, they are Presidents elected in times of real turmoil with a specific mandate to repeal what has gone before. The public's expectation is that these are Presidents who will develop new programs and policies, and in extreme cases this allows them to operate in a fashion relatively unconstrained by the institutional inertia built into the American political system. The most obvious example of a modern era 'reconstructive' President is Franklin Roosevelt. The severity of the Depression undermined the legitimacy of the established conventional wisdoms and the manner in which these wisdoms restrict political choice, giving Roosevelt the opportunity to redesign the political landscape in a radical fashion.

A more recent possible instance of a reconstructive President is Reagan. This is a more problematic case as only some elements of reconstructive politics were evident through the Reagan era. The late 1970s certainly did see a breakdown of the governing assumptions of the New Deal regime across political, economic and social questions, and Reagan was clearly identified with an ideology which repudiated the New Deal conventions (Anderson, 1988). On the other hand, his anti-government philosophy did not take over all elements of government. Most obviously the House of Representatives remained in Democratic hands which prevented the implementation of a New Right blueprint. Opinions thus vary on the extent to which Reagan did substantively change America (Pierson, 1994), but if nothing else there was a change in the rhetoric of politics with conservatism clearly becoming the 'in' ideology and centre-left liberalism the 'out' one. This climaxed in 1988 when Bush accused Dukakis of being a 'liberal' with little explanation deemed necessary of why, if true, this was a bad thing. Overall, then, the Reagan presidency was perhaps not a classically reconstructive one, but the 1980s changed the terms of political debate in a manner which was to have significant implications for Clinton.

The other models of presidential leadership which Skowronek describes are 'articulation', 'disjunction' and 'pre-emption'. Articulation is when presidents are faithful to the political commitments of their time and see their task as being simply to travel further down the path they inherited. This occurs most obviously when a reconstructive President is succeeded by someone from the same party on the basis that they will continue the same policies. Truman and Bush fit into this category of presidents who effectively rode the coattails of their predecessors. Disjunction, on the other hand, refers to presidents who try to pursue commitments based on a declining ideology. Jimmy Carter, for example, if sometimes rather half-heartedly, attempted to govern according to the New Deal precepts when it was apparent, or at least is in hindsight, that, for better or worse, those rules had lost their previously compelling socio-economic gravity and thus their political legitimacy. Neither of these two categories, however, really applies to Clinton. His intention was neither to articulate Reagan Republicanism nor to swim against the tide and return to New Deal Democracy. Clinton does, though, fit snugly into the pre-emptive category.

The aim of pre-emptive leaders is to build political support by projecting their own party's traditional strengths while appropriating, either by stealth or with due acknowledgment, some of the more popular ideas of their political rivals. The point is that pre-emptive leaders are operating in the general context of an inhospitable ideological environment and are thus limited in their capacity to shape the political world (Beland et al., 2002). For Clinton the series of humiliating defeats for Democratic presidential candidates through the 1980s and the limited nature of his own triumph provided ample evidence that he would have to operate within the limits of pre-emption rather than the freedom of reconstruction. Thus his claim was that he was a Democrat who recognized that there was no going back to the old days, good or bad depending on perspective, of the New Deal and Great Society. In a similar fashion to Eisenhower and Nixon, Clinton came to office at a time when the prevailing political climate was one which had been set by predecessors from a different ideological tradition; and like these two, Clinton largely chose to adapt to rather than confront this environment. So just as Eisenhower had not tried to repeal the New Deal and as Nixon had accepted the continued expansion of the American welfare state so too Clinton was bound to find an accommodation with elements of the Reagan legacy.

A further feature which was likely to make Clinton's task difficult, if in an intangible fashion, was the prevailing mood of cynicism about the political process. Some commentators have argued that the 1992 campaign was, relatively speaking, one fought over the issues and was, in this respect, a big improvement on the 1988 election (Quirk and Dalager, 1993; Foley, 1999). For all this, however, the general mood of popular disaffection was well illustrated by Ross Perot's garnering of 19 percent of the vote. This had helped Clinton get elected but the problem for the incoming President was to shape his agenda in this mood of negativity. A number of commentators noted how difficult a task he faced, even if he did come up with good policy, because of this cynicism, evident at both popular and elite level. One time Clinton pollster Stanley Greenberg noted a widespread mood of disillusion, 'People are not just politically estranged, they are increasingly negative, pessimistic, and depressed' (1995, p.9). W.D. Burnham noted that the political time was 'not particularly favorable to the realization of grandiose and integrated objectives' (1995, p.11). He added that Clinton's chances of defining a 'policy/public philosophy synthesis' were always going to be limited by the fragmentation of the American political structure which had been ongoing since 1968 (p.14). Stanley Renshon reflected that 'the major public dilemma' facing Clinton was 'the dilemma of public trust in public policy' (1995, p.6), while another analyst reflected on the difficulty of setting an agenda in an era which had witnessed 'a widespread loss of faith in the holy trinity of the old voter psychology: party, issues, and character' (Bennett, 1995, p.94). One of the most pessimistic essays in the wake of Clinton's victory came from Jean Bethke Elthstain who wrote, 'Despite rejoicing from media pundits about a postelection restoration of faith in government, ... the harsh truth of the matter is that voters are volatile, angry and deeply disaffected' (1993, p.112) Elsewhere the very titles of books left little to the imagination, representative examples being *Why Americans Hate Politics* (Dionne, 1992) and *Boiling Point* (Phillips, 1994).

Clearly then the cocktail of American politics in the early 1990s was made up of various ingredients which sometimes enhanced but mostly diminished the likelihood of Clinton being able to lead effectively from the front.

The Clinton, New Democrat and Third Way project

In some ways the very existence of the 'New' Democrats as an organized faction testified to the perception of centre-right Democrats that the party needed to develop a pre-emptive politics. In other words the New Democrats and the DLC saw the imperative as being to reconstruct the party so that it was no longer in a state of disjunction with the American electorate, rather than waiting for the electorate to see the light. The aim was nevertheless to develop this politics in a positive fashion with a coherent agenda of its own. The New Democracy then recognized that the time was not ripe for transformative change of the Roosevelt or even Reagan type, but there was an opportunity for a purposeful rather than simply cynical kind of pre-emption.

One obvious expression of Clinton's New Democracy was the promise that having a Democrat back in the White House would not lead to the return of Big Government. So too was the insistence that the choice was not between left and right, or liberal and conservative. Thus in his acceptance speech at the 1992 Democratic convention Clinton steered a course which attacked then President Bush but which also promised his own party had learned its lessons. He declared,

> [M]y fellow Democrats, it's time for us to realize that we've got some changing to do too. There is not a program in government for every problem. ...
>
> That's why we need a new approach to government. A government that offers more empowerment and less entitlement ...
>
> A government that is leaner, not meaner, a government that expands opportunity, not bureaucracy ...
>
> We offer our people a new choice based on old values. We offer opportunity. We demand responsibility. ... The choice we offer is not conservative or liberal; in many ways it's not even Republican or Democratic. It is different. It is new (Clinton, 1992, p.2129).

Regardless of the intellectual clarity of Clinton's thought, the point is that this speech tried to negotiate a path which attacked the Republicans for their knee-jerk anti-government rhetoric but which equally was careful to put aside the perception of the Democrats as a knee-jerk pro-government, liberal party.

On the other hand, while the effort was clearly to claim the ground of the political centre, Clinton and the New Democrats were keen to stress that they did not see themselves as a movement simply devoted to splitting the difference between left and right. Theirs was to be centrism with a cutting edge which moved the debate about policy issues and potential solutions *beyond* these historical categorizations. Indeed the constraints of the pre-emptive context were to be bypassed by forging a new political synthesis which recognized how the socio-economic and political environment had changed since the Democrats last controlled federal government, but which was ready to respond to the new circumstances and to break the Washington stalemate with bold new initiatives. Thus New Democrat writing is sprinkled with references to the need for a 'radical departure' (From and Marshall, 1993a, p.xv) and to the dynamism of 'the "vital center" of American politics' with its 'fresh agenda of big ideas' (From and Marshall, 1997, p.1). One effort intended to give some policy and philosophical substance to the 'newness' being claimed was the development of the notion of the 'Third Way', which positioned government as neither the problem nor the solution, a movement away from Reaganism and the stilted image of New Dealism. In short, government would act where necessary, but only where necessary; and, in turn, this efficient and targeted activism would restore popular respect for and trust in government. Undoubtedly then, this was a philosophy designed to leave a tangible legacy.

Some commentators, however, were always sceptical of the degree to which Clinton would be able to leave the straightjacket of pre-emption behind. Political scientist and expert on presidential politics Michael Nelson made the observation that at least in his first term Clinton was more likely to a 'President of Preparation' than a 'President of Achievement' because the 'confluence of conditions required for a Presidency of Achievement – an empowering election, leadership skill, and ideas – has not yet occurred for Clinton' (1993, p.145). Nelson's point was not that Clinton lacked ideas, indeed he says just the opposite, but that he did not have the sway and authority to get those ideas enacted (p.148). Nelson pointed out that Clinton's percentage of the eligible voting-age population, at 24 percent, was the lowest for any President since 1824. Furthermore, he added, 'Clinton's 370 electoral college votes compared unfavourably with the initial victories of all the century's other Presidents of Achievement: 435 for Wilson in 1912, 472 for Roosevelt in 1932, 486 for Johnson in 1964, and 489 for Reagan in 1980' (p.146).

In addition to the unconvincing size of his personal electoral mandate, other factors conspired to emphasize the limits on, rather than the reach of, Clinton's capacity to govern. First, Clinton's presidential victory had not produced any coattails effect for congressional Democrats. Thus, while their interests would obviously be best served by a successful Democratic presidency, they did not feel indebted to him. In fact not only had there been no coattails, but the Republicans had gained ten seats in the House with no partisan change in the Senate in the congressional elections. Together with Clinton's low poll, this gave the Republican leadership the opportunity to refute any notion that Clinton had a popular mandate which they should respect. Indeed, while no-one in early 1993 was predicting the scale of what would happen less than two years down the line, the GOP were clearly aware that any difficulties for the new President would exacerbate the normal turn against the party of government in the mid-term elections.

The likely impact of these factors in fact led the noted scholar on congressional affairs Gary Jacobson to forecast co-operation between the legislative and executive Democrats because the costs of failure could be high (1993, p.180). Others concentrated on the likely difficulties. Although the change in partisan balance in Congress had been limited, there were 47 freshmen Republicans in the House whose general ideological influence was to shift the party to the right. There was thus even more reason than normal to expect the 'out' party to oppose – leaving little room for bipartisanship. In Senate a relatively comfortable looking Democrat majority of 57 to 43 still meant that there was the possibility of Republican organized filibuster. Furthermore, not all congressional Democrats had been completely won over by the New Democrat message. Many remained old or liberal Democrats and the majority were more used to acting as an opposition to the White House rather than as a potential partner institution in government. In contrast to Jacobson, analyst Michael Foley suggested that the convergence of factors was bound to make presidential leadership even more problematic than usual because Clinton

> would need to rely exclusively on Democrats in a situation where his political status was weak, his party appeal was open to question, his public support was fragile and his experience in Washington politics minimal. Clinton would need to work hard at creating coalitions *within* his own party (1999, pp.26–7).

As will be seen, there was some truth and more besides in the arguments of both these respected scholars in the first two years of the first term. On some issues, notably the first budget, the administration did put together a Democratic majority in the face of uniform GOP opposition. On the key vote to ratify the North American Free Trade Agreement, on the other hand, most House Democrats voted against their President but Clinton was able to put together a winning coalition with Republican support. The anti-crime bill was backed by the majority of Democrats but needed a handful of Republican votes. Critically for the White House, however, the ability to get measures through by one means or another fell apart with the proposal for health care reform. Whether it was the administration's intention or nor, this came to be seen as the flagship legislative submission to the 103rd Congress and the unravelling and eventual disintegration of the ambitious plan dramatically undermined the record of legislative achievement built up in other areas. Thus the 1994 mid-terms were conducted amidst a sense that unified Democrat government had failed to address the Washington malaise, even though there had often been a significant degree of co-operation between the Democrats in the two branches. Of course the political and institutional dynamics all changed after 1994 when the GOP were in the majority in Congress; and, however successful Clinton was in outflanking Gingrich and company, the fact that he was dealing with an aggressive opposition which was looking to usurp the agenda-setting role could only reinforce the pre-emptive aspect of the Clinton presidency.

On top of this, the chief factor which propelled him into the White House – the state of the US economy – also promised to drag him down if he could not find some remedies which would turn things around quickly. The plight of the economy, however, was not the only area where Clinton was expected to improve American life. There were, for example, growing concerns about the condition of the country's health-care and welfare systems. In addition, Clinton would have to face up to the potential divisions and dilemmas likely to be thrown up by what might broadly be described as social and cultural issues such as crime, gay rights and the state of race relations in the US. The majority of this book is concerned with examining how Clinton acted in these different areas. It will assess the accomplishments and the failures – and analyse what they tell us about the capacity of the New Democrats and their Third Way to take American politics in a decisive new direction. The sections below provide brief introductions to these topics.

Economic policy

The state of the economy in 1992 was a mixed blessing for Clinton. Dissatisfaction with Bush's handling of the economy had been the primary issue driving the 1992 campaign and was thus the key factor in putting Clinton in the White House, but equally the forces which had consumed Bush did not appear to be either simple or irresolute foes which could be easily defeated. Growing inequality and the stagnation of median incomes were well established trends (Danziger and Gottschalk, 1995). In addition, the deficit issue, which had dominated

Washington life without being successfully addressed since the early 1980s, was given a sharper focus in the 1992 campaign by Ross Perot's concentration on the matter. The worry for the incoming President was that, although in the long-term deficit reduction might bolster economic growth and thus benefit middle America, in the short-term a serious effort at cutting the government's level of overspending was likely to require the unpopular combination of tax rises and spending cuts. Looking at the long-term data underlying both the general economic unease and the more particular specifics of deficit growth suggested that there were deep running problems which were not going to be easily corrected.

For all those with a vested interest in the success of the Clinton administration and the re-energising of the Democratic Party, however, economic progress was a *sine qua non* of political advance. In crude terms, of course, the success of Clinton's economic policy would depend on the pocketbook calculations of the voters. After the perceived hegemony of Reaganomics, however, there was a broader question for the Democrats as to whether Clintonomics would develop into an embracing economic philosophy, finally giving the party a coherent vision of economic policy for the first time since the faltering of what might be described as New Dealomics amidst the economic chaos of the 1970s. In other words, the Bush recession had given the Democrats the chance to re-establish their reputation for greater competence in economic affairs and it was vital to take it. Circumstances did not demand another FDR, but there would have been little patience with another Jimmy Carter.

As it was, as the Clinton era drew to a close, the plethora of 'good' economic news was reaching a startling level. The American economy was enjoying a period of boom of unprecedented length. The former director of the Congressional Budget Office, Robert Reischauer wrote, 'The performance of the US economy as of the summer of 1999 is superlative in almost every way' (1999, p.2). In its annual report issued in February 2000 the Council of Economic Advisers gushed about

> a 20-million-job increase in payroll employment since January 1993, the lowest unemployment rate since 1969, the lowest core inflation rate since 1965, the lowest poverty rate since 1979, rising productivity, significant gains all across the income distribution, and a Federal budget in surplus for two years in a row after three decades of deficit (p.21).

Not surprisingly, the President was eager to assert ownership of these good tidings. In his Economic Report to Congress he professed,

'These economic successes have not been achieved by accident' (Clinton, 2000, p.3). He then repeated what had become the White House's mantra in explaining, and thus claiming the credit for, this prosperity. According to this version of events, the administration's consistent pursuit of a three-pronged strategy was instrumental in generating growth. First, was 'a commitment ... to fiscal discipline' (p.3). Second, Clinton claimed, 'we have remained true to our commitment to invest in our people. Because success in the global economy depends more than ever on highly skilled workers, we have taken concerted steps to make sure all Americans have the education, skills, and opportunities they need to succeed.' Finally, he asserted, 'we have continued to pursue a policy of opening markets' (p.4).

For the administration this not only represented success, but it was success achieved through the implementation of a distinct Third Way agenda. Deficit reduction and trade liberalization created the climate and the scope for the market to flourish, while the investment in human capital gave individual workers the skills and opportunities sometimes denied to them in the free-for-all of the 1980s. In addition, efforts to make work pay gave extra incentives to workers at the lower end of the wage scale. As Clinton's presidency drew to a close, it was difficult for Democrats to be too critical of the administration's economic policy given the buoyant state of the economy. Some liberals, however, did protest that too much ground had been conceded to the wishes of business and Wall Street and that the investment agenda was clearly the least prominent element of the three-pronged Clintonomics design (Galbraith, 1996; Kuttner, 1996). A more obvious problem was that Clinton had simply not won his party over to a free trade agenda. Chapters 3 and 4 will examine the different aspects of the Clintonomics strategy, concentrating on the evolution of policy and what this tells us about the administration's priorities, both in terms of its economic and political choices, and how this set the framework for domestic reform.

Social policy

Clinton came to office promising two dramatic shifts in the direction of social welfare policy. Although the details of neither pledge was fully filled out during the 1992 campaign, the new administration was all but obliged to act to reform the US's health care system and also, as the campaign slogan put it, 'to end welfare as we know it'. Both of these were major tasks, but there was a general consensus that action did need to be taken. At the start of the 1990s the long standing worries of health care policy experts about the modus operandi of the health care system had shifted from the backburner to the front of the political agenda as popular opinion focused on the issue. There was also agreement that the existing welfare system, particularly as represented by the much disparaged Aid to Families with Dependent Children (AFDC) program, was dysfunctional and required urgent repair. Unfortunately, as was to become increasingly evident, consensus on the need for change did not extend to accord on what this change should actually comprise. Indeed, the Democratic camp was split over which of the two was the priority issue. To liberals, the new public consciousness on health care matters suggested that the time was at last ripe for the introduction of a system of national health insurance – presenting an opportunity which had to be seized at once. New Democrats, while they acknowledged that health care required attention, were more interested in pursuing welfare reform. In reality it was always manifest that the party was likely to be divided over the details of welfare reform as this was an area where there was a distinct New Democrat agenda which offended liberal sensibilities.

It is nevertheless possible to see the administration's initial attempts at reform in both areas as efforts to forge different types of social policy solutions to divisive problems. More specifically, although both came to naught (or worse), the Health Security Act and the administration's own, rather neglected, attempt at welfare reform known as the Work and Responsibility Act can be seen in this context as striving to achieve a Third Way blend. The HSA was an immensely complex plan designed to guarantee access to health insurance to all Americans while simultaneously introducing measures to control the dramatically spiralling burden that health care costs imposed on the US economy. It also aimed to do this while leaving the bulk of provision in the private sector. The WRA was presented as a manifestation of the 'new covenant' rhetoric of opportunity and responsibility. Welfare recipients would be required to make a genuine work effort but they and their families would continue to receive government aid so long as they did this. Clinton, however, was unable to sustain the political momentum necessary to build the legislative coalitions to materially further this agenda (Ferejohn, 1998). In the end, somewhat ironically, a version of welfare reform, which did leave liberals truly aghast, was enacted, but it was the failed attempt at health care reform which proved to be the most fractious and damaging issue for the Democratic party.

There were in fact other big issues on the DLC's social policy agenda, most notably the general theme of entitlement reform – including reform of the biggest government programs, Medicare and Social Security (Shapiro, 1992). This reflected not just fiscal concerns, but also a desire to redirect the one-way street nature of entitlements which gave eligible recipients rights without any obligations in return. As it was, however, the administration never made any serious effort at restructuring any entitlement program apart from AFDC and so the emphasis in this study will be on the stories of health and welfare in Chapters 5 and 6.

Cultural issues

Central to the New Democrat understanding of the political and electoral world was a sense that the Democratic Party's string of failures in presidential elections through the 1970s and 1980s owed much to the self-indulgence of liberal elites in the party who insisted on highlighting a series of controversial, and sometimes unpopular, beliefs on a range of what might be described as cultural or lifestyle issues, such as gay rights and abortion rights. In addition, New Democrats argued that liberals had shifted the ground on matters of racial equality away from the moral absolute of ensuring equality of opportunity to the much more questionable goal of promoting equality of result. Other parts of the 'limousine liberal' package which New Democrats felt damaged the party were the tendency to appear insufficiently condemnatory of criminal behaviour and a too dovelike approach to foreign affairs. The problem, as New Democrats perceived it, was not that liberals were always and inherently wrong on these questions, but that the promotion of these attitudes had added up to create an image of a party which cared for the various minority groups in American society and for those who had fallen foul of societal norms, but had forgotten about the majority who played by the rules and expected others to do the same.

This argument was made in an open and explicit form by two leading DLC lights, Bill Galston and Elaine Kamarck, in a 1989 pamphlet called *The Politics of Evasion*. This launched a scathing attack on what the authors called the myths of 'liberal fundamentalism'. In particular they accused liberals of ignoring the overwhelming evidence that 'Nixon's 1968 presidential campaign established the anti-liberal paradigm that has dominated American national politics ever since' (p.4). Thus liberals had insisted on steering the Democratic Party into the electoral rocks despite the warning lights flashed by the party's centrists and the evidence of the wreckage from the 1968, 1972, 1980 and

1984 presidential elections. This liberal hubris lasted through to 1988, but after the sinking of Dukakis's candidacy through the utterly explicit attack on his cultural liberalism the party finally turned to a candidate who promised to focus attention on the party's strengths and to apply a new realism in respect of its weaknesses. Thus the primary part of Clinton's promise was to focus on the thwarted *economic* ambitions of the 'forgotten *middle* class'. On the other hand, of course, cultural issues could not be ignored. Clinton's strategy here was to promise to deflect the 'L-word' attack by shifting away from some liberal positions where these had no popular support or overwhelming moral imperative. The success or otherwise of the White House's methods of defusing the cultural dimension in American politics will be explored in Chapter 7.

As Clinton left office there was little consensus even within the Democratic Party as to what all this amounted to. One thing which was clear was that the Democrats had lost ground in terms of their represenatation in Washington (Rae, 2000), but Clinton and New Democrat leaders were keen to proclaim their achievements and to stress the changes which had been brought to the American polity and society (From, 1999). According to this perspective, the Clinton era had seen significant and enduring change. Critics, however, were less convinced that Clintonism had developed an integrated vision of governance. They saw it more as series of ad hoc political choices some good, some less so – but not a new public philosophy to guide the Democrats forward (Faux, 1999). To such liberals the limits of Clintonism were highlighted by the strategy of triangulation put in place by the ubiquitous political consultant, Dick Morris. Triangulation was a classic statement of a cynical and manipulative version of pre-emptive politics which did not look to innovate but simply to find an electoral formula which would win as illustrated by the manner it simultaneously conceded considerable ground to the GOP while arguing that this showed how reasonable the administration was being in contrast to its extremist opponents. Still others agreed that significant changes had been wrought by Clinton, without being sure that these actually constituted something that would amount to an enduring legacy (Dionne, 2000a).[3]

New and old Democrats

Before embarking on the study of the Clinton years, however, the next chapter will focus on the emergence of the New Democrats as a major force within the party and the development of the New Democrat agenda. The chapter examines what the New Democrats disliked about the old ones and why they insisted that too much liberalism was costing the party dearly at the ballot box. It spends time too explaining why New Dealomics was perceived to have outlived its usefulness. Critically, however, it will emphasize that not all Democrats had converted to the New Democracy.

2
Redefining the Democrats

The New Deal era had seen the creation of a new political settlement in the US with the Democrats becoming the clearly ascendant party. This was a direct consequence of the deep Depression of the early 1930s. Republican president, Herbert Hoover, did little to alleviate the suffering caused by the economic chaos and consequently the voters turned to Democratic candidate Franklin Roosevelt in the November 1932 election. Roosevelt's promise was of a 'New Deal' to remedy America's woes. In its early days the New Deal was often a hit and miss affair, but what Roosevelt did succeed in doing was creating the impression that he was prepared to lead a federal government which would be active in seeking solutions. Fundamentally, it acknowledged that government did have a responsibility for the socio-economic well-being of the nation.

Thus there was some direct 'relief' and various employment schemes were set up. With an eye to the longer term, the administration pushed through the Social Security Act in 1935 which established the basic contours of the modern American welfare state including the old age insurance, unemployment insurance and Aid to Dependent Children programs (Berkowitz, 1991). Even though the economy remained in recession through most of the 1930s, this cocktail of activist policies met with majority voter support leading to the gelling of the so-called New Deal coalition. This in fact consisted of disparate blocks of voters, including pluralities from the following socio-economic and ethnic groups; blue-collar workers; trade unionists; Catholic and Jewish voters; ethnic minorities of southern and eastern European descent; the enfranchised African–American voters outside the South, and whites in the South. One way of understanding the full significance of the transformation this represented is to place this coalition in the context of 'party systems' or 'critical elections' and 'realignments'. These concepts, developed by political scientists, illustrate the manner in which an old political order is undone and a new one established (Key, 1955; Burnham, 1970). The change is not gradual but dramatic as significant numbers of voters shift their political identity in response to a new set of issues to which traditional responses appear inadequate. It is also important that these new identities are not a blip, but are enduring. In terms of the New Deal coalition this was certainly the case as the Democrats occupied the White House for 28 of the 36 years following Roosevelt's initial dramatic triumph. In addition, except for two brief periods in 1947–48 and 1953–54, the party enjoyed congressional majorities as well.

After Roosevelt's death in 1945, the New Deal became the Fair Deal under President Harry Truman. Truman's phrase was never popularized like Roosevelt's but his period in office did see the US move into prosperity and emerge quite decisively as the world's major industrial and economic power and the New Deal's social policy activism was reinforced. In fact, by European standards, neither the extent of government intervention in economic affairs nor the degree of social policy activism were expansive, but on their own terms New Deal policies did represent a significant move away from the pre-1930s prevalence of laissez-faire ethics. The permanency of the New Deal settlement seemed confirmed when Republican President Dwight Eisenhower made no serious effort at rollback during his years in office and as the 1960s dawned there were few obvious signs to contemporary liberal New Dealers of the anguish soon to come.

Indeed in 1964, sixteen years before Reagan's triumph, it must have appeared to the liberal community that the American right had been decisively vanquished. Lyndon Johnson's handsome victory over the ultra-conservative Barry Goldwater must have seemed to be a persuasive reaffirmation of America's faith in the principles of New Deal Democracy. Johnson himself was a classic New Deal politician (Johnson, 1964). Indeed the 'Great Society' was set to take the progressive project a step further. Government was to embark on new and ambitious undertakings to remedy some of the remaining injustices in American society. In hindsight, however, it is clear that Johnson's victory did not represent an extended commitment to liberal politics. Critically it emerged that the injustices to be tackled in the 1960s were different to those which had so immediately afflicted America in the 1930s, and there was not a full understanding of the direction in which the policies adopted in the Great Society program would lead (Davies, 1996). As early as 1966 the Republicans made significant gains in the mid-term congressional elections and in 1968 Democratic candidate Hubert Humphrey suffered a 19 point drop in support from Johnson's 1964 vote. Although not immediately apparent to all, this represented the beginning of the end for American liberalism in its existing format. Most obviously the hegemony of liberalish Democrats in presidential elections was over. Starting in 1968 the Democrats lost five of six presidential elections – with the only triumph being a disaster in disguise as it exposed the uncertain Carter administration to the disorder of the late 1970s, in turn leading to a further erosion of the credit Democratic presidents had built up in better days.

The strange death of liberal America

In truth it is possible to see that there were always enormous internal contradictions within the New Deal coalition which were likely to combust as the constituent elements became increasingly aware who their bedfellows were. The lynchpin of the electoral alliance had been the coalescing of the economic interests of various social groups who otherwise did not necessarily have a lot in common. Thus the New Deal remained successful so long as it stuck to its core message, but it became increasingly difficult to maintain this one-dimensional approach. Most obviously the fault line within the Democratic Party over civil rights for African–Americans was always likely to rupture Roosevelt's coalition. Through to 1960, mainstream liberalism had not really confronted the outstanding racial issues in America. Certainly as a party the Democrats had not unconditionally usurped the Republicans' historical position as the more forward looking on race issues. As Stanley Greenberg explains, 'The Democrats had fashioned a party of the people, a bottom-up party, but one created within a national political space that was largely and artificially white. As long as they could suppress the race issue, they could pretend that this fiction did not matter' (1995, p.101). Eventually, however, party leaders had to face up to the gaping hole in their efforts to promote greater social equity across the nation. In the end, with the civil rights movement forcing the matter to the top of the news agenda, the Johnson administration did take the major steps necessary and the 1964 Civil Rights Act and the 1965 Voting Rights Act did much to end the Jim Crow segregation laws and the disenfranchisement of blacks in the southern states. This, in and of itself, was bound to disturb the partisan loyalties of the white South, but problematically for the Democrats the white reaction against racial liberalism extended beyond both easily categorized racial issues and also beyond the borders of the formerly segregationist states. In particular the centrepiece of the Great Society, the War on Poverty, came to be seen as a program designed primarily to help poor blacks rather than the whole community (Carmines and Stimson, 1989; Edsall and Edsall, 1991).

It is, of course, too simple to say that Johnson's 61 percent of the vote in 1964 became Humphrey's 42 percent in 1968 just because of a backlash against the administration's progressive race policies. Most evidently, enormous tensions were generated by the war in Vietnam, and in political terms this only brought bad news for the Democrats. It was a Democratic administration which had ordered the involvement of so many American troops, but it was the Democrats who were divided over the war; and while it is impossible to second guess whether the Great Society might have fared better if Johnson had been able to concentrate on his domestic war rather than becoming obsessed with that abroad, the diversion of energy and funds was clearly damaging. Perhaps the riots across America's ghettos would not have appeared so threatening, and so easy for Richard Nixon to exploit as a 'law and order' issue in the 1968 election, if it had not been for the simultaneous horrors in Vietnam so vividly brought to America's television screens. Suffice to say, however, that, in the phrase used by Iwan Morgan and Allen Matusow, the liberal consensus which had prevailed at the start of the 1960s had 'unravelled' by the decade's end (Matusow, 1984; Morgan, 1994).

This should not hide the fact that there were important, enduring and popular additions to the New Deal legacy enacted in this period. Most notably the Medicare and Medicaid programs provided government health care to the elderly and the poor; the Head Start program provided pre-school education for underprivileged children, and during the Nixon presidency there were significant increases in the value of Social Security benefits which were subsequently index linked to rises in the cost of living (Berkowitz, 1991). While, however, these were all programs which brought political advantage to the Democrats they were subsumed by the negative factors which overwhelmed the party. For Democrats a critical question is whether these were problems which could have been avoided. To a considerable extent it would appear that they could not; but an analysis provided by some commentators at the time, which proved to be a forerunner to the type of argument advanced by the New Democrat camp, was that the disintegration of the New Deal was aided and abetted by some serious self-inflicted wounds as the national Democratic Party fell victim to a liberal fundamentalism. For example, while few Democrats would dispute that some political price had to be paid, and was worth paying, in order to correct the injustices suffered by African–Americans, some did argue that the subsequent development of racial liberalism, particularly the espousal of policies like bussing, was indicative of broader wrong turns taken by the liberals, particularly in the crucial period in the late 1960s and early 1970s.

The trials and tribulations of liberals and Democrats from 1968 through to the end of the 1980s have been well charted (Lengle, 1981; Polsby, 1983; Brown, 1991; Morgan, 1994: Mayer, 1996), but it is worth briefly reflecting on some aspects of the party's angst for the light they throw on the development of New Democrat thinking. In particular, exactly who were the New Politics liberals, why was the Democratic Party haunted for so long by the ghost of George McGovern, and when and why did the conventional wisdom decide that the essential economic message of the New Deal itself had run out of steam?

New Politics liberalism

To the New Democrats the 'L-word' rot had set in a long-time before the Dukakis debacle. The initial raison d'être of the New Democrats is perhaps best explained in a document, *The Politics of Evasion*, co-authored by William Galston and Elaine Kamarck (1989). In this the two authors, who remained very much at the forefront New Democrat thinking through the 1990s, maintained that the Democratic Party had lost its sense of direction over the previous twenty years by emphasising cultural issues rather than bread and butter ones. There was in fact little new about this type of analysis as various figures had given the same warnings in the early 1970s about the dangers for the Democrats of being seen as a party which appealed to intellectual elites, minorities and the poor but which had lost contact with white middle and working class Americans. Of particular import was the hostility of some Democrats to the emergence of Eugene McCarthy and George McGovern as standard bearers for the party. The objection was to these two as purveyors of a cultural liberalism which might have resonated with academic elites but which alienated working America.

The emergence of the New Politics, with its emphasis on a kind of social libertarianism and opposition to the American establishment's war in Vietnam, did reflect a different set of priorities from the more traditional New Deal values. In the context of their times Roosevelt, Kennedy and Johnson were all liberals inasmuch as they stood on what was then the centre-left of the American political spectrum, but their behaviour was not motivated by a desire for ideological clarity. They identified various socio-economic problems and determined that it was government's job to help resolve these. The primary aim was to improve the socio-economic position of working Americans within the framework of market capitalism. It was acknowledged that compromise was an inevitable part of the process. Advocates of the New Politics, however, challenged these assumptions on two fronts. First, they maintained that by the end of the 1960s America's overall prosperity had undermined the rationale of traditional Democratic politicians whose outlook had been shaped by the Depression of the 1930s. It was argued that as a result of this, people would become less concerned with economic affairs and that politics would increasingly revolve around social and cultural issues. Second, on these types of question there was little room for compromise. Critically, the contention was that opinion would become more liberal on these matters as the values of the 1960s student protesters permeated the American middle-class (Dutton, 1970). At the heart of this critique was a sense that old style New Dealers were too concerned with material progress for its own sake and that this led them to neglect broader visions about the quality of life.

To those who remained loyal to the New Deal tradition, however, this relegation of economic concerns to secondary status was potentially disastrous as it moved the Democratic Party away from its blue-collar base. In organizational terms those Democrats opposed to the New Politics rallied around the Coalition for a Democratic Majority. A key figure in this movement was Ben Wattenberg who had originally arrived in Washington to work as a speechwriter for Lyndon Johnson. His concern was that the party was alienating its most steadfast political constituency. In the summer of 1971 he wrote

> For many years of Liberal Democratic hegemony, it was the Republican Party that was perceived as the party of the elitist: the banker, the broker, the doctor. And it was the Democratic party that was seen as the party of the little man.
>
> That was the taproot of Democratic power. For the man who chooses the Presidents of this country is the man who bowls on Thursday nights. He is the man in his blue-work shirt. ... He is a man who is decidedly turned off as he watches the Democrats-of-Despair hand out the campaign buttons of the New Politics, buttons that read MEA CULPA (quoted in Crotty, 1978, p.227).

Perhaps the most significant publication by CDM types was *The Real Majority* by Richard Scammon and Ben Wattenberg (1970). The aim of this book was, so to speak, to save the Democrats from themselves. As the authors saw it, New Politics liberalism played into the hands of the Republicans by emphasising Democratic weaknesses and GOP strengths. Their fear was of the type of analysis presented by Republican strategist Kevin Phillips and his prediction of *The Emerging Republican Majority*. This contained the following observation.

> The great political upheaval of the Nineteen-Sixties is not that of Senator Eugene McCarthy's relatively small group of upper-middle-class and intellectual supporters, but a populist revolt of the American masses who have been elevated by prosperity to middle-class stations and conservatism. *Their* revolt is against the caste, policies and taxation of the Mandarins of Establishment liberalism (1969, p.470).

The Real Majority was concerned with how to keep potential defectors in the Democratic camp. Thus Wattenberg and Scammon did acknowledge that non-economic concerns were increasingly occupying the voters' minds, but they put a significantly different spin on this than their New Politics counterparts. They maintained that electoral victory in presidential elections went to the candidate and party which appeared to be in the political centre and that the New Politics liberals were tying the Democratic Party to a series of social issue positions on matters such as bussing and crime which were regarded by many voters as ultra-liberal. The two authors were particularly concerned that in their efforts to be sensitive on race issues, the Democrats were becoming associated in the public mind with being soft on crime. To this end they recommended that Democrats should not say, 'Crime is a complicated sociological phenomenon and we'll never be able to solve the problem until we've got at the root causes of poverty and racism.' Instead Democrats should have been saying, 'I am going to make our neighborhoods safe again for decent citizens of every color. I am also in favor of job training, eradication of poverty, etc' (p.286).

Others again were dismissive of this thesis, describing it as accepting the principles of Phillips' analysis and attempting to deal with the major issues raised through 'opportunism and cleverness, thereby reducing all of politics to gamesmanship' (Greenfield and Newfield, 1972, p.213). As will be seen through this book, the Democrats were still engaged in this type of debate twenty years later. In a number of ways the New Democrat critique elaborated at the end of the 1980s echoed that of the CDM. Wattenberg and Scammon argued that the New Politics liberals were perversely neglecting those issue clusters which won Democrats votes and were concentrating on other themes in a manner which provided more fertile ground for conservative politics (for an examination of the political and electoral weighting of issue clusters see Shafer and Clagget, 1995). In the late 1980s there were few references to the 'New Politics' but the essence of the argument was the same – that the liberal fundamentalists were alienating potential Democrats rather than wooing them. The liberals, on the other hand, despaired as the Clinton administration tried to resolve its first term problems by bringing in former Republican spinmasters David Gergen and then Dick Morris. This, however, is to jump too far ahead in the story.

McGovern and McGovernism

The most immediately compelling evidence to support *The Real Majority* thesis was the events of 1972. In this year the contest for the Democratic nomination illustrated both the state of fracture of the party and the confused condition of liberalism, and the general election finally provided crushing defeat. To disgruntled Democrats the most damning evidence of how unrepresentative McGovernism was came at the party's National Convention. Jeanne Kirkpatrick, then a Democrat but later a prominent Reaganite, published an article in an academic journal emphasizing the gulf between the views of McGovern delegates at the convention and rank and file Democrat voters. For example, she noted that while 71 percent of Democrat identifiers were strongly opposed to the bussing of schoolchildren in pursuit of racial integration only 3 percent of McGovern delegates were similarly hostile to the practice (1975). Given the obvious hostility to McGovern within his own party, it was easy enough for Nixon to repeat and develop the theme of these complaints during the general election campaign. In November McGovern carried only the state of Massachusetts and over one-third of Democratic identifiers voted for Nixon (Mayer, 1996, p.6).

After McGovern's catastrophic defeat, New Politics liberalism did not reappear in such an undiluted form again, but the discourse of the party had changed. Being a liberal no longer meant simply being a supporter of New Deal style economics. It also involved a re-evaluation of foreign policy attitudes, an emphasis on minority rights, a call for greater redistribution, and briefly in the mid-1970s an emphasis on environmentalism at the expense of economic growth. This in turn exacerbated existing schisms within the party, as those people who had previously traveled under the liberal label on the basis of support for the New Deal and the Great Society, such as Senator Henry 'Scoop' Jackson from

Washington state, now found themselves redesignated as centrists or conservative Democrats. One self professed 'center-right' Democrat, Ronald Radosh, writing in disillusion at the end of Clinton's first term, reflected on how the marginalization of Jackson reflected the reasons for what he saw as the downfall of the party.

> Scoop Jackson was, in retrospect, the very last of the old mainstream Democrats. He fought hard to hold together an eroding center, and he went down to defeat. The lessons he sought to instil, but for which his efforts went for nought, would haunt the Democrats for decades to come (1996, p.182).

Despite his disappointments, Jackson did remain a Democrat; others, however, often referred to as the neo-conservatives, finally abandoned the party complaining that while their views had remained constant the party which they once loved had shifted too far to the left.[1] Some even went as far as to claim that Reaganism was the new manifestation of old Democrat values. For example,

> In 1980, while the Democrats remained under the influence of... unrepresentative forces and ideas, the Republicans completed their usurpation of the abandoned Democratic tradition.... Reagan made this all but explicit when he not only quoted Franklin D. Roosevelt but offered a program that echoed in almost every detail the campaign on which John F. Kennedy rode to the Presidency in 1960 (Podhoretz, 1981, p.28).

This is an extremely dubious assessment of both Kennedy's call to arms and of Reaganism, but the point is that it stands as an effective statement of how disillusioned some former Democrats had become with the direction the party had taken during the 1970s.

The defeated Democratic candidates of the 1980s, Mondale and Dukakis, were not McGovernicks but Dukakis in particular fell victim to the Republican rhetoric that he was a limousine liberal. Ironically, in some ways Dukakis tried to run a campaign based on New Democrat prescriptions, inasmuch as he eschewed ideology by arguing that the election was not about making a choice between left and right but was about choosing the most competent person for the job. This message, however, made little headway and Dukakis was in the end defined less by what he said than by what the Bush campaign said about him (Edsall, 1988). By concentrating on selective and emotional issues like the Massachusetts furlough program and the pledge of allegiance, the Bush team created an image of their opponent as someone who was soft on crime with questionable patriotism – culminating in the 'L-word' tag. As Wilson Carey McWilliams reflected, 'Where Democrats once ran against Hoover, Republicans ran against McGovern in 1988, and George Bush argued repeatedly that "neighborhood Democrats" should prefer him to a leadership dominated by "the remnant of the '60s"' (2000, p.58). The manner in which Bush did this so successfully confirmed to the growing New Democrat movement that for a Democrat to win the White House the party could not again nominate a candidate who could be so easily lampooned on social and cultural issues. The party's problems, however, were becoming more complex.

Moving beyond the New Deal

Bush may have turned the 1988 election round, after polls in the spring and early summer suggested that Dukakis might be a real threat, by caricaturing his opponent as a 'bleeding heart', but blaming 'limousine liberals' for all the party's presidential level woes was conflating too many problems. Perhaps even more disturbing than the rise of cultural liberalism was the undermining of much of the substance of the New Deal's socio-economic agenda which brought into question the fundamentals of FDR's legacy. It was on social and economic welfare questions where the New Deal had been strong. Losing because people preferred Republicans on the death penalty and defence was one thing, but losing because of uncertainty about how to pitch a Democratic economic message was another. The crux of the matter was that the New Deal's success had been based on an American version of Keynesianism which, by the end of the 1980s, was perceived to be past its sell by date.

American Keynesianism had always been more limited that the west European version, but it had shared the hypothesis that government could, and therefore should, intervene to beneficial effect in socio-economic affairs and this working assumption had provided the original and most enduring appeal of New Dealism. That is, the disparate elements of the Democratic majority had been brought and kept together by the sense that New Deal activism had brought prosperity and had been instrumental in creating the mass middle class. In short it was economic considerations and the extent to which the Democratic Party satisfied these which kept the populist and liberals elements of the New Deal coalition together. This is not to exaggerate the economic coherence of the New Deal. Much of what President Roosevelt did in the 1930s was hit and miss rather than a calculated effort to devise an alternative economic strategy to laissez faire, and it was not really until the 1960s that an administration began to recognize intellectually the possibilities of deficit financing to generate economic growth (French, 1997). What the New Deal did do, however, was create an expectation that government *could* and therefore would act to sweeten the economy, and in political terms it established the Democrats as the party of the 'common man'. Thus, in the long-term, the most disruptive feature of the 1970s for the Democratic Party was the emerging sense that government had lost control of the economic agenda. That is, in the most basic terms, the stagflation of the 1970s undermined the assumption that government knew what it was doing. More particularly, the credibility of the idea that government could manipulate the economy through the use of fiscal and monetary policy was severely damaged. In the late 1970s the Carter administration had floundered in its efforts to respond to ever mounting economic problems leaving the way open for Reaganomics – an explicitly conservative economic and political experiment.

The question for the Democrats was how to forge a credible 'we're on your side' message which would bring the so-called Reagan Democrats back into the party's camp. President Carter was much vilified for his 'malaise' speech in mid-July 1979, a time of economic troubles and severe energy shortages, when he suggested that American society engage itself in a period of introspection. This was attacked as a sign of weakness and internal angst when the country wanted leadership, and indeed the tone of the speech was a political misjudgement; but if the so-called 'misery index' figures had not been so miserable then there would have been no need for the speech in the first place – and the misery index was not about cultural values but unemployment and inflation.[2] Moreover, in the language of the Reagan era, government had mutated into Big Government which had taxed and regulated away American competitiveness.[3]

Some analysts put all of this together and came up with a gloomy picture indeed. Writing in July 1988 political commentator William Schneider made the following observation when previewing the forthcoming presidential election.

> The Democrats cannot win an ideological election anymore ... too many voters have shifted from the pro-government to the anti-government side. They identify as taxpayers, not as the beneficiaries

of public spending, and they are more likely to see government as interfering with them than as protecting them (1988, p.32).

It was this type of interpretation of what happened in 1988 which augmented the growing New Democrat demand to move the party away from its impulse to turn to government to provide the answers to America's problems. Moreover the changes in the economic structure as the country moved from mass manufacturing employment to mass service employment and the so-called phenomenon of globalization were perceived as undermining the basic tenets of New Dealism that government could have a decisive effect on the US's economic well-being.[4] Increasingly the language of the 'Information Age' economy was invoked by New Democrats to argue that there had to be a shift in attitude which recognized that government's role was best confined to enabling those displaced by economic transformation to respond to the changes, rather than intervening (in what could only be a forlorn effort) to stop the displacement from happening in the first place. Thus by the start of the 1990s the New Democrats were calling for a significant overhaul of the party's thinking, starting effectively with first principles.

The rise of the New Democrats

The presidential election results of the 1980s illustrated the depth of the Democratic Party's problems at national level as Reagan and Bush were able to tag their opponents as being too liberal on a series of cultural and value issues where, regardless of the merits of the argument, being perceived as liberal was not a vote-winner. Moreover, on those issues where being liberal (even if not actually using the term itself) had traditionally served the party well, that is on social and economic policy, there was an uncertainty over whether New Dealism remained either politically credible or intellectually relevant; and in trying to formulate a response to the self-confidence of Reaganism there was initially much confusion. According to one study the various elements of the party 'had literally lost their collective head and were not able to find the stability and identity they so frantically sought' (Arden, 1988, p.x). There was no organizational structure to bring order and no faction in the party was dispassionate enough to command the respect necessary to give it a voice of authority. There was some comfort from the 1982 mid-term elections when the normal turn against the party in the White House helped the Democrats secure gains of 26 seats in the House, but the 1984 results were thoroughly demoralising.

It was in the wake of this that the DLC was formed in 1985, but there was no immediate hint that this new faction would be able to impose itself any more successfully than any of the other groupings within the party which engaged in the post-defeat recriminations; and there was ample evidence to fuel the various arguments. The manner of Mondale's loss made it easy for all factions to find vindication for their perspective. Essentially, however, there were two primary contentions. First, liberals maintained that Mondale had run the meekest of campaigns, conceding ground to Reaganism at every turn, without ever articulating a positive message which might have energized a groundswell of support (Kuttner, 1988, pp.21–32). In particular liberal-left commentators strongly rejected the idea that the result itself represented a rejection of liberalism.

> [T]he mistake the Democrats made in 1984 was not their alleged 'reaching down' but the fact that they did not 'reach down' nearly enough. On economic issues, the Democrats offered the voters almost nothing in 1984. Though Mondale spoke incessantly about the values of work and self-discipline, he became the first Democratic nominee in many years to fail even to put forward a major jobs program. Nor did he couple his call for tax increases with a program of popular economic revitalization' (Ferguson and Rogers, 1986, p.36).

Second, and in distinct contrast, centrist and conservative Democrats maintained that Mondale, whatever he said during his campaign, was too weighed down by baggage from both his own liberal past and also by the image of the Democratic Party as one which pandered to a series of special interest groups, but which paid little heed to the wishes of mainstream, middle-income, middle-class, Middle America. William Galston, who had in fact been Mondale's issues director, explained the party's problems in the following fashion

> ... the concept of the national interest advocated by Democrats for half a century was dissolved into a myriad of benefits for specific groups – the so-called special interests. Citizens who did not regard themselves primarily as members of such groups felt left out entirely (quoted in Kuttner, 1988, pp.27–8).

In truth, in the narrow context of what happened in 1984, it was unlikely that the Democrats could have nominated anyone and adopted any tactics which would have unseated Reagan, but this dispute provides an important indication of the state of the debate between the opposing wings of the Democratic Party in the mid-1980s. It was in this environment that the DLC was born, but while its centrist aims were immediately apparent, there were, at first, several liberal members of Congress who affiliated themselves with the group, as they too agreed that the party needed to rethink (Hale, 1995). It was not really until after the 1988 elections that the DLC began to aggressively market itself both organizationally and ideologically. This was a response to the disappointment of 1988 when the Democrats appeared to throw away a winning position. One DLCer who did make a bid for the Democratic nomination was Senator Al Gore from Tennessee. Gore's candidacy, however, made strategic mistakes and never really threatened Dukakis once the latter had established front-runner status. It was in the light of this that the DLC's leadership decided that if the organization was to make a difference it had to be more uncompromising in promoting its centrist perspective and to make a more determined effort to capture the 'head' of the party, something best symbolized through success in the presidential nominating process (Baer, 2000, pp.120–42). One important step was taken in 1989 with the establishment of the Progressive Policy Institute. Although formally a separate organization, this was easily recognisable as a think tank arm of the DLC. This gave the DLC a forum though which New Democrat ideas could be more coherently developed and then pushed into the political arena.

One of the most significant early publications of the PPI was *The Politics of Evasion* (Galston and Kamarck, 1989). This was a fierce attack on 'liberal fundamentalism' and, as such, illustrated the DLC's more confrontational style in the context of the Democratic Party's internal ideological angst. The authors' central contention was that liberal activists had distorted the party's message in the pursuit of ideological purity and that if the Democrats were alienating a majority of voters on cultural and social issues such as crime, then they were not going to get across their more appealing message on 'economic and social progress' (p.27).

[A]ll too often the American people do not respond to a progressive economic message, even when the Democrats try to offer it, because the party's presidential candidates fail to win their confidence in other key areas such as defense, foreign policy and social values. Credibility on these issues is the ticket that will get Democratic candidates in the door to make their affirmative economic case. But if they don't hold that ticket they won't even get a hearing (pp.27–8).

Denouncing liberals, however, was not, by itself, enough. The New Democrats had to provide an alternative agenda of their own if their call for centrism was not to be easily dismissed as warmed over moderate Republicanism. As Jon Hale reflected, the task was one of 'differentiating…from both left and right sides of the political spectrum without appearing to be simply posturing in the middle, as was too much the tendency of the early DLC' (1995, p.223). The founding of the PPI was one step towards developing a fuller blueprint, and this heralded a concerted effort to push New Democrat ideas as the way forward for the party. These ideas were given a public airing at the DLC's annual national conventions in 1990 and 1991. The 1990 conference resulted in the 'New Orleans Declaration' (DLC, 1990) which brought together many of the ideas which were to become part of the standard New Democrat lexicon. Thus there was more emphasis on being tough on crime and less on the rights of minorities than had been the case in the Democratic platforms of the 1980s. Moreover, there was also a shift in socio-economic policy representing a move away from the prescriptions of New Dealomics. That is, the 'politics of entitlement' was to be replaced by 'a new politics of reciprocal responsibility' and there was to be a downsizing of the state's role in the new economy (p.8). Government was to aid and abet economic growth and to re-skill dispossessed workers rather than to intervene directly.

These themes were further elaborated at the May 1991 conference in Cleveland. In his generally favourable account of the DLC, Kenneth Baer describes this as 'a seminal event in the history of the New Democrats' as it categorically established their alternative path for the Democratic Party and provided a forum for Bill Clinton, then Governor of Arkansas and DLC chairman, to advertise himself as a potential candidate for 1992 (Baer, 2000, p.177). The manifesto produced this time went by the title 'The New American Choice' (DLC, 1991). The repeated emphasis was on the need to steer a course which would restore American competitiveness, provide fair reward and security to American workers, improve educational opportunity, and strengthen the family. The controversy was in the proposed means rather than these ends. Fundamentally government was to be less prominent in achieving these goals than liberal Democrats would expect. This was reflected in the statement, *'We believe the mission of government is to expand opportunity, not bureaucracy'* (p.9). Presaging some of the major conflicts of the Clinton presidency, the document urged that America 'use its enormous market power to expand fair and free trade around the world' (p.18). There was also an attempt to stress the New Democrats' affinity for the traditional family unit rather than countercultural alternatives. This was expressed in the statement that 'new approaches should emphasize individual and parental responsibility, strong families and the moral and cultural values that most Americans share' (p.26). The message that the DLC hoped to get across was that, through them, the Democrats were once again fit to govern. In his introduction to 'The New American Choice' Bill Clinton noted that it showed that 'the Democratic Party is willing to stand up for the interests of ordinary people again.' He continued

> If we want to be a national party, we've got to have a message that touches everybody, makes sense to everybody, and goes beyond the stale orthodoxies of "left" and "right." A message that resonates with the hopes and dreams of ordinary Americans. That's what the DLC has set out to do (p.3).

If, however, the DLC were to really make an impact then it was clear that a recognized New Democrat had to make a serious bid for the party's presidential nomination. This is not to say that the nominee's ideological stance tells all that there is to tell about the party's ideological stance, indeed far from it, but the presidential candidate is certainly the most easily identifiable marker of the party's position at a point in time. Thus, after 1988 the DLC leadership decided that its primary efforts should be directed towards the 1992 primary process,[5] and the person to carry the New Democrat torch was Governor Clinton (for a detailed discussion of the evolution of the DLC's strategy and the courting of Clinton by DLC leaders see Baer, 2000, pp.160–92). On the other hand the presence of a convincing New Democrat candidate in the primaries was only the first step – with two major problems to be overcome if the overall project was not to be further stalled. First, actually winning the nomination, and then second winning the White House. Ironically, however, the fact that the latter task seemed so daunting in mid-1991, when potential candidates had effectively to declare their hand, helped Clinton in his pursuit of the nomination; yet, by the time of the general election campaign, the political dynamic had changed to such an extent that President Bush looked less like an invincible incumbent and more like an uncomfortable *pro tem* manager waiting to be relieved of responsibility.

Winning the White House

1. The nomination

American party processes had fundamentally changed between 1968 and 1972 when the primaries switched from being 'beauty' contests which candidates could avoid and still take the nomination, to being the only route to the nomination. The transformation occurred as a result of the turmoil within the Democratic Party in 1968 when, in order to appease the McCarthy and Kennedy insurgents, the Humphrey camp agreed to set up an investigation into the process of delegate selection.

At first few realised how far reaching the recommendations of the Commission on Party Structure and Delegate Selection (better known as the McGovern-Fraser Commission) were likely to be; and even fewer realised how far it would empower the party 'amateur' activists at the expense of the so-called party regulars 'who regarded themselves as political 'professionals'' who represented the various constituent groups of the New Deal coalition (Shafer, 1983). The 1972 battle for the Democratic nomination, however, made it immediately apparent how the new system was likely to lead to a prolonged display of ideological agonies on the public stage and the possible nomination of a candidate who would excite many activists but alienate much of the electorate. Through the rest of the 1970s and the early 1980s there were was considerable tinkering with the rules of delegate selection mainly in an effort to at least give some influence back to the party establishment, but the fundamental rule of binding primary (and caucus) results has remained intact. Most commentary on the nature of the reforms has emphasized the downside for the Democrats inasmuch as it has been the party most plagued by internal primary strife, which has undermined the efforts of the eventual candidate in the general election (Crotty, 1978; Polsby, 1983).[6] The rancor of 1972 has perhaps not been repeated, but the open nature of the primary process did have further disruptive effects. In 1976 Governor Carter was as close to being a genuine 'outsider' as the political system allows, and his selection as party candidate would surely not have materialised under the previous nomination format. His non-Washington credentials probably in fact served him well in the aftermath of Watergate, but certainly did not when he got to Washington and had to deal with the city's Congressional barons. Four years on, the internal party challenge by such a senior figure as Senator Ted Kennedy, if poorly organized, did illustrate the depth of dissatisfaction within the incumbent President's own party. Furthermore, Senator Gary Hart's vibrant campaign for the nomination in 1984 reinforced the impression that eventual nominee Walter Mondale was not a man of the times.

The concern for the DLC in 1992 was that the primary process still gave added weight to the views of party activists who were notably more liberal than the general electorate. The dilemma, at least as understood by the DLC, was that only a New Democrat could win the White House in competition with the Republicans but that New Democrats were distinctly disadvantaged when in internal party competition. Hence the DLC's decision to plan their strategy for 1992 very soon after the 1988 election. They could not control external factors, however, and one of these was who else would run. Clinton was seen as better standard bearer for the New Democrat cause than anyone had proved to be in 1988 but there were other potential Democratic heavyweights who might provide serious competition. Among the names often touted as potential candidates were Senators Sam Nunn (who was a strong DLCer), George Mitchell, and Bill Bradley as well as Congressman Dick Gephardt. Clinton's path was certainly eased as these declined, and the difficulties posed to Mondale and Dukakis by Jesse Jackson were also avoided. Increasingly the Clinton camp's concerns focused on whether New York Governor Mario Cuomo would run. This would have meant the entry of a charismatic and high profile liberal who might well have been able to energise the party's liberal activists. Eventually, after some hesitation, Cuomo announced that he would not be running leaving, Senator Tom Harkin from Iowa as the only significant challenger from the liberal-left of the party (Cook, 1991).[7] Other challengers were the former Senator from Massachusetts Paul Tsongas, Senator Bob Kerrey of Nebraska, Governor of Virginia Douglas Wilder, and former Governor of California 'Jerry' Brown. This was generally regarded as something of a second string field and, due in large part to DLC help and organization, Clinton raised the most early money and gained frontrunner status.[8] Nevertheless, he had to tread carefully. He had to be sure that his New Democrat stance did not alienate the party's base (Cook, 1992b).

As it was, this problem was largely resolved in the campaign's early stages. Wilder's campaign was short-lived, and Kerrey (who could have challenged as an alternative voice of the New Democracy) also soon pulled out. Critically so too did Harkin – which meant there was not really an established liberal contender in the field. This pitted Clinton against the idiosyncratic Brown, who appealed to some environmental liberals but had few friends among the more traditional bastions of the

New Deal, and against Tsongas who *ran to the right* of Clinton.[9] This allowed (or forced) Clinton to appeal to the party's liberal wing as well as centrists and moderates.

After clinching the nomination, however, Clinton made a major avowal of his New Democrat faith with his choice of Vice Presidential candidate. Traditionally this is a time for balancing the ticket either geographically or ideologically, or both. Clinton did neither in picking fellow white Southern male and like-minded DLCer, Senator Al Gore. This came as a relief to some Clinton supporters who were concerned that the candidate was in danger of going too far in appeasing the liberal-left. For example, a June editorial in *The New Republic* magazine, which had become increasingly New Democrat in its outlook, worried that Clinton was conceding too much ground to the 'liberal interest groups that have cost the Democrats the last three elections.' It urged him to use the Vice Presidential pick to re-establish his centrist credentials by choosing Gore because, in selecting 'someone who will give the party's left sleepless nights, ... he will be showing the party that he is truly a new voice in the democratic conversation; and he will be showing critical independent voters that the Democrats are no longer the problem but part of the solution' (The New Republic, 1992b, p.8).

Clinton further reinforced the centrist message in his speech formally accepting the nomination at the party's national convention. This reflected a number of key New Democrat themes, such as when he talked of cutting the number of bureaucrats and increasing the number of police officers. Indeed the 1992 National Convention was in many ways a triumph of DLC orchestration, as even the disagreements illustrated Clinton's distinctiveness from recent Democratic candidates for president. Thus Jesse Jackson gave an impassioned speech in which he offered several criticisms of the Clinton–Gore ticket, but this served as much as anything to highlight that Clinton had created some distance between himself and the party's left wing. Another sign that the New Democrats had extended their influence came with the party's 1992 platform which contained a number of typical New Democrat refrains. It stated, for example, 'We believe in an activist government, but it must work in a different, more responsive way', and it had to be one which was 'more efficient, flexible and results-oriented ... ' The platform continued 'We reject both the do-nothing government of the past 12 years and the big government theory that says we can hamstring business, and tax and spend our way to prosperity. Instead we offer a third way.'[10] The platforms are not things that too many voters pay too much attention to, but they are an important statement of the party's intent to activists, and so the New Democrat tone of this document was significant. For Baer it represented an explicit triumph for the DLC as it was 'noticeably more centrist than ever before and was tailored to win back voters who had deserted the Democratic Party in national elections' (2000, p.202). DLC executive director, Al From, reflected, 'These candidates, combined with this platform, mean this party really has changed' (quoted in Elving, 1992, p.2075); and this did seem to be a message which much of the public took from the convention as opinion polls showed that four in ten respondents agreed that Clinton and Gore were a different kind of Democrat (Hale, 1995, p.228). The next question was whether Clinton could translate his primary success into a general election victory.

2. The general election: A New Democrat campaign?

The standard answer as to why Clinton was able to win was that the voters were focused on the faltering state of the economy, with President Bush accused of indifference to the problems of ordinary Americans and more concerned with international matters – a moment highlighted in the second television debate of the campaign by the contrasting answers Bush and Clinton gave to a question about how they had been affected by the recession (Germond and Witcover, 1993a, pp.9–12). Two political scientists who have studied the DLC in depth, however, both argue that although the poor performance of the economy gave the Democrats the opportunity of winning the White House it did not guarantee this outcome. That is, if the Bush team had been able to repeat the trick of 1988 and pin the 'liberal' label on Clinton, then Bush might still have won. According to Jon Hale, therefore, 'Clinton's New Democratic credentials' were critical in establishing 'a level playing field' which prevented a rerun of 1988 (1995, p.228). Baer is even more emphatic, stating

> Bill Clinton would not have been able to win the election if he had not run as a New Democrat, addressing the problem of cultural breakdown, the perceived practical failures of government, and public doubts about the welfare state (2000, p.203).

According to this analysis, the GOP were not able to turn the election into a referendum on liberalism as in 1988, as Clinton did not appear 'weak', as Dukakis had done, on cultural values – especially on the death penalty.

Others, on the other hand, asked whether Clinton ran as a New Democrat at all – or at least questioned the importance of the New Democracy's contribution to the triumph. Indeed some liberals claim his success to be due to his liberal campaign. In one exchange about the nature of Clinton's campaign, liberal commentator Jeff Faux debated with Will Marshall of the PPI. According to Faux, 'If it turns out that Bill Clinton truly is a New Democrat, then he was elected on the basis of bait-and-switch advertising' (1993, p.21) and adds that it was the 'liberal coalition – labor, environmentalists, minorities, fundamentalists, gays' which provided 'the shock troops of Clinton's political army' (p.23). In a rather different interpretation Marshall puts Clinton's success down to his efforts to portray himself as 'a "Different Kind of Democrat", one who at last understood and sympathized with "the forgotten middle class"'(1993, p.11).

In some ways this debate does somewhat miss the point, as in truth Clinton probably did what he needed to do to win. In the primaries his pitch as the centrist, non-liberal, candidate was somewhat changed by the manner in which his main challenger, against whom he had to define himself, had staked out the conservative turf – at least on socio-economic policy. This left Clinton in the unexpected position of being the candidate favoured by many liberals. In the general election campaign Clinton did sometimes use the rhetoric of populist liberalism in his attacks on Bush's economic policies, but where he did toe the New Democrat line was in his constant emphasis on helping the middle-class rather than talking about the poor. In addition, on the major floating danger issue of the cultural dimension, Clinton was for the death penalty and generally promised to be tough on crime, thus avoiding Dukakis/Horton syndrome. He did take the liberal side of the divide on abortion and gay rights, but did not allow the campaign's focus to stray too much onto these questions. Furthermore, although this is difficult to quantify, Clinton was also surely helped by the end of the Cold War. Bush's foreign policy triumphs and Clinton's draft dodging and lack of gravitas for someone about to take charge of the Armed Forces would likely have carried more weight had a nuclear showdown still been on the agenda.

Overall then Clinton did pick and mix old and New Democrat themes as it suited the campaign and he did make promises which the different sides of the coalition could relate to. Thus health care was balanced by welfare reform and deficit reduction was balanced by stimulus and investment proposals. Sometimes particularly problematic issues were dealt with somewhat ambiguously. Thus Clinton did eventually come out in favour of NAFTA which was an anathema to the unions, but he tried to diminish the starkness of his support for liberalising trade by talking of how he would insist on all sorts of environmental safeguards and protections for American workers threatened by cheaper labor abroad. All of this, however, was not in itself reprehensible in the context of an election campaign. Certainly it was political behavior which fitted well with one part of the DLC's mantra – that was to find an agenda which could win. After winning, however, the bigger questions lay in wait.

3
Clintonomics I: Deficit Reduction and Free Trade

Without question Clinton's trump card when playing the game of assessing his presidency was the much improved state of the US economy; and he was particularly keen to emphasize that the prosperity of the 1990s had not happened by accident but resulted from the administration's deliberate policy choices which had constituted a consistent and coherent approach. The next two chapters will examine the different aspects of this approach and ask whether there was a identifiable attempt to implement a distinctive, Third Way, economic strategy in the aftermath of Reaganomics. Furthermore, to the extent that there was a discernible Clintonomics, to what degree did this satisfy the Democratic Party's various factions? This chapter will concentrate on the efforts to reduce the deficit and promote free trade while the next will look at the human investment strategies, broadly defined, and at the specific efforts to 'make work pay'.

Candidate Clintonomics to presidential Clintonomics

The economic issue served candidate Clinton well in 1992 but it did not take too astute an observer to recognize that different elements of the Democratic Party had quite different ideas about what the economic priorities were which, in turn, reflected quite different perspectives on the nature of the modern economy. That is, after the Carter years witnessed a meltdown of the governing assumptions of the American version of welfare state Keynesianism, it was evident that defining a Democratic economic agenda in the 1990s was going to involve different groundrules than had been the case in the 1960s and 1970s. The idea of re-energizing the old New Deal economic agenda was widely deemed impossible due to the Reaganomics legacy of deficit and debt, the emergence of the post-Fordist/post-industrial economy and the impact of trade and capital globalization. However, even though there was general acknowledgment that these changed conditions meant that Clinton would have to provide a different sort of economic leadership from his Democratic predecessors, there were significant disagreements over whether policy should bend to accommodate these changes or whether it should fight to reverse their consequences.

The most compelling concern for the incoming administration in 1993, however, was that the economic data suggested that a formidable task lay ahead whichever approach was adopted. The long-term statistics behind both the general economic unease and the more particular specifics of deficit growth indicated that these were deep rooted problems which were not going to be easily remedied (Phillips, 1994). The critical issues were the stagnation in the living standards of middle-income Americans and the related evidence that the rewards of economic growth were being ever more unequally divided (Edsall, 1984; Phillips, 1990; Frank and Cook, 1995; Schwarz, 1997). The real-life fall-out of the dispiriting economic data gave candidate Clinton considerable scope to play the champion of the middle-class, but the task for President Clinton of actually fulfilling this role was going to be more problematic. For example, while the growth in income inequality was due in some degree to the tax and spend priorities of the Reagan years, disconcertingly, the greater share of the disparities appeared to be caused by market dynamics which increasingly rewarded an elite for their skills but not the masses for theirs (Danziger and Gottschalk, 1995).

Thus even if Clinton was prepared to use public policy tools to reverse the policy direction of the Reagan era, it was unclear how much this would change things; and, if public policy meant spending money then this would itself be immediately problematic – regardless of merit – because of the state of the public finances. Clinton inherited a record deficit of over \$320 billion – amounting to 5.2 percent of GDP, which, on existing baseline figures, was predicted to rise to \$350 billion in fiscal year 1997 when Clinton would presumably be running for re-election. The worry for the new President was that, although in the long-term deficit reduction might bolster economic growth and thus benefit middle America, in the short-term a serious effort at cutting the government's level of overspending was likely to require the combination of tax rises and spending cuts – a policy mix with little obvious political appeal.

A further, and increasingly controversial, issue was the future direction of US trade policy. Clinton had taken a 'softly, softly' approach to this during the campaign, but in office he was going to have to face up to the question of where the Democratic Party now stood in relation to trade and protection questions. Since the 1970s significant parts of the Democratic coalition had become increasingly protectionist, reversing the general trend towards trade liberalization favoured by the party in the earlier New Deal period (Destler, 1992, pp.173–9). This meant that the party was divided across the economic dimension. To New Democrats the priority issue was the budget deficit coupled with promotion of free trade: to liberals, more in the New Deal tradition, it was the need to promote economic growth through increasing public investment and creating the climate to foster private investment in order to create more jobs, while protecting existing ones from low wage competition outside the US.

In 1992 Clinton had been able to appease both wings of the Democratic Party by attacking the Bush administration for failing to deliver on both job creation and deficit reduction, without having to explain in too much detail how he would reconcile government pump-priming of the economy with cutting overall government spending. He had promised a stimulus, a middle-class tax cut and policies to encourage long-term investment; yet, he was also committed to significant deficit reduction over a four year term. On top of this he had offered qualified support for the NAFTA treaty negotiated by President Bush but yet to be agreed by Congress, implying that his full backing was dependent on changes guaranteeing greater protection for American workers and the environment. Thus Clinton had campaigned using a combination of old and New Democrat themes. The uncertainty about quite how President Clinton would elucidate this agenda once in office was exacerbated by the manner in which efforts to devise an economic program which he could implement in tandem with Congressional Democrats only really began with his election. Through the Reagan/ Bush era, Democrat leaders in Washington had become accustomed to opposing presidential initiatives rather than developing a strategy of their own. This resulted in the onus very much lying with *Clinton* to be the architect of any new, post New Deal, direction for the Democrats in economic policy (Wetherford and McDonnell, 1996, pp.412–3). The problem was that the clear delineation of Clintonomics as *Democratic Party* economic policy was bound to illustrate the degree of divergence from that, or any other, particular line within the party.

The triumph of deficit reduction

It was because of the various and potentially divergent policy directions promised during the campaign that the choice of Clinton's economic policy team and the nature of the first budget were so critical. How was he going to square his campaign circle? There was thus either consternation or relief when the selection of the leading members of the economic team suggested a greater emphasis on the deficit reduction than public spending. In particular, those business and financial leaders whose main concern was the deficit were happy to see Clinton edge towards a fiscally conservative stance as indicated by his nomination of Senate Finance Committee chairman Lloyd Bentsen as Treasury Secretary, Robert Rubin as chief of the new National Economic Council, with deficit hawks Leon Panetta and Alice Rivlin heading up the Office of Management and Budget (Starobin, 1992). There were of course some liberal figures appointed, most notably Robert Reich as Labor Secretary and also Laura D'Andrea Tyson as head of the Council of Economic Advisers – but these were not the senior economic positions in the administration. It was also clear that the newly elected President saw a need to befriend Alan Greenspan, the Republican chairman of the Federal Reserve Board, whose obsession with keeping inflation in check made him wary of policies which might in any way overstimulate the economy (Starobin, 1993). According to perspective, this first tranche of appointments and Greenspan's influence were either a signal of Clinton's quick acquiescence to the agenda of Wall Street and corporate America (Akard, 1998, pp.192–4), or were vital in saving Clinton from his own more self-destructive liberal impulses (Tatalovich and Frendreis, 2000, p.46).

1. The 1993 (FY 1994) budget revisited

One particular feature of the credit-claiming exercise, which developed as economic conditions improved, was the manner in which the White House publicly resurrected its first economic and budget plan of 1993 in an attempt to portray this as the key moment in changing the nation's economic fortunes. Part of this was undoubtedly political point-scoring as, with no Republican support, it was the first major bill since 1945 to pass without a vote from the minority party. This, in effect, meant that the argument over the budget's contents was one conducted within the confines of the Democratic Party. In the end, the passage of the legislation was interpreted as a triumph for the White House, but proper examination of the evolution of the plan from its first formal appearance in mid-February to its final angst-ridden passage in early August shows that there was much tinkering with the original design in the legislative process as the project became a cause of angst within Democratic ranks.

In its initial form, the Clinton budget contained five priority themes. First, the deficit was to be reduced to a little over $200 billion by 1996, entailing a cumulative reduction of approaching $500 billion from existing baseline predictions over the course of the presidential term. Second, extra revenues were to be raised through a combination of sharply increased taxes on the wealthy, a general new energy tax, and higher taxes on corporations. The top individual tax rate was to be raised from 31 percent to 36 percent for individuals earning over $115,000 and for couples earning over $140,000. Those with an income of over $250,000 were also to pay a surtax which would bring their effective rate up to 39.6 percent. In addition, higher income retirees were to have 85 percent of their Social Security benefits taxed, up from 50 percent. One early campaign theme – the call for a middle-class tax cut – was quietly dropped. The President also proposed a broad-based energy tax on the heat content of fuels known as the BTU tax. It was claimed that this would raise nearly $73 billion over five years. Further-more, corporations with a taxable income of over $10 million would be taxed at a new rate of 36 percent, up from 34 percent. Third, there were to be cuts to both entitlement spending, such as Medicare and Medic-aid, and appropriated discretionary spending to the tune of a total of nearly $190 billion over five years. Fourth, on the stimulus and invest-ment side, so-called empowerment zones were to be established in a number of depressed areas which would offer tax breaks and other incentives for businesses to set up there and, more generally, invest-ment was to be encouraged through a series of tax breaks to small and new businesses. Finally, the Earned Income Tax Credit scheme for the working poor was to be expanded (Hager, 1993; Novak, 1993a).

The first critical test for the bill came in the House of Representatives where it squeaked through by a 219 to 213 majority with 38 Democrats voting against. At this stage Clinton's proposals were relatively intact, although it was acknowledged that some crucial conservative and moderate Democrat votes had been brought onside by the administra-tion through an agreement that there would be major changes to the BTU tax and further cuts in entitlement spending once the bill was dis-cussed in Senate. In addition, the House's deliberations had revealed a series of tensions. First, that there was a block of conservative Democ-rats who took the Republican line that what was needed were fewer tax rises and more spending cuts and who were not going to be a party to the Clinton budget. Second, that those Democrats elected from mar-ginal districts were particularly jittery about voting for the bill. Most of this group still voted with the President, but did so, nervous of future accusations that they were tax hikers. Third, that although liberals felt they had little choice but to support the package and were keen on some aspects, there were elements that they too did not like, notably the cuts in medical programs. Finally, that the Clinton loyalists were infuriated by their colleagues who seemed prepared to down his presidency almost before it had left the ground. At this stage the Republican show of unity and the number of Democratic dissenters was ominous, as the Democrat majority in Senate was even less reliable, and critically there was only an 11 to 9 Democratic majority on the crucial Senate Finance Committee where one defection could potentially kill the whole deal.

The make-up of the SFC, particularly its Democratic contingent with members from the big energy producing and consuming states, meant that the BTU tax was a non-starter. The problem was that this left a $70 billion-plus hole in the budgetary mathematics, and the attempts to fill this exposed a series of rifts. One alternative was to increase the tax on transportation fuel but this was not going to make up the revenue lost through scrapping the BTU tax. Attention thus turned to further possible spending cuts or a scaling back of some of Clinton's tax credits and breaks. Given that all the Democrats on the SFC virtually had an individual veto, discussions were bound to be tense. Particularly problematic for the administration's efforts to nudge the protagonists towards a compromise was the presence on the SFC of Oklahoman David Boren. He was not alone in his doubts about elements of the plan, but he, even more than fellow sceptics and New Democrats such as John Breaux from Louisiana, was prepared to flout his concerns and antagonize liberal Democrats. Thus Boren led the way in proposing extra cuts in Medicare and Medicaid and in suggesting the reduction or even elimination of the EITC expansion and empowerment zones. This outraged those House liberals who had been unhappy with the scale of health care spending cuts but who had found some comfort in the EITC and the empowerment zones.

In the end, the Senate agreed on a package which differed from the House version of the budget in significant ways. Most problematically, on the revenue side, the BTU tax was replaced by a 4.3 cents a gallon gas tax which left around $50 billion to be made up in other ways in order to hit the deficit targets. Thus, in order to compensate, the EITC expansion and the investment tax breaks for new and small businesses were scaled back, the empowerment zones were eliminated, and Medicare cuts were increased. Even so, six Democrat Senators voted against and the measure was passed only on the casting vote of

Vice-President Al Gore. Even after this torment, however, it was clear that there was more anxiety to come for the administration. The compromises made to get the package through Senate had infuriated many Democrats in the House, especially those in the Congressional Black Caucus and liberal factions. The House–Senate conference committee thus promised and duly delivered another round of Democratic bloodletting (Hager and Cloud, 1993a). The mathematics of the initial votes in the two chambers meant that in effect every 'Yes' voter from the first time around had a potential veto over the process (Hager and Cloud, 1993b). Thus every grievance had to be negotiated and in particular some way found of reconciling Boren and the CBC (Cloud, 1993a). This reflected a more general frustration amongst House Democrats at having to draft a package that would satisfy Senate mavericks, who seemed quite willing to flout any general consensus on what an acceptable compromise would look like. For its part, the White House staked out its priorities as being an aggregate $500 billion in deficit reduction,[1] 'fairness' in taxation – meaning a minimal hit on the middle-class but including an energy tax of some sort, a generous EITC expansion and the creation of the empowerment zones, some measures to encourage job creating investment, and no more Medicare cuts than the $58 billion over five years in the Senate package (which was up from the $50 billion agreed by the House).

Following these general guidelines, the conference committee finally managed to report out a bill at the beginning of August which the administration could credibly claim was an evolution of its February starting point. The report saw most of the original tax raising proposals included in a recognizable form. Individual income tax rates on the wealthy went up as Clinton had demanded. The cap on the Medicare tax of 2.9 percent at $135,000 was removed. Wealthy social security recipients were to be taxed on more of their benefits.[2] The top marginal corporate income tax rate was raised, though to 35 percent rather than the 36 percent first mentioned. The BTU tax was replaced by the 4.3 cents per gallon gas tax and some of the EITC expansion cut back in Senate was restored. The empowerment zones were brought back in – although again with a smaller budget than the original bill had called for. Medicare cuts were set at $55.8 billion. The main area of sacrifice proved to be the tax break agenda Clinton had desired to promote investment. This had in fact been eroded at each stage of negotiation, as it had been overtaken by the deficit agenda and it proved easier to sacrifice it than to make specific further cuts in identifiable programes such as Medicare and Medicaid. In the end this compromise did do just enough to satisfy just enough Democrats that they should support the package and give their new President the chance to govern. Thus in two agonizing votes for the administration the House supported the package on August 5th by 218 to 216, and the next day the Senate approved, but once again only on the casting vote of Gore.

At the end of this saga, however, it was unclear what the consequences of victory in this budget battle would be. Few predicted that five years on, the President would be able to herald it, whether justifiably or not, as a key moment leading to sustained non-inflationary growth and balanced budgets. Even the administration made no such claims in the summer of 1993, accepting as 'fact' projections from all the established sources that the deficit would once again start to climb after 1997. At the political level, while the budget's passage had been vital for the administration, it was far from clear that it was to the medium-term benefit of the wider Democratic Party. Popular opinion seemed less than completely convinced of the merits of what eventually emerged. This was due, partially at least, to a concerted assault by the Republicans and other interested parties opposed to particular elements of the plan. That is, although sidelined in Washington, the GOP had been active outside the beltway in running down the whole project and, as the Democrats squabbled, the Republicans made political capital by portraying the plan as a reversion to 'tax and spend' type by the Democrats. Thus even before the conference report was settled, the Republican National Committee and the National Republican Congressional Committee had used radio attack advertisements in the states and districts of eight Senators and over forty House members who had voted in favour of the budget plan the first time around. Other groups, opposed to specific tax aspects of the plan, ranged from the American Energy Alliance, which spent over $1 million in its campaign against the BTU tax, to the National Restaurant Association, which objected to a cut in the deductions allowed for business meals (Novak, 1993b).

After the final vote, Republican leaders were quick to mock the outcome. Then House minority Whip Newt Gingrich declared that it would lead to a 'job-killing recession' and, playing a version of class politics of their own, they declared that the middle-class would be hit by the tax rises (Hager and Cloud, 1993d, p.2122). The White House denied this, insisting that less than 2 million of the nation's 115 million income tax payers would pay extra, but there was worrying evidence for the Democrats that the GOP had succeeded in shaping the popular perception of the tax hikes. A Gallup poll in August found that when asked, 'Who do you think is going to pay most of the taxes

in this plan – wealthy Americans or middle-income Americans?',
68 percent replied that middle-income earners were going to bear the
brunt. In contrast only 22 percent got the message that it was the rich
who were being squeezed the most.[3]

For the administration this aftermath to its efforts must have been
hard to swallow. With no support from the party of fiscal conservatism, Clinton had forced through a sizeable deficit reduction package
relying completely on Democrats, many of whom were unhappy at the
straightjacket they had imposed on themselves. The restrictive nature
of the budget was illustrated by the effective freeze on discretionary
spending set in place until fiscal 1998. This freeze, which had been relatively undisputed through the budget process, was on total spending
rather than on individual programs, but, given the difficulty in elimi-
nating or even making sizeable cuts in existing programs, it in effect
meant that there was little prospect of money being forthcoming to
fund any major new initiatives through discretionary spending during
the Clinton first term and beyond. The effect of this freeze was seen by
the end of 1993, as the administration planned its second budget to be
presented to Congress in February 1994. As Clinton and his team tried
to find more money to finance AIDS research and the Head Start program, they were forced into looking to cut the federal contribution to
mass transit subsidies, low-income heating assistance and other education programs – all traditional Democratic favourites – in order to com-
pensate (Novak, 1994). Thus to the White House the conservative
taunt, that the budget represented a return to old-time Democratic
spending excesses, must have been galling in its misrepresentation of
reality and distance from the truth.

In reality the 1993 budget did represent something different, at least
for a new President still with ambition to define the economic agenda
rather than simply react to it, as in aggregate it was a 'tax and cut'
package – hardly a recipe traditionally designed to ignite political
enthusiasm. For all the pain caused, however, by this attempt to do the
right thing as defined by Wall Street, Alan Greenspan and media elites
there was little political reward. In immediate terms of course the budget remained in deficit and therefore continued as a target for Republican criticism. As Dick Morris expressed it, 'There is no political
substitute for zero in the game of deficit reduction' (1997, p.159).
Furthermore, while the economy was turning around it did so only
slowly and not by enough to reap any rewards in the 1994 mid-
term elections. The irony was, however, that while Clinton gained little politically from his own efforts to better balance the books he was

able to exploit Republican efforts to do so to help resurrect his presidency.

2. Train wreck: the budget and the 104th Congress

As with almost every other aspect of political life, the groundrules of the budget process were re-written by the GOP's capture of Congress. The President's budget was now little more than a symbolic gesture but the overall budget process did offer the White House the opportunity to pit its wits against the newly Republican Congress and to try to win back some of the political initiative lost in November 1994. Furthermore, the administration's response to the Republican budget proposals was likely to be critical to the continuing evolution of Clintonism in general and Clintonomics in particular. The newly installed Republican majorities saw their task as being to oversee a major downsizing of government – and at the core of this project was the commitment to reshape the federal budget. It was in this context that Clinton had to decide whether to stand defiant in defence of the role of government and the value of public spending, or go with GOP flow and accept significant cuts to programs which Democrats had nurtured for many years and others which owed much to his personal initiative since he became President.

At first sight, the long-running struggle which developed between the White House and Congress over the plans for fiscal 1996 might suggest that Clinton chose the former path, but this would be to oversimplify. Through 1995, Congress and the White House reached an impasse over the budget with the President vetoing the overall budget reconciliation bill produced by Congress as well as some of the appropriations bills covering particular areas of discretionary domestic spending. This led to the commonly evoked image of a train-wreck with the very process of government threatening to come off the rails as many non-essential government services were shutdown because no money was authorized to fund them. The good news for Clinton was that clear majorities believed that Congress was the principal at-fault driver in this crisis, and the administration was particularly adept at exploiting popular fears that Medicare and Medicaid were likely to be serious casualties of the GOP's runaway spending cut train. On the other hand, the administration's own sense of direction was far from consistent and it is important in analyzing the budget wars between Clinton and the 104th Congress to tease out for separate evaluation the short-term political calculations and the longer-term consequences for budgetary policy. Thus although at times Clinton made a great show of refusing to go to the GOP's desired final destination and was prepared to countenance a crash, he did take some significant GOP-inspired detours on the journey.

Overall, as the wrangling continued into the spring of election year 1996, it became evident that the immediate *political* struggle, as measured by popular opinion, was clearly being won by the White House. Close analysis, however, suggests that while Clinton did stand by some important points of principle, and while the GOP were thwarted in their attempt to implement the Contract with America's blueprint, the broad *ideological* issue framework, as measured by substantial shifts in policy position, was determined as much by Congress as by the President. By the end of 1995 Clinton had agreed that the budget needed to be balanced; yet he continued to make political capital by denouncing the GOP's plans as unreasonable and extremist even as he edged towards their position.

The White House's budget, while it played little part in determining the year's budgetary outcomes, did provide the first salvo in the budget war and showed that the administration was willing to use the budget arena as a political battleground. The President was well aware that his budget plan would be effectively dead on arrival in Congress but, perversely, this potentially gave him some fiscal leeway, providing the opportunity to use the budget as a political tool rather than as a necessarily coherent and binding piece of economic policy. Thus Clinton came up with what he called 'the Middle Class Bill of Rights' which included proposals for a $500-per-child tax credit for children up to the age of 13 and a measure offering a $10,000 tax deduction for any college, university or vocational program. When asked why the administration had changed tack and offered a combination of tax cuts and only relatively limited new spending cuts Alice Rivlin, who had become OMB director, replied that the deficit was under sufficient control, but perhaps more tellingly acknowledged that there was frustration within the administration that 'we got no credit' for what had been done (Shear, 1995, p.359).

These proposals met with little enthusiasm in Congress. Republicans ridiculed the budget, while few Democrats made serious comment; and of those that did some of the more prominent were disappointed deficit hawks such as Senator Bill Bradley who admonished the President for fumbling the deficit football. As a piece of political maneuvering so soon after an electoral repudiation, however, Clinton's budget was modestly skilful. The GOP had promised both to make significant tax cuts and to balance the budget by 2002. If they were not, however, simply to repeat the fiscal ineptitude of the 1980s, this would require major cuts to existing programs. Clinton had given the Republicans no political cover for these cuts, leaving them to say where spending surgery could be carried out (Hager, 1995a). Furthermore, in calling for the various tax credits, Clinton had followed the GOP lead but with a distinctly populist slant allowing him to claim that his was a responsible tax cutting scheme targeted at middle-class families whose standard of living had remained stagnant even during the first two years of his presidency. The Republican proposals, in contrast, were portrayed as irresponsible and as of primary benefit to those who were already doing very well for themselves (Rubin, 1995a). This was thus an early example of the strategy of 'triangulation' at work. Clinton was not once again to be caught short by insisting on taking the high road of long-term policy planning in the short-term political hothouse. It was thus a sensible tactic to let the GOP leadership and the new congressional majorities, which were in any case filled with a fervour to transform, take the lead.

For the Republicans the 1994 elections were an endorsement of their attack on Big Government, and the aim of producing a balanced budget over seven years combined the virtue of fiscal prudence with an opportunity for government-bashing. It was always clear, however, that operationalizing this budget balancing, anti-government philosophy was going to be problematic; and the difficulties stemmed at least in part from the fact that the GOP, for all their rhetoric, were not prepared to downsize the biggest government benefits program of all – the so-called 'third rail in American politics' – Social Security. They also declared that there would be no further cuts in the defence budget. On top of this, interest payments on the national debt had to be paid. Unfortunately for the budget cutters these were the three biggest single items of government expenditure and together constituted over half of federal spending. Therefore, in order to get the numbers to balance, dramatic reductions were going to have to be found elsewhere. The problem was further exacerbated by the ideological insistence of some, particularly House freshmen, on delivering a sizeable tax cut. Speaker Gingrich was having no backtracking, and so, despite having admitted that there was no logic to the choice of 2002 as the year for balance, he insisted that the GOP leaders in the House would produce a plan to reach budget balance by that date (Hager, 1995b). Not surprisingly, hitting the numbers produced dispute within GOP ranks and a protracted process, but to general Democratic surprise both House and Senate did come up with budget resolutions which were arithmetically credible.

It was, however, the details of these plans, and particularly the manner in which they aimed to curb health care spending, that at last gave the Democrats a common theme, as they attacked the scope of the cuts and accused the GOP leaders of trying to fund tax breaks for the rich by slashing away at programs for the vulnerable and middle-class, especially Medicare – a Big Government program not too far behind Social Security in public affection (Rubin, 1995b). The other stand-out feature of the GOP plans was a proposed complete structural overhaul of Medicaid. These suggestions provided the Democrats with an easy target, and defending health care programs happily combined principle with good politics.

Ironically, however, at the same time as the White House turned up the rhetorical volume it trimmed its own wings and moved ever closer towards the GOP's position. Thus in mid-June, Clinton embraced the concept of a balanced budget plan but insisted that this be done over a ten year rather than seven year period. This announcement infuriated liberal Democrat House member David Obey from Wisconsin who remarked, 'Most of us learned some time ago that if you don't like the president's position on a particular issue, you simply need to wait a few weeks' (Hager, 1995c, p.1715). Republicans were equally unamused, accusing Clinton of playing with the numbers, particularly as his calculations were based on economic forecasts from the OMB which envisioned a much more optimistic scenario, thus requiring less spending cuts, than the CBO which was the source for the Republican leadership's predictions (Hager and Rubin, 1995a).[4]

In their frustration, the Republican leadership decided to take Clinton on earlier than anticipated by attaching provisions to a stopgap funding bill which Clinton had already declared unacceptable (Hager and Rubin, 1995b). This prompted a veto and the first government shutdown. The shutdown began on 14 November and lasted six days with around 800,000 government workers furloughed. After this the rhetoric became more barbed, even as Clinton took further steps towards the GOP's starting position. On 6 December Clinton vetoed the Republicans' full balanced budget package which led to the second shutdown affecting nearly 250,000 workers and lasting for 21 days; yet at the same time he put forward his own version of a balanced budget plan over a seven year period. The GOP's response was to accuse Clinton of acting in bad faith by continuing to use more optimistic forecasts.

The critical jury in this battle were the voters, and while it would seem unlikely that the public were happy with either the executive or the legislature, opinion polls showed that significant majorities thought that the Republicans in Congress were more responsible than the Democrat in the White House. An ABC–Washington Post poll in January 1996 found that 50 percent of respondents blamed the GOP against 27 percent blaming the President.[5] Media coverage focused on government workers who could not pay their mortgages and Clinton was very aware of the need to make it look like the GOP's decision to enforce the shutdown. In his 1996 State of the Union address he introduced a government employee from Oklahoma City who had been involved in the rescue effort after the April bombing who had not been paid due to the shutdown (Hershey, 1997, p.213).

Overall then Clinton's triangulation strategy had paid off, reviving his presidency and inflicting what turned out to be permanent damage on Newt Gingrich. Clinton got the credit for being willing to deal with the deficit in a moderate manner. This credit would have been much more deserved in 1993, but it came only when Clinton was able to play himself off against the perceived extremism of Gingrich. What was more confusing, and perhaps more fundamental, was quite what Clinton's actions said about his attitude towards the government programs threatened by the Republicans. Certainly there were areas of significant principle where Clinton was not prepared to give way; for example, Clinton had no truck with the GOP plans to turn Medicaid into a state run block grant program. The White House insisted that Medicaid would remain a federal entitlement. Furthermore, while the administration agreed to some cuts in Medicare, it would not countenance the scale of reductions proposed by the Republicans. In addition, while the administration did try to create some room for tax cuts, these never approached the levels demanded by the GOP. On the other hand, Clinton's position by the end of the year was quite different from where he started it. The degree to which he, and it should be said many congressional Democrats, had shifted and come to embrace at least the concept of budget balance was obscured by the fact of the shutdowns and the heat of the rhetoric surrounding these, but in hindsight, the distance that Clinton traveled is more evident than it was at the time. As Pierson notes, 'Against the backdrop of anything other than the Republicans'...proposals, this...represented a fundamental shift in policy, implying deep cuts in public spending' (1998, p.165). So Clinton made political capital by appearing to stand up for programs at the same time as agreeing to scale them back. This behaviour was evidenced again in the next budget setpiece in 1997 when the White House and Republican leadership did reach agreement on a plan to secure balance by 2002.

3. 1997: Balanced budget

In August 1997 Clinton signed two bills, the Balanced Budget Act and the Taxpayer Relief Act, which laid out a program of both spending and tax cuts leading to a balanced budget by 2002. Two key reasons accounted for the ability of the two sides to reach agreement this time around. First, in political terms the primary factor was the intervening election. The fact that divided government was now the result of the same election cycle meant that neither side could really claim a mandate over the other. Second, in fiscal terms the task of reaching balance was eased considerably by the changed, and significantly improved, budgetary situation. That is, as a result of better than expected economic growth, government's revenues had gone up and its projected expenditures had gone down. Thus the meeting of minds was able to take place on friendlier terrain. This helped the first substantial agreement emerge in early May on the shape of the budget resolution (Hager, 1997b). This, however, only gave the broad outline, and there was some further turmoil as the actual details were filled into the spending and tax reconciliation bills (Taylor, 1997).

On the Democratic side the focal point of opposition was House Minority Leader Dick Gephardt. His complaint echoed the Democratic rallying cry of the 1995 saga – that services were being cut in order to finance a tax cut for the rich. At this time it was widely thought that Gephardt was a likely contender for the 2000 Democratic nomination and it was thus assumed that part of his personal strategy was to distance himself from the White House, and Al Gore in particular, while appealing to the Democratic Party's base (Koszszuk, 1997a; 1997b). In truth, though, the very fact that the White House was bargaining with GOP leadership illustrated that this deal was not being constructed around the party's liberal wing. Obviously Clinton did not want to drive a wedge between the administration and a major congressional player, but equally there was no chance of a bipartisan agreement on Gephardt's terms, and such an agreement was the priority. As negotiations progressed, there were moments when it looked as if the deal might fall apart (Hook, 1997), but in the end the final margins were overwhelming in both chambers. The spending portion of the reconciliation bill passed by 346 to 85 in the House and by 85 to 15 in Senate, while the tax portion went through by margins of 389 to 43 and 92 to 8.

Thus, few Democrats resisted, even though the deal was clearly more conservative than any of the other packages drawn up in the 1990s (McGrory, 1997; Pierson, 1998). For example, the tax cuts agreed included two conservative favourites; first, a reduction in the rate of capital gains tax from 28 to 20 percent, and second, an increase in the estate tax exemption from $600,000 to one million dollars. A $500-per-child tax credit was also introduced, although Clinton did succeed in focusing this on the middle class rather than the wealthy (Elving and Taylor, 1997). Further to the income bias of the tax cuts, there was little elsewhere that was redistributive about the plan. That is, unlike in 1993 there was no expansion of the EITC to ease the pain for the least well-off caused by cuts in programs serving their needs; and while there were some new education initiatives, the spending on these was geared mainly to appease the middle class. Overall the spending cuts totaled $263 billion over five years, including a reduction of $115 billion in estimated Medicare spending with further caps imposed on discretionary spending in the long-term. On the plus side for Democrats, $24 billion was set aside for extending health care coverage for the children of low-income uninsured parents, although initially this owed more to the efforts of Senators Kennedy, Daschle and Republican Orrin Hatch than to the White House.

For all these numbers, however, in the aftermath of this deal there was general agreement amongst budget experts that this was a relatively minor piece of the puzzle compared to the efforts of 1990 and 1993, which of course congressional Republicans had opposed because the measures increased taxes (Broder, 1997a).

Freeing up trade: a cause of Democratic angst

As the reviews of the Clinton administration gather, there is a consensus that one area where he did show strong and consistent leadership was in promoting a free trade agenda (Nitschke with Tully, 2000; Kessler, 2000). While, however, the administration did aggressively push for trade liberalization, it constantly did so against the wishes of a majority of congressional Democrats. Indeed, perhaps more than any other single area of policy, the disputes within party ranks over trade issues revealed a division between New and old Democrats which remained unresolved at the end of Clinton's presidency. There was not a simple split in congressional voting because many were influenced and pressured as much by local concerns as national ideological ones (Avery, 1998), but differences in attitude between either welcoming or mistrusting easier conditions of trade marked a significant division. Moreover, the line-up of economic interest groups tells much of the story with the voice of organized labor, with its ties mostly to old-style Democrats, consistently opposed to the administration's efforts. The

White House, on the other hand, was happy to take heed of the New Democrat insistence on a more pro-business approach and thus lined up alongside the big corporations. From a New Democrat perspective the division was forcibly expressed by a PPI senior fellow, Joel Klotkin, writing at the end of 1993.

> Our opponents in the party are often identified as liberals. In reality, they are as reactionary as Republicans. They simply seek to preserve a different version of the past.
>
> This is clearest in economic terms. Liberal Democrats to a large extent reflect the forces of the old economy...
>
> ...they want to turn the clock back to the 1950s when America's economy...could more or less go its own way...They ignore the fact that our economy is increasingly linked with the global economy; in 1960 only 8 percent of our national income was tied to the international trade system; today that figure is roughly 25 percent (1993, p.26).

The alternative case has often been argued by Jeff Faux, based at the liberal Economic Policy Institute, who maintains that the real danger of globalization is the manner in which it declares itself to be an inevitable process against which resistance is futile.

> The expansion of international competitive forces has narrowed the domestic economic debate in America...The question of what economic policies best support social progress has faded before insistent demands for reducing private sector costs. The values of social solidarity are under attack. The public sector itself is more and more held in contempt as a drag on national competitiveness (1995, p.x).

These contrasting views came into stark conflict in the first year of Clinton's presidency when he called on Congress to ratify NAFTA, which extended the free trade agreement already existing between the US and Canada to include Mexico.

1. NAFTA

As with the economic plan, the media portrayed the vote on NAFTA as a 'win or bust' one for the administration, and the expectation was of another close run thing, particularly in the House. In the end, the agreement was approved in mid-November by the seemingly comfortable majorities of 234 to 200 votes in the House and 61 to 38 in Senate;

but these winning margins do not tell the whole story. Most immediately, the President had to rely heavily on *Republican* members, as deep divisions were manifested within the Democratic Party (the House tally of 234 'Yes' votes included 132 from the GOP).

The irreconcilable arguments within Democratic ranks over NAFTA reflected quite different and competing views on the best way forward for the American economy in an era of increasing trade globalization. The trade pact was designed to eliminate all tariffs on goods produced and sold in the US, Canada and Mexico from the beginning of 1994. Not all tariffs would be removed immediately, but the vast majority would within a ten year spell, with a few remaining for fifteen years. The agreement also stipulated that there could be no discrimination against investors from the other countries. There was little consensus, however, on what the costs and benefits of these changes would be for the US economy. The 'yes' camp insisted that the lowering of trade barriers would create a 'win–win' situation; that is, in the long-term it would result in a positive-sum game in which both the US and Mexican economies would benefit. The 'no' camp, while agreeing that the easing of trade restrictions might lead to improved corporate profits on both sides of the border, emphasized that this might well not be to the benefit of the ordinary worker.

At the forefront of the opposition were the unions who argued that the pact would cost American jobs as employers based in the US went south to Mexico in order to profit from the lower wage costs. Attached to this was the fear that even if jobs were not lost directly, there would be a depression of American wages due to an unchecked influx of cheap Mexican imports which would force employers in the US to seek any means to reduce their costs. In addition, environmentalists, like organized labor a part of the old Democratic coalition, argued that American businesses would relocate because of the laxer environmental regulations in Mexico or call for an easing of regulations in the US to level the playing field. On the other side, the administration and other champions of NAFTA maintained that the agreement would create jobs by opening up the Mexican market with all its potential for rapid expansion. Supporters further argued that the environmental lobby ignored both the commitment of the US and Mexican governments to cleaning up the border between the two countries and also that an improvement in Mexican living standards, generated by NAFTA, would lead to a reduction in the country's sanitation hazards.

Important though this set of proposals was in itself, the passion generated by arguments over the pros and cons of NAFTA, and particularly the extra emotional edge which was evident among opponents, was fueled by the still uncertain state of the economy in 1993. Economic statistics might have suggested an economy in recovery but this was not yet a job-creating recovery and nor was it one which had begun to raise the living standards of the majority of the population. For many of those who already felt themselves to be losing out as a result of the process of economic transition, the prospect of intensifying competition with a low-wage economy and making it easier for businesses 'which had shown little compassion for their workers through the downsizing of the 1980s' to relocate there was not an enticing one. In short, NAFTA really brought to life and gave form to the deep-seated worries about the stagnation, and for many the decline, of living standards which had taken place over the previous twenty years.

For Clinton, trying to make the argument that freeing up trade was in fact a way to reverse this process of stagnation, the big macro-economic considerations were complicated by micro-politics – with some of the damage self-inflicted. Support of NAFTA *was* consistent with his long-term ideological development. He was by nature a free-trader, and advocacy of this position was certainly part of his claim to be espousing a New Democrat outlook. On the other hand, he knew that many in his party took a much more protectionist stance, and when President Bush announced the completion of the NAFTA negotiations in August 1992, candidate Clinton was circumspect, saying that he would need time to study the deal before making a commitment to it. Eventually, in early October, Clinton made a tepid endorsement of NAFTA but emphasized that he would be keen to see some side-agreements added to the body of the text which would allay the fears of labor and environmental groups (Cloud, 1992). While, however, this straddling of the issue may have made good sense to candidate Clinton, it did not serve him well in the long-run as it encouraged the idea that there was something wrong with NAFTA which he was going to do something about.[6] Significant change, however, was always most unlikely. The main body of the text could not be amended unless all parties agreed to renegotiation. This would in effect mean starting from scratch which neither the Mexican nor Canadian governments wanted. Thus the most that could be done would be to add some supplemental clauses, perhaps eking out some protection for particular industries against the impact of the free trade zone.

In fact as President, Clinton's first NAFTA imperative was to delay debate on the issue so as not to confuse the partisan politics of the budget plan with the cross-cutting politics of NAFTA. Since it was clear that some of those Democrats who were loyalist on the budget were going to break ranks on NAFTA, it was important for the administration that the budget and trade be seen as independent elements, to be dealt with separately, rather than as co-equal parts of an overall economic package. The administration did manage to get Congress to think about the budget and economic plan before turning its collective mind to trade, which was critical for legislative success, but it clearly meant that Clinton's encompassing vision of economic strategy was not shared by the majority of either congressional party. This meant that when the budget was passed, Clinton was well aware that the Democrats-only strategy which had just carried the day could not be repeated on NAFTA. Thus he was faced with the task of building up a comprehensive economic program on the back of quite different political, and hence Congressional, coalitions. The inherent difficulties involved in having to operate in this manner were further exacerbated with respect to the NAFTA debate by opinion polls showing that slight majorities of the public opposed the measure.[7] Indeed for a period some of his New Democrat advisers worried that this combination of factors was leading Clinton to second-guess his position.[8]

One complicating dynamic in the build-up to the vote was that many Democrats, under strong but conflicting pressures, held back from taking a definitive position until as late as possible (Box-Steffensmeier et al., 1997). One person whose attitude was assumed to be critical was Gephardt, as the Democratic House leadership was already split with Speaker Tom Foley from Washington behind NAFTA but with the Majority Whip, David Bonior from Michigan, a strident opponent (Germond and Witcover, 1993b). Gephardt had established a reputation as a tough talker on trade issues and his scepticism about the Bush negotiated deal was well known. Through the early summer Gephardt said little as the administration negotiated its supplemental side-agreements, but in late September he announced that these did not do enough to correct the flaws in the overall package. With deep splits within Democratic ranks inevitable, the administration did try to win over as many waverers as possible by launching into a sustained lobbying and bargaining blitz (Cloud, 1993b; Drew, 1994, pp.338–54; Livingston and Wink, 1997).

As with the budget battle, the political aftermath of the NAFTA battle was confusing. The overall alignment of political forces which emerged during the debate, pitting the administration, Republican leaders, and business executives against 'unlikely alliances of opponents' ranging from 'farmers worried about imports of Canadian wheat and afraid of new competition from Mexican sugar to workers who see their jobs being exported to Mexico to supporters of Ross Perot' had little long-term future in the broader political and economic framework (Stokes, 1993, p.2472); but their very incoherence demonstrated that implementing New Democrat ideas had not established any new political order. Furthermore, it was evident that however much the administration and business tried to define its opponents as fighting a cause already lost, the real passion was on the side of the anti-NAFTA coalition. This strength of feeling was captured by Bonior's emotive last ditch appeal to his party colleagues in the final House debate on the measure. He implored them to reject the agreement and demanded to know of them, 'If we don't stand up for the working people in this country, who will?' (Cloud, 1993c, p.3177).

Clinton, on the other hand, heralded the vote and said that 1993 would 'go down in the history books as a watershed for trade liberalization', with NAFTA ratification accompanied by the completion of the Uruguay round of the General Agreement on Tariffs and Trade and the beginning of negotiations with East Asian and Pacific Rim countries about establishing yet another free trade zone. The administration insisted that expanding exports was vital to creating 'the kind of high-wage, high skill jobs the country needs' (Clinton, 1994, p.6). The fact that the administration won the NAFTA battle, however, did not mean that the free trade wars were over in the party.

As it was, the next potential struggle never really materialized since the Uruguay Round of GATT was ratified relatively painlessly in a lame duck session of Congress just after the 1994 elections. This certified the formation of the World Trade Organization and overall 'reduced a record number of trade barriers and included a record number of countries' (Destler, 1999, p.75). Outside Congress the usual suspects, including labor unions, environmental groups, and figures as diverse as Ralph Nader, Ross Perot and Pat Buchannan, rallied against the GATT pact; but on Capitol Hill there was little of the sound and fury which had surrounded NAFTA, with even Gephardt onboard for the administration (Benenson, 1994a, 1994b).

2. Fast track

The issue of fast track authorization, however, showed that many Democrats were far from reconciled to the globalization agenda. The so-called fast track procedure was one by which Congress agreed to limit its own capacity to intervene in the detail of trade negotiations between the US and other countries. Fast track represented an acknowledgement that if Congress were to sift through all the items of trade pacts signed by the President before ratifying them then the process might be never ending. Through granting fast track authority to the White House, therefore, Congress agreed that it would vote only on whether or not to approve the whole of a final trade package presented to it. In other words, Congress could assent to or veto a trade agreement negotiated by the President, but could not amend it. Fast track authority was first extended to the White House in 1974 and subsequently renewed five times. The administration's intention was to ask for renewal of fast track along with GATT ratification but decided against this in order to ensure the smooth passage of GATT.

After this the White House struggled to find a form of words which it could include in a further extension of fast track which would placate unions and environmentalists without upsetting business. The problem was that, while the former group demanded clauses which referred to protecting the environment and enhancing labor standards, the potential inclusion of such provisions sparked business opposition. In the end Clinton finally opted to push for fast track in the fall of 1997 without these types of qualifications, which immediately meant that many Democrats would resist. Through the summer and fall of 1997 both business and labor lobbied intensively (Neal, 1997), and the DLC threw its weight behind the quest for re-authorization (From, 1997b). When it became apparent that up to 80 percent of House Democrats would oppose the administration, however, Clinton opted to pull his request (Harris, 1997). A year later Newt Gingrich in fact pushed the issue onto the floor in order to illustrate Democratic divisions in the build-up to the 1998 mid-terms. The motion failed by 243 votes to 180, with only 29 Democrats in favour (Destler, 1999, pp.76–81).

3. Trade with China

The next trade topic to pit the administration against the House Democratic leadership was the question of whether to grant China permanent normal trading relation (NTR) status. The issue arose after a deal struck in November 1999 between the Chinese government and US Trade Representative Charlene Barshefsky. This agreed that the US would support Chinese entry into the WTO in return for China opening up its market to American companies. Congressional consent was not needed for China to join the WTO, but if US business was to get the best from the deal, then it needed to be sure of China's permanent NTR status rather than be hampered by the existing arrangement which demanded annual reauthorization (Nitschke, 1999). It was immediately

clear that many Democrats would be opposed to such a change in policy, especially as trade issues with China were complicated by human
rights concerns. Business, on the other hand, quickly stated its support for
the agreement and its intention to lobby Congress hard (McCutcheon
and Nitschke, 1999).

As with all these trade stand-offs, the real concern for the White
House was what would happen in the House. The vote on making permanent China's NTR standing took place there in late May 2000, with
Clinton working alongside the Republican leadership to ensure passage.
In the end the vote went Clinton's way by 237 to 197, with Democrats
splitting 138 to 73 against amidst clear signs of an old versus New division. Prominent New Democrat, James Moran from Virginia, thought
the result an encouraging sign 'that when we put our minds to it, we
can govern from the center out' (Nitschke with Tully, 2000, p.1252).
Opponents were frustrated but insisted that the size of the 'no' vote
showed that there were continuing and unresolved concerns about the
manner of globalization. The Senate vote did not take place until September. There were some worries (or hopes) that Senate might amend
the House version which would mean that the matter would have to
go back to the House, but in the end this did not happen and the
vote was 83 to 15 in favour – with eight of the 'no' votes in fact coming from Republicans. The pressures from outside Congress were
revealing. Big business spent millions on lobbying, with the high technology sector in particular beginning to exercise its political muscle
(Nitschke, 2000). The unions, on the other hand, while determined in
their opposition were less threatening towards straying Democrats than
they had been after the NAFTA vote – as they concentrated their energies on recapturing Congress in the 2000 elections (Foerstel, 2000).

Conclusion

In its original form the economic program advanced by Clinton in
1993 was an attempt to craft an agenda reflecting the various concerns
of his party. The ill-fated stimulus package (discussed in the next chapter), with its neo-New Deal/neo-Keynesian approach, appealed to liberals, while the budget, with its overall deficit reduction yet targeted
investments, drew praise from New Democrat sources. PPI economist,
Robert Shapiro, for example, noted, 'In submitting his new economic
program, President Clinton has passed his first test of presidential character. A subtle, New Democrat vision provides much of the program's
basic architecture' (1993, p.8). As it was, however, the stimulus fell by

the wayside, and then the actions of New Democrat types in the Senate disrupted the attempt at a policy symmetry within the budget as the investment elements of the package were either eliminated or watered-down. Once the debate was set up as a conflict between hitting the deficit reduction targets or keeping the investments, the latter came to play second-fiddle. Overall then, there was a conservative shift in the balance of the economic program which, in turn, had longer term ideological implications with which the administration, as manifested by subsequent budget dealings, ultimately seemed content.

The White House's consistent support for freeing up trade was an important demonstration of its capacity to step outside of the traditional Democratic fold in terms of both policy direction and political coalition building, but it would surely have been better for Clinton if he had managed to persuade more within the party to sign on as 'different types of Democrat' seven years on. One aspect of the free trade debate was the manner in which it was implied that opponents were little more than commercial Luddites (Glassman, 1997); but Gephardt, Bonior et al. did not see themselves as the reactionaries in the battle over globalization and they clearly resented the notion that they were swimming against the tide of history. What is interesting is that the choice was framed as a clear-cut one – there was no room for a third way on free trade. This, however, was not necessarily so. The administration could have adopted a strategy which would have championed free trade while at least attempting to insert clauses in trade agreements which referred to workers' rights in both the US and its trading partners.[9] Indeed, as Dionne notes, this could have served the dual purpose of pursuing free trade while creating a distance between Democrats and Republicans on the issue, to the former's advantage.

> By embracing open trade linked with real social protections, Clinton could give himself a cause and the legacy he keeps ruminating about. He would give Americans something to chew on: not protectionism vs. free trade but free trade with equity vs. free trade without rules (Dionne, 1997a, p.A27).

This may have been how Clinton would have liked to proceed (Destler, 1999, p.79), but it was not the course the administration chose to adopt when subjected to corporate pressure.

Thus on both fiscal and trade policy the divisions between New and old Democrats were consistently apparent, making it manifest that Clinton's overall vision of economic development was not shared by all within his own party. It is important to understand, however, that Clinton and the New Democrats insisted that there was significantly more to their 'Third Way' in economic thinking than simply deficit reduction and free trade. Principally the administration claimed that, despite its emphasis on fiscal responsibility, it did find sufficient funding to implement the third leg of its agenda which was a strategy of investment to privilege those Americans left out of the Reaganomics prosperity. Implicit in this was some homage to a more traditional Democrat program of mild redistribution of the rewards of economic growth, although it was clear that this would preferably be achieved through indirect means. The next chapter will take up this story and offer some conclusions about the overall political sense of Clintonomics.

4
Clintonomics II: Leveling the Playing Field?

In its first annual report Clinton's Council of Economic Advisers reflected on the combined impact of shifts in the nature of the economy and the public policies pursued by the Reagan and Bush administrations. 'In concert, the market and the government produced the greatest disequalization of incomes since at least before World War II.' It continued

> This Administration sees the combination of stagnating average incomes and rising inequality as a threat to the social fabric that has long bound Americans together and made ours a society with minimal class distinctions. Although the underlying forces of the market are vastly more powerful than anything the government can do, the right kinds of policies can make a difference (Council of Economic Advisers, 1994, p.26).

This statement, with its reference to the 'underlying forces of the market', constituted a stark acknowledgement of how the Clinton economic team saw its room for maneuver limited by pressures it felt that it could not control; and in prioritizing 'responsible fiscal management' and free trade, the administration quickly signalled that it was not going to battle against the conventional wisdom as defined by the dominant bastions of the business community. On the other hand, it did express a willingness to use public policy tools at least to engage in some skirmishes on the fringes in an effort to do something to redress the imbalances which had been integral to American economic development through the Reagan-Bush era. The weapons to be used were expanded investment in human capital and changes to 'make work pay' for those at the bottom end of the income scale. When translated into policy this meant exploring a number of different avenues. In the long-term the administration put its faith and its intellectual stock in the idea that the best way of tackling inequality is through education and training to level the playing field by equalizing opportunity. More immediately the aim was to pacify organized labor's anger over trade liberalization by extending government help in the redeployment of workers displaced by foreign competition. The primary method of increasing the rewards of low wage work was to be EITC expansion.

It was in these aspects then that Clintonomics intended to remedy the harm done to many Americans by the transformed nature of the economy since the prime of the New Deal era. Thus, while Clinton and the New Democrats bowed to the conventional wisdom by accepting that nothing could, or should, be done to reverse the tide of the 'new economy', there was still assumed to be incumbent upon government some responsibility to help those tossed around by the rougher waves of these seas. In other words, it was acknowledged that there was a downside to the generally beneficial phenomena of globalization and what might be termed technologization for some of those who had been secure in the old economy; and there was an appreciation that workers caught in this trap deserved assistance in retraining and re-skilling so that they could re-engage with work without slipping too far down the economic ladder.

Robert Reich, writing about how this gave a distinctive dimension to Third Way thinking, explained the rationale in the following manner.

> It's a win–win catechism: governments should not try to block change. They should not protect or subsidize old jobs in old industries or keep unemployed people on the dole. Instead, governments should embrace economic change, but – and here's the sharp break from Reagan and Thatcher – they should do it in a way that enables everyone to change along with the economy (1999, p.48).

Certainly, taken together and at face value, the public commitments to improving and expanding access to education, to retraining and to increasing the take home pay of lower wage workers represented the 'opportunity' side to New Democrat and Third Way policies. In this context, while the deficit reduction and trade liberalization strategies fitted comfortably with the prevailing economic wisdom as developed through the 1980s, the investment strategy was a more liberal call to arms. It did still, however, reflect a limited policy framework inasmuch as the human capital approach was a supply-side model which would provide workers with skills, but not actual jobs. On the other hand, one of the administration's first actions was to propose a stimulus package, which in principle if not scale, did echo earlier Democratic eras.

A flirtation with demand-side: the stimulus package

The 1960s and 1970s had seen a number of government led employment initiatives, notably the Manpower Development and Training Act, the Economic Opportunity Act and the Comprehensive Employment and Training Act. These had involved increasing sums of government funding but had resulted in uncertain economic benefit and diminishing political returns (Mucciaroni, 1990). Whatever their flaws, however, they did represent a government commitment to intervene directly to help the least well-off. After its enactment in 1973, CETA in particular, increasingly functioned as a public service employment programme providing, at its peak, '739,000 public service jobs' accounting for '12 percent of unemployed workers' (Weir, 1998, p.271). Indeed at the time of its reauthorization in 1978, changes were made which were 'clearly designed for the economically disadvantaged' and which reflected 'a clear and, in principle, measurable objective ... to increase the earned income of those who participated' (Franklin and Ripley, 1984, p.20). Overall CETA expenditures came to over 55 billion dollars before it was eliminated in 1981 (p.22). The program's existence was always mired in controversy as it was often deemed disorganized and wasteful, but its demise was not just a reflection of these concerns but also of the fundamental ideological hostility of the Reagan administration to this type of government intervention.

The point about these programs is not that they were unequivocally successful, far from it, but that they represented a belief in both the economic need for and the social worth of government policies consciously designed to remedy the unequal outcomes produced by the free market. Such beliefs became increasingly unfashionable, however, through the 1980s and, in addition to ending the flagship CETA program, the Reagan administration also oversaw the decline of other benefit and training programs. Margaret Weir highlights the impact of tightened regulations which reduced eligibility for unemployment benefit and for what was known as trade adjustment assistance (TAA), a benefit which aided workers displaced by new or an expanded volume of imports arriving as a result of new trade agreements. 'The nadir was reached in 1984, when only 28.5 percent of the unemployed received unemployment insurance, and trade assistance spending had been cut by 97 percent' (Weir, 1998, p.272). By the time Clinton came to office, 'government had few active policies to assist workers in adjusting to economic change or to reduce growing economic inequalities. Labor market policies remained either passive or remedial' (p.273).

Clinton, of course, had never proposed a reinvention of Keynesian spending policies but the campaign rhetoric had promised immediate action to reduce unemployment. Once in office, one of Clinton's first major initiatives was to try to make good on this promise by pressing for a spending bill which was almost Keynesian in design, if not in scope. The plan, which was to appropriate an extra $16.3 billion in 1993 and also to spend $3.2 billion more from the transportation trust funds, was advanced for immediate congressional consideration.[1] The influence of the deficit hawks ensured that this was downsized from the response to the unemployment problem implied in the campaign. Nevertheless, pressure from figures such as Robert Reich and the political aides, notably George Stephanopoulos, Paul Begala and James Carville, who felt that to renege on the promise of job creation would offend too much of the Democrat constituency, secured some action. Clinton insisted that even the scaled down plan gave 'the chance here to create half a million new jobs and do things that are good that need to be done' (Woodward, 1994, p.157). More specifically Panetta maintained that the new spending would directly fund 200,000 permanent new jobs and 150,000 summer jobs, with a further 150,000 jobs being indirectly created. In the faintest echo of the New Deal's public works programs, the majority of the jobs to be directly created were in construction, with the indirectly funded jobs arising from proposed new spending in a variety of areas including health, education and aid to the homeless. The comparison to New Deal style efforts should not be overstated. The money proposed in 1993 was enough only to repair and improve existing infrastructure – it was certainly not enough to fund fresh projects. It was, however, a recognition of the plight of the construction industry with its unemployment rate of 14.3 percent in January 1993 compared with the overall rate of 7.1 percent (Healey, 1993a). The bill also included $4 billion for unemployment benefits.

Republicans, however, were immediately on the attack, declaring that the bill contained too much pork. Perhaps even more ominous was the guarded response from some Democrats. For example, Senator Boren warned

> It would send the wrong message to the country ... If the first thing they see us do is pass a stimulus package, it's going to destroy our

credibility. A lot of us will be extremely uncomfortable with voting more money for anything before we lock in deficit reduction (quoted in Woodward, 1994, p.150).

In the House the bill in fact passed comfortably with 'only' 22 Democrats breaking ranks. It was always clear, however, that getting the bill through Senate was going to be more problematic and in the end the stimulus package's undoing was Clinton's failure to bring any moderate Republicans onboard. Rallied by Senate Minority Leader Bob Dole, the Republicans launched a filibuster which neither the Democratic leadership in Senate nor the White House could break.

In some ways Clinton was a victim of his own rhetoric. Republican obstructionism in Senate, at a time when the President might have expected to still have some political mileage left through the 'honeymoon' factor, was made easier to defend by the fact that opponents of the stimulus bill could almost claim to be protecting the President from himself. That is, the stimulus spending was easily portrayed as being inconsistent with the administration's insistence that it was determined to bring down the deficit. In fact the size of the package meant that its contribution to the deficit would have been minimal and it was perfectly intellectually consistent to maintain that in the long-term the economic boost which would have resulted from the stimulus bill would have generated the extra revenues needed to bring down the deficit, but the White House never made this case with any great conviction. At one point, in an effort to place pressure on the Republicans, Clinton did stress the importance of providing employment as he protested against Republican tactics by declaring, 'The Senate's got a swimming pool, doesn't it? Doesn't it? And it was built with taxpayers' money, and somebody worked, somebody had a job building it' (Healey, 1993b, p.909). This appeal to the old-time New Deal philosophy cut little ice with Republicans however – indeed it probably aggravated them. They retorted that the bill was simply a reversion to type by a Democrat President who was using public money to buy off Democrat special interest groups.

The irony was that what once might have traditionally been seen as the more populist part of Clinton's agenda was washed away by the insistence that he concentrate on the more austere element. The message did not get across that this was spending designed to fulfil the growth part of the economic equation. For liberals this was especially frustrating because, while opinion polls found little support for increasing public spending, they also showed pluralities who thought that job creation to deal with unemployment was a higher economic priority than deficit reduction.[2] After the demise of the stimulus bill there was no further effort at such direct demand-side economic intervention to create work. Instead the emphasis switched to a supply-side strategy to prepare and improve people's capacity to compete for the better jobs, and to ensure that less skilled work was more adequately rewarded in order to guarantee proper incentives to participate in the labor force.

Increasing investment and expanding opportunity

The demise of the stimulus bill was a disappointment to the administration but was probably of more political than economic significance because, even if it made good policy sense, spending $16 billion was not going to fast forward the recovery dramatically. In political terms, however, the proposal had encouraged important parts of the core Democrat constituency who were anxious that Clinton quickly demonstrate that deficit reduction was not the administration's sole concern. In crude terms then, the stimulus was an appeal to liberals. New Democrats were keener on education, training and work incentives; yet, even the pursuit of this agenda was quickly undercut by the rationale of fiscal conservatism.

The difficulty for the White House was making the case that increasing funding in some instances was compatible with the goal of overall deficit reduction. Implicit in the 1993 budget was that a distinction should be drawn between investment and current spending. This could have been done formally by establishing a capital budget which would have flagged up the intent to pursue long-term goals and may also have 'reframed the deficit issue, calling into question the apocalyptic scenarios associated with government borrowing' (Pierson, 1998, p.147). The new President, though, did not seriously consider this device and was unable even persuasively to articulate the value of his own proposals which implied that investment would lead to economic growth which would lead to a higher government revenues thus reducing the deficit. In a world of political soundbites this was a complex argument to make, and the prevalent atmosphere remained one in which any new outlays were seen only in the immediate context of a zero-sum game between spending and deficit reduction. This, inevitably, restricted the possibilities of the investment strategy effectively imposing a 'pay-as-you-go' modus operandi. Nevertheless, the administration was always keen to stress its investment successes and the importance of these to its overall economic vision.

Education: creating a level playing field

All politicians come to office promising to improve the national education system. For Clinton, however, actually delivering on this promise was critical if his administration was to fulfil its Third Way vision. That is, one of the more consistent mantras of those claiming to champion the Third Way is to point to education as an effective, and in the long-term *the most effective*, means of promoting human capital investment. This emphasis is so pronounced because educational reform serves the purpose of both equalising economic opportunity for individuals while at the same time promoting the state's own interests by providing a better educated workforce which will spur on the new economy. Candidate Clinton put it this way, 'Putting people first demands a revolution in lifetime learning because education today is more than the key to climbing the ladder of economic opportunity; it is an imperative for our nation' (Clinton and Gore, 1992, p.85). One of the key documents in the development of DLC thinking, *The New Progressive Declaration*, declared that 'knowledge is the new wealth of nations' and it called upon 'government' to 'be a catalyst for a new public educational system that will be the foundation of equal economic opportunity in today's world as well as a necessary condition for our nation's continued economic and political leadership in the 21st century' (Marshall et al., 1996, p.14).

For all this grand rhetoric, however, the nature of the American education system means that the scope for federal government to organize a fundamental restructuring is limited, even if there is the political will to do so, as 90 percent of funding for schools is provided at state and local level. Nevertheless, Clinton did come to office with a commitment to expand educational opportunity from pre-school to college. This was an area where he came with some form from his days as Governor of Arkansas where he had made education reform a priority and had, in the process, demonstrated that he was not afraid to face down the teaching unions in his pursuit of change (Maraniss, 1996, pp.409–16).

Overall there were four chief elements to the administration's plan. First, to expand the Head Start program for disadvantaged pre-schoolers. Second, to establish a series of national goals and standards for the country's high schools with a greater emphasis on checking actual student achievement rather than simply annual progression. Third, to help those students not going on to college after high school move more smoothly into work. Finally, to improve access to college for those students deterred from further study by the cost.

To an extent each of these objectives was fulfilled through 1993 and 1994 (Stanfield, 1994). The programs, however, were initially generally modest in scope and the chances of expansion diminished significantly after the Republican capture of Congress. As it was, new tax credit measures to encourage participation in post secondary school activity were enacted in 1997 and, in the budgetary scramble in the build-up to the 1998 mid-term elections, Clinton did push through extra money for teacher recruitment.

One program which Clinton promised to extend was Head Start. This was set up in 1965 and specifically targeted children from low-income families for pre-school classes. This survivor from the War on Poverty was a popular program which had never been funded in a manner which reflected the compliments paid to it. Here the administration did manufacture a considerable boost to funds as the allocation of $2.2 billion in fiscal year 1992 was increased to $4.4 billion in fiscal 1998. All the same at this point it still only served 40 percent of eligible children (Kirchnoff, 1998). Sympathetic critics also point out that the program 'has only vague performance standards' and finds it hard to hire well-qualified teachers because of the poor salary structure (Ravitch, 1999, p.291). Ravitch, a PPI senior fellow, in fact argued that the administration had taken the easy route to Head Start reform by simply looking to increase numbers on the program, rather than engaging in a serious effort to overhaul its variable structure (1998). Furthermore, a 1995 study showed that while Head Start was of identifiable long-term benefit to white children, its usefulness for African-American children was often quickly undermined because of the low quality of the elementary schools many subsequently attended (CEA, 2000, pp.148–9). This in turn emphasized the need to improve standards in elementary and secondary schools.

To this end, the administration designed the Goals 2000: Educate America Act which was signed into law at the end of March 1994. The aim of the program was establish clearer targets for both student achievement and teacher quality. At the time of its passage it included such grand objectives as raising high school graduation rates to at least 90 percent and making American students the world leaders in mathematics and sciences. On a more practical level the focus was on ensuring that state and local education authorities were concentrated on setting standards, improving accountability and co-ordinating their various agencies. In a 1998 report reviewing the progress made as a consequence of the program, Secretary of Education Richard Riley claimed, 'Goals 2000 is fulfilling its historic mission of helping schools to raise academic standards.... This is a fundamental change in the very structure of American education, and it is helping to prepare our nation's young people for success in the 21st century' (US Department of Education, 1998, p.1). The fuller report went on to detail some evidence of improvement in the key areas identified by the legislation, notably state methods of assessment of student performance, actual student performance, accountability processes, teacher preparation and ongoing development, community and parental involvement, and state and local co-ordination of improvement efforts (pp.15–26). While progress was identified across the board, the report acknowledged that change was often difficult to bring about and that fulfilling 'the promise of high standards for all children' remained 'a monumental task' (p.26).

Another, and distinctly New Democrat, element of the administration's strategy was its support for so-called 'charter schools'. These are public schools which are freed from many standard regulations in exchange for a promise to meet certain performance criteria. Decisions about whether to allow the formation of charter schools and, if so, how strictly to monitor them are made by the states. In the 1998–99 academic year there were more than 1,200 charter schools across 27 states and Washington DC (Ravitch, 1999, p.278). The perceived advantage of these schools is that they are less weighed down by bureaucracy and have a greater incentive to achieve, as they will lose their charter if they fail to meet the agreed standards. This is in contrast to regular public schools where there is no punishment for even consistent poor performance. Sceptics, however, doubt the efficacy of this trade-off, pointing out how difficult it is in practice to hold schools accountable in a meaningful manner. In the summer of 1998 Richard Rothstein noted that while a few charter schools had had their licences revoked for financial mismanagement, none had been penalised for 'measured academic performance... since charter schools began in 1991' (1998, p.49). This at least brings into question the idea that there is genuinely extra pressure on charter schools to perform. Furthermore, even if the alleged benefits are actualized in a high percentage of charter schools, these would still only cater for a tiny percentage of America's schoolchildren. That is, while Clinton wanted to double the number of charter schools to around 3,000, this would still represent only a fraction of the nation's 85,000 public schools (p.47).

One administration project which did focus on a relatively marginalized group was the School-to-Work Opportunities Act of 1994. The aim of this was to help those students leaving high school, but not going to college, move into work. Enacted in April 1994, the bill granted funds to states to set up vocational learning programs. The guiding idea of integrating the worlds of school and work was reflected by the fact that the initiative was administered jointly by both the Departments of Education and Labor. Overall, it is difficult to criticise the principle behind the School-to-Work initiative. In targeting those without post-high school qualifications it set out to aid a social group who, the income data showed, had been left behind since the start of the 1980s. On the other hand, as with Goals 2000, whatever the inherent virtues of STW, the program was only ever going to have a modest impact because of its limited funding. In its first three years of operation $695 million was awarded in implementation grants – not perhaps a negligible sum but certainly not one to transform the life chances of a large, but often neglected, group of young Americans (Riley and Reich, 1996, p.1).

The area of educational reform where the administration had most immediate impact was in improving access to higher education, particularly for those potentially scared off by the cost. The evidence from the 1980s and continuing through the Clinton years strongly suggests the advantages enjoyed by college graduates in the labor market. According to the CEA there was a clear correlation between educational inequality and wage inequality.

> Between 1979 and 1999 the real median weekly wages of comparable male college graduates aged 25 and over who worked full-time rose by almost 15 percent, ... Despite a 6 percent increase since 1996, the earnings of full-time working males with only a high school diploma fell by 12 percent over the same period (CEA, 2000, p.135).

Such aggregate data can, of course, disguise a multitude of complicating factors but it did lead to a number of White House initiatives. Foremost among these was the National Service Act, which effectively provided grants to people in exchange for community service. This was very much a pet project for both Clinton and the DLC as it combined the themes of community participation and educational opportunity. In the end, however, while Clinton celebrated the passage of the legislation in September 1993 the actual sums appropriated were well down from his initial requests. In particular, while the administration had hoped to award grants of up to $10,000, the limit was set at $4,725 per year for two years (Zuckman, 1993a). Another early effort to improve funding opportunities for students was the direct loan program. This allowed students to borrow from the federal government which could offer better repayment packages than banks and the guarantee agencies.

Further measures, enacted in 1997, were the HOPE Scholarship program and the Lifetime Learning tax credit. In 1999/2000, 5.9 million were eligible to benefit from the HOPE Scholarships which offered a tax credit of up to $1,500 for the first two years of college for those enrolled on a half-time or more basis. The credit was phased out for couples earning between $80,000 to $100,000 and single people with incomes between $40,000 to $50,000. The Lifetime Learning tax credit applied to 20 percent of the first $5,000 in costs for adults looking to re-educate or re-skill themselves with eligibility for the same income groups as the HOPE program. More specifically targeted at low-income families are Pell grants which provide direct assistance for post-secondary education. The maximum value of these rose from $2,300 in 1993 to $3,300 in 2000 (CEA, 2000, p.156).

In the final analysis, judgment as to whether Clinton's efforts bore fruit depends on how success is measured. There was some evidence of improvement. This included the increase in the number of states applying assessment standards to measure student progress in essential subjects, partially as a consequence of Goals 2000. There was also some indication of progress by students in the highest poverty schools as gauged by the National Assessment of Educational Progress in reading and math tests (US Department of Education, 2000, p.2). Perhaps the most quantifiable success for the administration came in its efforts to increase access to higher education. Here there was a notable increase in federal government aid. The National Service scholarships had provided help to over 150,000 students by 1999. In 1998 there were further improvements in the repayment terms for those using the direct loan program established in 1993. Furthermore in fiscal 2000 the budget for the HOPE Scholarships scheme was nearly $5 billion with $2.4 billion set aside for the Lifetime Learning tax credit. Overall, according to the administration, while 43 percent of students benefited from federal grants and loans in 1992, this had increased to 59 percent in 1999 (US Department of Education, 2000, p.11).

Important qualifications do, however, need to be made. For example, the expansion of Head Start was significant, but at the end of eight years of Clinton's presidency still less than half of eligible children were enrolled in the program. The Goals 2000 and STW scheme did break new ground and the latter in particular drew attention to a somewhat neglected group, but the actual sums set aside for the new programs were small and so any impact was bound to be limited. The best hope is that the programs demonstrate their worth and so serve as markers for future developments. Reflecting on the 1993 and 1994 round of reforms, Stanfield commented that at least Clinton had attempted to do something in an area where the long dominant sentiment that 'something' needed to be done had not previously provoked much tangible action (1994, p.1304). Not surprisingly, however, there were still many concerns about the quality of America's education system, particularly at elementary and secondary level, at the end of the Clinton era. That politicians had a sense of public anxiety was reflected in the manner that both Bush and Gore promised further action through the 2000 campaign even though there are clear limits to the federal government's authority in this area.

Retraining

The second part of the strategy to equalize economic life chances was to make sure that people who wanted to work were not excluded from the labor force because their skills were obsolete. This was a goal which accorded with two prevailing ideas about how the 'new economy' worked. First, that while it did offer plenty of opportunities it also increased the likelihood of workers having to move around from one job to another as the old economy expectation of a job for life diminished. Thus workers would need to be equipped with a variety of skills. Second, the already accumulating evidence strongly suggested that, while there was still plenty of low skilled work available, workers without skills were unlikely to enjoy significant fruits for their labor, while those with the in-demand abilities would be remunerated handsomely. Furthermore, 'retraining' is one of those buzzwords which, particularly when expressed as a vague principle, receives widespread applause.[3] The problem, of course, comes with actually designing programs which are effective. For the Clinton administration this difficulty was exacerbated by the different expectations of how retraining was to be funded and organized. In the atmosphere of 1993/4 no significant new money was going to be allocated to training so any developments would largely have to involve a juggling of various existing schemes.

The most coherent effort to put together an overall package from what was already around came in 1994 with the proposals for a Reemployment Act. This set out to bring together several existing programs aimed at displaced and unemployed workers, including TAA, with a total budget of $13 billion over five years. The aim was to get any worker who was deemed to be permanently laid off due to a change in government policy or corporate restructuring into a retraining scheme and to provide some income support for the time of their participation (Kellam, 1994). The training and income benefits would have been an entitlement to all qualified applicants, with those eligible including workers displaced by military base closures and defence cuts, clean air legislation and NAFTA (Wells, 1994). There was tepid business support for this measure but, ironically, the unions objected to the plan partially because they did not want to see TAA, which largely benefited union members, eliminated as a stand alone program. In the end there was simply not the political dynamic to push this bill through, as the full House Ways and Means Committee never got around to giving it due consideration (for a discussion of the Reemployment Act see Weir, 1998, pp.284–7).

More generally, the struggle to find funds for retraining programs, particularly in the crucial early months of the administration, is well captured in Robert Reich's account of his time in the cabinet as Secretary of Labor (1998). Essentially Reich describes how job training had no strong supportive constituencies. Even potential supporters, such as union leaders and liberal Democrats, were sometimes unsympathetic if they thought that the promise of job training was an effort to deflect attention from more fundamental economic decisions. Reich, for example, recounts a meeting with Representative William Ford from Michigan, as the vote on NAFTA neared. Reich had gone to try to persuade him to support a reemployment plan, but Ford's response was categorical, *'"No! I will not give Bill Clinton a fig leaf for his NAFTA"'* (p.126). At the same time as being unable to rally likely allies, the sceptics within the administration made it clear that money could not come from other areas of government. Again Reich recalls a conversation with then Treasury Secretary Lloyd Bentsen in March 1993. Reich is pleading the case for a tax credit (rather than direct subsidies) for parents to send their children to college or for adults to learn new skills. His suggestions, however, for cutting tax breaks for executive pensions and health plans or reducing tax concessions to insurance or oil and gas companies in order to offset the costs of his own proposal meet with a negative response (pp.89–92).

Indeed the debate about how to set up training programs was marked by a growing tension between old and New Democrats. Those in the old camp preferred to stick with a traditional model of training provision, but the New lobby argued that workers should be given training vouchers in programs which devolved more organization down to the states. In fact after the Republicans took control of Congress, the administration and moderate congressional Democrats worked with Republicans to fashion legislative proposals to consolidate various existing programs into a voucher based block grant format. However, although both the House and Senate passed bills, they were not able to reconcile the differences in conference committee and so no action was taken. In the end, the administration was probably relieved by this as the proposal would have cut overall spending by up to 20 percent (Weir, 1998, pp.291–4). As it was, money set aside for education and training funding through 1995 and 1996 dropped and then recovered slightly so that by 1997 spending on employment programs was down by 6 percent from its 1994 level (Weir, 1998, p.294). On the other hand, the administration was able to point to some signs that retraining did provide more than cosmetic help. The 1999 CEA report estimated that 600,000 dislocated workers had participated in training and adjustment schemes in 1998 – and the evidence from the previous year offered these workers some encouragement. That is, of those workers who had engaged with the schemes in 1997 '71 percent … were employed and had earnings on average, of $10.39 per hour, or 94 percent of their previous wages' (p.128).

In fact, in a little heralded measure, a revamp of the nation's training structures was enacted in August 1998 in the Workforce Investment Act. The aim of this was to streamline various support services to workers while giving considerable autonomy to Work Investment Boards effectively run by local business communities. Following the New Democrat line, the WIA also created Individual Training Accounts. These are intended to give workers information on the cost effectiveness of different training providers so that each worker can make the right choice for his or her self, in turn putting pressure on the providers to give the best service possible. By the end of Clinton's term, however, there was little evidence of what effect the WIA will have, if any, in the long-term.

Making work pay

The determination to do something to help those in low wage jobs was a response to the growth in inequality since the late 1970s. It is important to note here that the primary problem, even as identified by many Democrats, was not inequality per se – surveys show that Americans are less concerned with the distribution of income than the citizens of other western industrialized nations (Burtless, 1999, p.140); that is, what was of concern about the increase in inequality was not so much that the rich were getting richer faster than the poor but that the poor were not getting better off at all. According to Mishel and Bernstein while the real income of the worst-off 20 percent of American families increased by 3 percent annually from 1947 to 1967, the equivalent group from 1979 to 1989 saw its income drop by 0.4 percent annually with a precipitous further decline in the following two years of 3.1 percent annually (1993, pp.43–7). A CBO study, released in late 1990, showed that from 1977 to 1990 the top 20 percent of families had, in real terms, seen their income rise and the percentage of their income paid in income tax decline. In contrast the bottom quintile of families had experienced the exact opposite effect as their real income went down but the percentage of earnings paid as tax went up (Kosterlitz, 1990, p.2952).

Not all of the poorest American families were of course working families, but equally many were, and it was not just the liberal wing of the Democratic Party which thought it unjust that people worked harder for less in return (Levitan et al., 1993). As it was, the administration's preferred method of implementing its pledge of making sure that the working poor – in other words the unquestionably *deserving* poor – got a fairer deal was through expanding the EITC, which was effectively a tax rebate for low income working families. As noted in the previous Chapter, the EITC became something of a political football in the negotiations over the first Clinton budget, but the White House was firm in its resolve to extend the program significantly. In 1992, 14.1 million families received an average tax credit of $921 through the EITC. At the time it was estimated that the changes incorporated in the budget would mean that by 1996 17.9 million families would receive an average credit of $1,400 with the further projection that in the year 2000 19.1 million families would benefit to the tune of an average $1,565 (US, 1996a, p.809). This meant that by the mid-1990s EITC had become the biggest specific anti-poverty government cash program.[4] In their study of inequality, Danziger and Gottschalk noted that this was a 'substantial' enhancement of the program which would 'substantially offset the decline in real wages over the past two decades for workers at the bottom of the earnings distribution who work year-round and reside in families with children' (1995, p.159). The 1993 change did also for the first time allow childless workers to claim some small sums.

The EITC in fact started life as a New Democrat style solution to low pay and was intended to be a substitute for an increase in the minimum wage (Rauch, 1989).[5] As it was, however, both old and New Democrats were quite happy to take credit for both EITC and the more old-fashioned Democrat response to low wages when congressional Democrats exploited election year nerves to persuade enough Republicans to support raising the minimum wage from $4.25 an hour to $5.15. Clinton had never been a great champion of the minimum wage but he did propose such an increase in the 1996 State of the Union address. This gave added momentum to the efforts of those like Senator Ted Kennedy who used various procedural devices to tie up Senate business and intimidate reluctant colleagues by pointing to polls showing 85 percent support for the increase (Sinclair, 2000, pp.89–90). As it was, the measure was passed overwhelmingly by margins of 354 to 72 in the House and 76 to 22 in Senate, although many Republicans and New Democrats were only brought onside after a series of tax breaks were granted to small businesses which would be affected. Nevertheless it was estimated that this would benefit 10 million workers (Rubin, 1996). To liberals such as Reich this rise was welcome but long overdue (1998, pp.326–9). Measured in constant 1996 dollars the high point of minimum wage value had in fact been in 1968 when it stood at the equivalent of $7.21 an hour, and it still had as high a commensurate value as $6.38 in 1978 (US, 1998a, p.438). This decline in the real worth of the minimum wage can also be measured if it is calculated as a percentage of the average hourly earnings of non-farm workers. Thus in 1968 it was equal to 54 percent of average hourly earnings and was still at 44 percent in 1978. By 1996 it had dropped to 34 percent (US, 1996b, p.429). So, while welcome, the 1996 increase did not restore the minimum wage to a level even close to its previous peaks.

Conclusion

In sum, attempting to judge the administration's efforts to help America's workers, and particularly the least well-off amongst them, presents a classic case of deciding whether the glass should be seen as half-full or half-empty. In particular, perception is distilled by the timeframe used. Should comparison be restricted simply to 1993 and 2000 – or should a broader span be considered? Take as another example the story of hourly wage rates. Measured in constant 1982 dollars, the 1998 average hourly earnings in private non-agricultural industry was $7.75 – this being the highest figure of the decade and an improvement on the rate of $7.39 an hour when Clinton took office. On the other hand, this looks less flattering when set against the peak figure which in fact came in *1973* when hourly compensation was *$8.55* (CEA, 1999, p.382).

A further interesting tale emerges from looking at the administration's most explicit interventions to alter the distribution of wealth – the changes to the federal income tax code. According to one study, changes to the tax code enacted in the 1990s (including the 1990 budget agreement) resulted in personal income tax reductions for all but the top 1 percent of earners. For lower income families the EITC and for middle-income families the $500-per-child tax credit adopted in the 1997 budget package were important gains, while the highest earners were hit by a rise in the top regular rate of income tax from 28 percent in 1990 to 39.6 percent (McIntyre, 2000).[6] These statistics would suggest some attempt to strike back at the shift in wealth in the 1980s. Once again, though, the picture changes if the starting point for the comparison is the mid-1970s rather than 1990, due to the steep reductions in top tax rates made between 1977 and 1985 (Mishel et al., 1999, pp.91–118).[7]

Much of the above is difficult data to interpret with any finality. In its 2000 report, the CEA claimed that 'the evidence on inequality suggests that policy has been doing the right things' and added, suggesting a more optimistic outlook than in the quotation used at the start of this chapter, 'We remain masters of our own fate' (CEA, 2000, p.40). On the other hand, there was little sign of a return to the era of steady growth and diminishing inequality of 1945 to 1975 (Thompson, 1994). The President himself was, not too surprisingly, keen to present the most fulsome portrayal of his administration's efforts to befriend those who had not been invited to the economic party during the 1980s. In his 2000 *Economic Report*, Clinton claimed that

> ...even as we maintained fiscal responsibility, we expanded our investments in education, technology and training. We have opened the doors of college to all Americans...So that working families will have means to support themselves, we have increased the minimum wage, expanded the...(EITC),...and invested in making health insurance coverage available to millions of children (Clinton, 2000, p.4).

In a literal sense all of these claims were true, but in reality the overriding emphasis on deficit reduction immediately put the squeeze on Clinton's ambitious investment agenda. The 1993 budget saw some spending measures enacted but hopes of using this as a springboard were to be dashed. The administration was left with the choice of doing little or attempting to implement its New Democrat agenda by sacrificing programs dear to the hearts of supporters of the older version. As the administration contemplated its options at the start of its second year in office the pay-as-you-go budget rules and caps on discretionary spending effectively ruled out major investment in education, health, job training, and transforming the welfare system unless it could come up with serious savings elsewhere (Angle, 1994).

Furthermore, an important part of the overall fiscal story which is sometimes neglected is the manner in which the deficit reduction target itself shifted through the 1990s. When Clinton came to office few categorically called for, and even fewer expected, a balanced federal budget by the end of his presidency. This was partially because the fiscal and economic forecasts were considerably off-line, but it also reflected a consensus that while the deficits of the mid-1980s to early 1990s were at a damagingly high level, it was not necessary actually to balance the books in order to create the conditions for economic growth. Deficit reduction, therefore, was seen as a means to an end but not as an end in itself; however, the manner in which deficit reduction gave way to budget balance which in turn gave way to *debt* reduction suggested that restricting spending had come to be interpreted as a virtue in its own right regardless of the broader economic and social policy picture. There was in fact some speculation in the aftermath of the 1997 budget deal that, despite the immediate conservative triumph on tax and spending matters, the deal was potentially of longer term benefit to the Democrats as it took the deficit issue, which had so inhibited innovative policy development, off the table (Brownstein, 1997). This is not how matters played out, however, and while the Clinton years did see some increased spending on existing programs and some new investment initiatives, particularly in education, these did not match the stated intentions of the 1992 campaign. Indeed, bizarrely, as a result of what Teixeira and Rogers call the 'New Austerity', which insisted on the sanctity of the budget surplus, it turned out that increasing spending became more difficult, *even as the fiscal picture began to improve* (2000, p.152). Apart from the degree of self-congratulation, the politics of surplus seemed little different from that of deficit in terms of getting new initiatives off the ground. Thus, although the administration continued to tout its investments strategy as integral to its Third Way approach, the reality is that investments, however much they fitted the bill of preparing people for life in the information age economy, consistently lost out to the competition from fiscal austerity. One indication of this is that, according to the CBO, federal spending as a percentage of GDP dropped from 21.5 percent in 1993 to 18.7 percent in 1999 (Parks, 2000, p.229).

Certainly it is clear that, even to the extent that the initiatives championed by Clinton did make a difference, they were only a limited part of the initial investment agenda. Perhaps most obviously, the health care reforms which were actually enacted pale against the ambition of the failed Health Security Act. (Health care issues will be discussed more thoroughly in the next chapter, but Clinton's plan was the most ambitious of his presidency in terms of improving *economic security* for low income working American families.) Furthermore, the one-off economic stimulus plan of 1993 was lost and much of the investment funding contained in the original version of the first budget was stripped out in order to accommodate the meeting of deficit reduction targets. Thus did campaign promises, such as that to establish the 'Rebuild America Fund, with a $20 billion federal investment each year for the next four years', quickly evaporate (Clinton and Gore, 1992, p.9). Overall, even though the investment spending was portrayed as a means of improving long-term economic performance, the anti-deficit message was overwhelming. Reich reflected that while seen as one of the main accomplishments of the first year in office, the first budget 'cut the deficit but left almost nothing for new public investment' (1998, p.150). Weir is particularly scathing about the administration's efforts to build political support for this part of its program, noting that 'Neither the intellectual nor political groundwork had been laid for the investment strategy' (1998, p.279). Thus at the end of the 1990s, despite all the historic evidence pointing to the value of government interventions, 'the case for public contributions to economic growth has all but vanished from public life' (Brinkley, 1997, p.42). Clinton himself highlighted that much of his investment agenda remained unfulfilled when, in 1999, he embarked on a tour of poverty stricken areas which had not been embraced by economic growth (Broder, 1999; DeParle, 1999). Furthermore, in May 2000 he commenced a two day 'Schools Reform Tour' by calling for more federal spending to help poorly performing schools and to improve access to after school programs and summer education classes in low-income areas (Babington, 2000).

Overall, while it would be unfair to deny the administration its successes and its consistent commitment to the investment and making work pay agenda, there was in actuality considerably less evidence of the successful implementation of this supportive and activist side of the Third Way economic policy equation than of the more conservative side dedicated to deficit reduction and free trade.

5
The Politics of Health Care

For all the debate and division over the deficit and free trade, the Clinton proposal which would have most immediately affected the US economy and reached into numerous areas of American society was the Health Security Act. The HSA proposed a revamp of a sector which devoured over one-eighth of the country's GDP. The battle to accomplish this opened with a flourish in September 1993 with Clinton's address to Congress in which he explained the rationale for taking on such a big task (Johnson and Broder, 1997, pp.3–31). This display of presidential bravado, however, was not a prelude to what followed. Almost exactly a year later a last ditch attempt to salvage something from the legislative wreckage surrounding the issue collapsed. Two months on from this, the GOP captured Congress laying to rest the prospect of any near-term fundamental, progressive overhaul of the American health care system. Indeed not only had Clinton failed but the manner of this failure had undoubtedly contributed to the Republican success. This painful episode stands out as a, possibly the, defining event of the Clinton years. Certainly nothing on this scale was even thought about, let alone attempted, subsequently. The reform effort had been lampooned as Big Government, regulation gone mad, liberalism; and even those sympathetic to Clinton's goals damned the administration for the way in which it had proceeded.

The HSA, however, is not the whole story of the politics of health care in the 1990s. Its demise was, without doubt, a policy failure and political disaster which severely undermined the administration's credibility; yet, having cost Clinton so dearly in 1993 and 1994 it was, ironically, health care issues which were instrumental in restoring a *raison d'être* for his presidency through 1995 and 1996. That is, it was in standing up to the Gingrich led effort effectively to begin dismantling the existing government-run health care programs that Clinton once more found his political voice, a popular cause and common ground with most Democrats.

In the end then, the very different Clinton and Gingrich endeavours, respectively to restructure and to dismantle government's role in the provision of health care, led them and their parties into the political quagmire. In hindsight both seem to have made extraordinarily expensive political errors of judgment. The potential rewards of success, however, were great and so it should not be too surprising that they were lured into their grand undertakings. That is, for both, health care seemed to offer the opportunity to fulfil key policy and political goals. For Clinton health care reform appeared to be a good cause around which all Democrats could rally especially as they were so divided on the other critical social policy measure of welfare reform (Skocpol, 1995a, p.68). Furthermore, if Clinton had managed to push through reform which guaranteed all, or at least very nearly all, Americans some form of health insurance coverage and which also contained the overall burden of health care costs imposed on the American economy, then he would have demonstrated that government could simultaneously do good deeds and also encourage efficiency. This would potentially have resurrected the idea that government-led initiatives could do much to improve the quality of American life at a time when trust in federal government's capacity to get things right was at a low ebb.[1] Moreover, successful health care reform would have had a positive impact on other key areas of the administration's agenda. For example, the cost containment measures would have helped bring ever spiralling public health care expenditures under control – thus easing the budget deficit. In addition universal coverage would have removed one of the major disincentives for people to leave the welfare rolls and move into low wage jobs with no health coverage. For Gingrich, the temptation was almost a reverse image. If the Republican efforts to cut back and disperse Medicare and Medicaid had been implemented then two of the biggest federal government sponsored programs would have been downsized, signalling the further retreat of the American welfare state.

After the failure of these radical efforts a third version of health care reform emerged which did result in some legislative action. This was reform on a case by case basis illustrated by the Kassebaum-Kennedy Act of 1996 which was designed to improve the portability of insurance for workers changing or leaving jobs which had previously provided their insurance. In addition the Children's Health Insurance Program (CHIP), introduced in 1997, expanded access to health coverage for low-income children under 19 years of age.[2] Whatever the benefits of these reforms, however, they did not satisfy the ambitions expressed by Clinton in 1993 when he set out to make sure that all Americans were covered by a health insurance scheme while also bringing medical inflation under some control.

The problem of reform

Retrospectives on the health care effort have tended to portray it as a doomed initiative – categorizing it variously as noble, foolhardy or plain dangerous. Furthermore, while there is disagreement as to why the plan fell by the wayside, there is consensus that the fact that it did so was greatly damaging to the Democratic Party in the 1994 elections, and, indeed, that the injury went beyond these immediate electoral considerations and haunted the administration through to the end of its days. In the blunt words of one-time pollster for the President, Stanley Greenberg, 'The health care defeat was catastrophic for Democrats' (1995, p.308). The politics of the episode also amply illustrate how difficult it was always going to be to instigate substantive change on a complex topic in a Third Way manner.

Indeed one of the primary lessons from the whole affair was that there was little agreement about what actually constituted a New Democrat or Third Way style reform, or perhaps even more fundamentally what was a legitimate project for the Third Way to tackle at all. That is, while the administration clearly thought that the mechanics of the HSA, the so-called 'competition within a budget' formula, was a carefully crafted centrist approach which it would be able to sell as an acceptable compromise to the various interested parties, critics dismissed the whole enterprise as misconceived. One particularly prominent school of thought held that the reform effort was a reversion to old-fashioned Big Government liberalism which, along with other early mis-steps such as the gays in the military affair, undid the administration's carefully cultivated New Democrat image. For example, in their analysis Quirk and Cunion maintain that the plan and the administration's unwillingness to water down the commitment to universal coverage reflected a 'drift toward liberal, partisan positions' (2000, p.216). Crucially this was the line which the New Democrats outside the administration, at least as represented by the DLC, also deemed appropriate.

The New Democrat analysis of events depicts the health reform effort as one which began by legitimately latching on to important concerns and which initially did try to negotiate a compromise solution. The contention, however, is that the plan went off the centrist track promised in the campaign and, as drawn up by Hillary Clinton and Ira Magaziner, ended up following a liberal route which in itself provides the primary reason for the ensuing political crash. Critically, while DLC type New Democrats paid homage to the principle of universal care, they clearly identified cost issues as the priority. For example, the PPI's 1993 guide to the new President, *Mandate for Change*, said that the debate about how to guarantee access 'is *not* the most important choice. Far more fundamental is the choice of how to restrain our health system's runaway costs' (Rosner, 1993, p.108).

According to this perspective then, the decision to set the stall out for universal coverage, which Clinton declared to be non-negotiable, was one which dictated that the Clinton plan started life in left field. The PPI's Will Marshall commented that Clinton's insistence on comprehensive coverage and nothing but this was part of the 'old time Democratic religion' (quoted in Cloud, 1994, p.19). This in turn meant that any political, and crucially legislative, coalition would have to be built from the liberal wing inwards to the centre. This conflicted with the preferred New Democrat strategy of encouraging bipartisanship by building coalitions from the centre out. According to New Democrats this latter type of coalition building would have allowed moderates from both parties to hitch themselves to the wagon; in contrast, starting on the left antagonized centrist Democrats and made it most unlikely that many Republicans would be brought onboard. At first, New Democrats were temperate in their criticisms of the Clinton plan and credited him with trying to find the middle ground. After the plan was unveiled, however, they did express concern that it afforded 'lavish guaranteed benefits to politically important constituencies' and as such 'has many of the earmarks of a new entitlement program' (From, 1993b, p.22). The passage of time reinforced this viewpoint. Writing in a PPI volume in 1997, the think tank's health care analyst David Kendall, somewhat oversimplifying the complexity of the 1993 plan, wrote, 'Without question, the historic setback Democrats suffered in 1994 was due in part to public apprehension about the Clinton health plan – an effort to secure universal access to health insurance through a new federal entitlement' (p.57). As it was, by the time the Health Security Act was in its death throes, the DLC had, in effect, publicly opposed the administration's efforts by rallying behind the much more limited proposal put forward by Representative Jim Cooper from Tennessee and Senator John Breaux of Louisiana which did not resolve to establish universal coverage (Baer, 2000, p.216).

The time seemed ripe

Thus the New Democrat version of history is that the health reform effort was overambitious in scope and misguided in detail; and clearly, whatever its intentions and expectations, the administration got it seriously wrong, inasmuch as no legislation was enacted and a high political price was exacted for this failure. Nevertheless, for all the wisdom and twenty–twenty vision provided by the lens of hindsight, the early 1990s *had furnished more than sufficient evidence* to justify legislative action in the health care arena. When Clinton revealed his plan, there was widespread anticipation that some version of reform would be enacted coupled with, or rather driven by, a sense that this was what the public wanted when faced with overwhelming evidence of the failures of the existing health system. Simply put, the health care system was costing too much and providing insurance to too few. Furthermore, as will be explained below, the Clinton plan was not designed to 'socialize' medicine and was by no means the favoured method of the liberal-left for achieving substantive reform. What it did set out to do was tackle the two outstanding issues of cost and access.

The broad heading of cost in fact covered different types of concern. The overarching problem was the rising overall burden that health care related expenses imposed on the American economy, as an ever higher proportion of the country's GDP was consumed by the medical sector. In 1960 national health care expenditures accounted for 5.1 percent of US GDP. This had risen to 7.1 percent in 1970 and then to 8.9 percent in 1980. In 1990 it was 12.2 percent, and had already reached 13.4 percent by 1992 (Patel and Rushefsky, 1999, p.162). To better understand the practical repercussions of these figures it is worth looking at how they translated into cost increases for both the private and public sectors. In 1992 a clear majority of Americans received their insurance as a consequence of either their own or a family member's employment.[3] The problem for employers was that the cost of providing this insurance was rising at an unsustainable rate. Mark Peterson explains it thus, 'Between 1970 and 1989, employer spending on wages and salaries, controlling for inflation, went up just 1 percent, but for health benefits, it rose 163 percent' (1998, p.183); and then things got worse as 'From 1989 to 1990, the cost to employers of providing employee health benefits rose 46.3 percent' (Patel and Rushefsky, 1998, p.27).

In the public sector the two major government run programs had experienced similar escalations of outlay. Medicaid, which is paid for out of general revenues with the overall expense shared between federal, state and local governments, had cost $5.3 billion in 1970. This had climbed to $24.8 billion by 1980 and further risen to $71.7 billion by 1990. Remarkably, this figure had already jumped to $101.6 billion by 1992, with the federal government footing $65.4 billion of this bill (Patel and Rushefsky, 1999, p.59). In 1990 Medicaid consumed 30 percent of federal money passed to the states. In 1993 this had risen to 39 percent, but even this aid left the states on the point of being overwhelmed by the expense of the program (Patel and Rushefsky, 1998, p.41). Medicare, the health care program for the elderly, is in fact funded by a separate payroll tax paid into a trust fund. This, however, was predicted to be rapidly nearing bankruptcy due to the increasing number of enrolees, their increased life expectancy, and the consequent increase in demand for care in terms of both volume and expensive medical technology. In 1970, there were 20.5 million Medicare enrolees. In 1980 there were 28.5 million and in 1990, 34.2 million. This translated into costs of $7.5 billion in 1970, rising to $36.8 billion in 1980 and up to $111 billion in 1990. In a similar fashion to Medicaid this rate of growth further exploded in the early 1990s such that costs in 1992 amounted to $135.8 billion (US, 1996b, Table 163, p.115). A further feature was the manner in which the public interpreted the ongoing debate and fed this back into their own calculations. In particular, in the context of the economic downturn at the start of the 1990s, many, perhaps insecure in their jobs, worried that if they lost their existing insurance package they would not be able to buy into another scheme. This, in turn, leads into the second big issue, that of the number of uninsured people in the US.

The data here is simpler to summarize, although the detailed picture is again a complex one. The starkest statistic is that in 1993, 39.7 million Americans, amounting to 15.3 percent of the population, lacked health insurance coverage. Disturbingly, this had risen from 31 million, constituting 12.9 percent of the population, in 1987 (US, 1996b, Table 173, p.120). Perhaps just as tellingly, over a 28 month period beginning in early 1992, only 73 percent of the population had insurance coverage for the entire time with nearly 5 percent never being covered (Table 175, p.121).

A profile of the uninsured was given in a Census Bureau report, published in the aftermath of the collapse of the Clinton plan in 1995. Of the insured population in 1995, 70.3 percent were covered by private insurance with 13.1 percent covered by Medicare, 12.1 percent by Medicaid and 3.5 percent by a military health plan.[4] The number of uninsured, however, had risen again to 40.6 million, constituting

15.4 percent of the population. However, the relative effectiveness of the government-run schemes in helping particular sections of American society was illustrated by the fact that less than 1 percent of over 65 year olds did not have some sort of cover. On the other hand, despite the existence of the Medicaid program, other vulnerable sections of the community suffered disproportionately. Most immediately, the poor were twice as likely to be uninsured as the non-poor, though there was a curious twist to this figure (US, 1996c, p.1). That is, while among the general working aged population workers were more likely to be insured than nonworkers, ironically, because of the Medicaid eligibility rules, poor workers had higher uninsured rates than the nonworking poor. This leads to the important point that 22.4 percent of part-time workers and 16.4 percent of full-time workers were uninsured (p.2).

The significance of this is that it demonstrates that the uninsured could not simply be dismissed as the 'undeserving' or workshy. Indeed, according to one study of the uninsured in 1990, 49.3 percent were full-year, full time workers, with a further 36.4 percent employed part-time (Mishel and Bernstein, 1993, p.402). A 1993 survey found, 'the overwhelming majority of the uninsured have no coverage, not by choice, but because they cannot find employers willing to provide them insurance, and lack the financial means to purchase their own health benefits, with many of them uninsurable at any cost due to chronic illness' (Laham, 1996, p.22). The most obviously 'at risk' group were those who worked for employers who did not offer a health benefits package to their employees. Such workers could of course buy their own insurance, but for most such an option was unrealistic due to the prohibitive cost. One reason for the increase in the number of people working in such 'at risk' jobs was the change which had taken place in the fundamental make-up of the US economy. That is, service sector jobs were less likely to offer health insurance than manufacturing ones, and so the shift from manufacturing to service sector employment added to the overall health insurance problem (Patel and Rushefsky, 1999, p139).[5] Thus the health care reform effort needs to be understood not simply as a 'social' issue but also as an economic one – with the potential primary beneficiaries being low-income working Americans.

The contrary outcome of this combination of problems is that the US 'spends substantially more on health care than any other nation' yet is 'the only advanced industrial democracy with a significant share of its population which is uninsured' (Laham, 1996, p.25). The same point is made by Patel and Rushefsky. 'The United States spends 40 percent more money per capita on health care than any other Western industrialized nation' but 'remains the only industrialized nation in the world that does not provide a basic health benefit package to all its citizens' (1998, p.23). A further irony was suggested by Paul Krugman – as improvements in medical technology had made health care more expensive so insurance premiums had been pushed up in turn driving more people out of the system. Thus, perversely, it could be argued that improving medical technology had worsened the nation's health (Krugman, 1994, p.72).

In other words, many Americans were left out of the insurance system, the number was increasing and it was quite obvious that there was no possibility that the system was about to correct itself. Thus, if universal coverage was deemed to be a desirable outcome, then some sort of new regulation was necessary. Furthermore, at least in the early 1990s, regardless of how many people were or were not insured, there seemed equally little possibility that the health care industry was about to impose cost control on itself. In short, the system was not about to jump, so it had to be pushed; and while health care reform thus posed an enormous challenge, it was one which if successfully accomplished promised tangible rewards.

In political terms the potential of these rewards had apparently been illustrated by the dramatic come from behind victory of Harris Wofford in a special Senatorial election in 1991 in Pennsylvania. Despite the fact that he had been appointed to the Senate following the death of the Republican incumbent, John Heinz, the Democrat Wofford was little known and was expected to be easily defeated by his well known opponent Richard Thornburgh, both a former state Governor and US attorney general. The polls in the summer of 1991 suggested that the race would be little more than a formality; yet in November, Wofford won with 55 percent of the vote. Most significantly, all the evidence was that this remarkable turnaround was due to Wofford's decision to campaign on the issue of health care reform which seemed to crystallize the latent political weight of the issue. In particular it suggested that it was not just the already uninsured who wanted change, as Wofford had won votes across the class and partisan spectrum (Hacker, 1997, p.11). The economic downturn which began in 1989 was clearly making white-collar and professional workers, who had previously taken their health coverage for granted, increasingly aware of their vulnerablity to losing this protection (p.19). Overall to Democrat leaders, eager to gauge and profit from the public mood, the Wofford story and a succession of opinion polls showing how health care was ranked as one of the most important issues suggested that here was an issue with a potentially significant political pay-off.

Indeed the political class was so convinced of the popular demand for action that even President Bush advanced plans for reform in February 1992 with a proposal based on tax credits and vouchers for families earning up to $70,000 per annum. There was never a serious effort to pursue this, but when Clinton got to office he had little option but to attempt to carry out his campaign pledges. *Putting People First* had promised that a future Clinton administration would act decisively to change the organisation of health care funding and delivery because it was unacceptable to persevere with a system which 'leaves 60 million Americans without adequate health insurance and bankrupts our families, our businesses, and our federal budget' (Clinton and Gore, 1992, p.107). The campaign treatise further promised to 'take on the bureaucracies and corporate interests' in order 'to make health care affordable and accessible for every American' (p.108). On the other hand, there was also a commitment to 'preserve what's best in our system: your family's right to choose who provides care and coverage, American innovation and technology, and the world's best private doctors and hospitals' (p.107). Thus the primary message was about the need for reform and the determination to implement it, but there was also reassurance that this was not going to lead to the 'socializing' of American medicine. Once in office, actually announcing a policy prescription to reconcile these various requirements was deferred, as Clinton's promise to put a plan in the public realm within one hundred days was abandoned due to a combination of the protracted budgetary saga and the reality of the complexity of reform. Thus, as the health care task force led by Hillary Clinton grappled with the complexities of overhauling an industry integrated into countless aspects of American political and economic life, the formal release of the blueprint was put off until the fall. This abeyance and the protracted length of the plan, illustrating the sheer scale of what was being proposed, added to the daunting political task ahead.

Devising reform: finding the centrist option

One thing which did not cause the delay was deciding which of the various models of system reform to use as a starting point. Clinton had settled on, if not elaborated on, 'managed competition' during the campaign. As a campaign tool this was attractive, as it promised a system overhaul while leaving the principle of health care delivery embedded in the private sector intact. This allowed Clinton to parade as a reformer, but not one who was going to 'tax and spend' his way to a solution. In a setpiece campaign speech in late September 1992 Clinton described his plan as offering, 'personal choice, private care, private insurance, private management, but a national system to put a lid on costs, to require insurance reforms, to facilitate partnerships between business, government, and health care providers' (quoted in Skocpol, 1997, p.45). In short, managed competition appeared to be a New Democrat response to the talk of a health care crisis. This was especially the case if its methodology was compared to the alternatives on offer.

The managed competition concept was in fact a relative newcomer to the debate on how to reform the health care system. Indeed one of the leading exponents of this approach and a principal designer of the HSA, Paul Starr, noted that at the start of 1992 it was 'not on the menu at all' (1994, p.xiv). At this point the best known plans for achieving universal coverage were the 'single payer' and 'play-or-pay' designs. The most passionate long-time advocates of reform were of course liberal Democrats and these were their preferred schemes as they were more straightforward and more radical than managed competition. The favourite of House liberals in particular was the so-called 'single payer' plan which was in place in Canada. This would have largely undone the private insurance system and funded care through ear-marked taxes. In order to ensure universal coverage, everyone would get a national health card guaranteeing access to what would effec-tively be a government run system. Costs would be contained as hospi-tals and other care providers would have an overall budget within which they would have to operate. 'Play-or-pay' was a less radical, but nevertheless bold enough proposal. This would have left employers with the choice of either providing insurance for their employees or paying money into a government fund which would then be used to help pay for coverage for the remaining uninsured. The conservative response was to attack these schemes as respectively 'tax and spend' and anti-business. Their solution relied on the type of tax credit scheme which had been tentatively put forward by President Bush early in 1992. This, however, had little attraction to Democrats as it made no claim to universal coverage (or in fact cost control). As it became clear that health care was to be a significant issue in the 1992 race, play-or-pay garnered much attention as a workable option, but Clinton quite quickly embraced the emerging principles of managed competition as a means of achieving the Democrats's various goals (Skocpol, 1995a, pp.69–70).

The starting premise for major reform was that the private sector had not delivered universal care and was not going to do so of its own accord. The problem was in devising a framework which would achieve the two goals of expanding coverage *and* imposing cost containment. Although it was left unspoken, the inescapable consequence of *simultaneously* pursuing these aims was that someone somewhere was going to be squeezed. Indeed this was not so much a zero sum as a negative sum game. That is, the conundrum was to get greater numbers, meaning people, on one side of the equation while reducing the figure, meaning money spent, on the other. In short, however much it tried, the administration was not going to be able find an answer to the health care puzzle which all sides would find agreeable. One way of understanding the difficulties that were always likely to surface for the administration is to think of the extant health care system as a version of the Gordian knot. The solution favoured by liberals was to follow Alexander's example and to cut through the layers of complexity by imposing the single payer system. This would leave quite clear sets of winners and losers and would thus have distinct battlelines. It was, however, perceived to be too radical a solution and while it would have mobilized much of the party's base it was not regarded as a realistic legislative prospect. In choosing managed competition, the administration decided instead to attempt to untie and then re-fasten the knot in a sort of similar, but sort of different, reconfiguration. Not surprisingly then this resulted in an immensely complicated proposal.

At over 1300 pages, the HSA comprised a wide range of regulatory codes and supervisory agencies. It was desperately complicated, but promised to provide universal coverage through a mandate on employers to provide insurance for their employees and through subsidies to the poor and remaining workers without insurance. Insurance would be bought through so-called 'health alliances'. These, set up by the states, would effectively act as purchasing agencies. They would sort through various plans offered by insurers and providers and then offer their subscribers a choice from a set of recommended plans. An important part of the overall design was that employers would pay 80 percent of the cost of the premium with the remainder picked up by the subscribers. The point of this was to give people a financial stake in the type of plan which was chosen. In addition Medicare would largely continue in its existing form but Medicaid would be eliminated. The plan aimed to combine a series of objectives; first, the continued dominance of the private sector in both funding and care provision; second, regulation to ensure that everyone would be covered in one way or another; third, the retention of choice between different types of insurance and care plans; fourth, incentives for savings of scale and efficiency, and also, if necessary, overall cost containment through limits on the growth of insurance premiums for the health alliances (Patel and Rushefsky, 1999, pp.271–4. For a detailed account of the development of the ideas behind managed competition see Starr, 1994, and Hacker, 1997). The strategy was outlined by Walter Zelman, one of the inner circle who designed the HSA.

> [T]he Health Security Act…draws on many competing proposals. But its goal is not to merge them into a lowest-common-denomina-tor political compromise; rather, it is to draw on the best of compet-ing ideas to create a new, higher-level synthesis, and in doing so to overcome the ideological and political deadlock that has marked the reform debate over the past decade. In this way, the Health Security Act attempts to achieve…a "bridge to compromise" (1994, p.11).

The political calculation was that there was enough in the plan to keep the big players onside and, whatever the later conventional wisdom about the inevitability of failure, there was a general sense at the time that significant reform was likely in the 103rd Congress (see, for exam-ple, Peterson, 1998, p.221). So why did this carefully crafted attempt at a centrist reform agenda come to be traduced as just another example of Big Government liberalism?

Attacking the Clinton plan

Before moving on to discuss the specifics of the health care debate, it is important to remember that this did not happen in a political vacuum. Factors only tangentially related to health care and others which had no relation to the issue but which affected Clinton's standing played their part in the demise of the HSA. The announcement of the plan had already been damagingly delayed by the budget battle and even after it was formally made public it temporarily played second fiddle to the immense effort to get NAFTA ratified. Then when the administra-tion really wanted to concentrate its energies on health in late 1993 and early 1994, it was forced on the defensive over the Whitewater affair. Finally the last gasp efforts to resuscitate reform in the summer of 1994 clashed with the bitter fight over the anti-crime bill (see Chapter 7). In reality once legislative deliberation had carried significantly into 1994, the chances of decisive action, particularly if this depended on bringing moderate Republicans onboard, were reduced by the day as the 1994 mid-term elections approached. Thus the combination of a crowded legislative agenda, scandal, and an intensifying partisan atmosphere all contributed to undermine the prospects for reform; and, as was increasingly evident, the administration could ill afford even minor external hiccups if it was going to win the day on the HSA. In the end the administration's gamble that the complex formula contained in the legislation would bring onboard moderate and conservative Democrats, and possibly some moderate Republicans because of the commitment to cost control and continued reliance on the private sector, while winning over single payer liberals because of the promise of universal coverage, did not pay off. In short the plan lacked enthusiastic supporters but had plenty of raging opponents.

That this would be the case, however, was not immediately evident. The administration was aware of the need to set the agenda for the public relations battle in order to rally reform's boosters and marginalize antagonists. An internal White House memorandum from Mike Lux, in charge of public liaison for the plan, to Hillary Clinton in May 1993 explained the strategy, 'The trick in passing health care reform has always been in part to *figure out a package that can draw some business and provider support, while exciting the people who should be our base*' (quoted in Peterson, 2000, p.159). In this context Clinton's speech to Congress was well received by both elites and the wider public and the momentum seemed to be with the reform advocates; and at first it did appear as if the HSA's terms had managed to spread the pain in a manner which isolated the plan's enemies. Small insurance companies, who would be effectively put out of business, and those companies who would be hit by the new employer mandate were always going to be in opposition, but initially some of the business community, at least as represented by the leadership of the US Chamber of Commerce responded favourably to the plan. Those companies that already offered their employees coverage saw the mandate as a means of equalizing the burden. However, as the clamour from small businesses generally and small insurers in particular – led respectively by the National Federation of Independent Businesses and the Health Insurance Association of America – grew louder, so the overall attitude of companies and their umbrella organisations turned more hostile, as illustrated by the Chamber of Commerce's about-face (Judis, 1995). The notorious Harry and Louise advertisements exemplified the message by playing on the fears of the haves that their costs would go up and their range of choice of care provider down.

What must have been shocking to the administration was the speed with which these antagonistic messages got across and how quickly the initial positive reaction was replaced by one of doubt and pessimism about how the plan would work. In September polls showed the public supporting a broad outline of the plan by a 2 to 1 margin; yet by the end of October opinion had already shifted to an even split (Schneider, 1993a). An important factor in explaining this turnaround was undoubtedly the very complexity of the plan. Regardless of the merits of the arguments being made for and against the HSA's provisions, it proved much easier for its opponents to articulate their case than for supporters to find a winning soundbite. For example, while the administration struggled to explain the nature and role of the health alliances, the bill's enemies found it easy to portray them as potential bureaucratic monsters who would severely restrict consumer choice.

In a prescient article first published in 1993, Theda Skocpol, looking back over earlier efforts at health care reform, predicted that the administration's expectation that the debate about reform could be won on merit by focusing discussion on the relative strengths and weaknesses of alternative operating systems was unfounded, as a more likely scenario was a bitter ideological struggle.

> If past battles over health insurance turned out to be very ideological, leaving the rational reformers mystified and demoralized, it is very possible that this could happen again during the 1990s. Once again, proponents of universal health care coverage may be becoming overly complacent, assuming that rationality and logic will inevitably triumph. Most reformers are placing their faith in technically complicated insider bargaining, overlooking how ideological and politically charged the debates about health care reform are likely once again to become (1995b, p.281).

In hindsight, however, it was not just the level of opposition from potentially injured parties and ideological opponents of any state intervention which was so devastating, but also the relatively muted support from champions of reform.

Part of the problem was that many single-payer liberals saw their task as being to bargain the administration to the left, which meant that even the strongest advocates of universal care spent much time sniping at the HSA rather than praising it. Perhaps, however, more damaging in terms of actually advancing the legislation in Congress was the scepticism from centrist, DLC type, Democrats as they jumped on the bandwagon denouncing the HSA as a Big Government project. In this context a particularly important development was the reform proposal known as the Cooper plan, after its leading sponsor Representative Jim Cooper from Tennessee. He had been an early advocate of the managed competition approach to reform as it emerged at the start of the 1990s, but he felt that the administration had made too many concessions to the single-payer block. In particular he disagreed with the employer mandate and the imposition of direct controls on insurance premiums. Thus, even as the health care task force deliberated through 1993, Cooper made it clear that he did not like the direction it was taking. His opposition was further reinforced by the fact that, although still a junior member of the House, Cooper was planning a run for Senate in 1994 and was particularly sensitive to the wishes of for-profit hospitals and insurance companies who were providing funds for this campaign (Johnson and Broder, 1997, pp.309–14).

It was two weeks after Clinton's speech to Congress that Cooper released details of his own managed competition plan which, without an employer mandate, he estimated would provide insurance to 60 percent of the then uninsured. Amidst considerable publicity Cooper issued statements which sabotaged the administration's efforts to portray the HSA as the compromise solution. According to Cooper it was *his* bill which was 'squarely in the middle' of the competing versions of reform. Furthermore, emphasising that he had Republican support, Cooper contrasted his 'bipartisan proposal' with the administration's position (Johnson and Broder, 1997, p.314). The not so subtle message was that the HSA was out in left field. In addition, Cooper's credibility was enhanced by the fact that he garnered support from those business and insurance interest groups who were so hostile to the HSA. This all added up to suggest that the message of the Harry and Louise advertisements, that there was a better way to reform than the Clinton plan, carried some weight.

As it was, the Cooper plan made no more progress than the HSA but to some of Cooper's backers his intervention more than served its purpose. That is, in hindsight it is clear that a number of those who attached themselves to his effort did so more because it was not the Clinton plan than because of any real virtues which they saw in it. In his review of events Paul Starr, a pivotal figure in designing the HSA, summed it up thus, 'Most of the initial business backing for the Cooper plan seems to have been expedient. Business interests backed Cooper when they feared the worst; they lost interest when the feared alternatives evaporated' (1995, p.28). Cooper himself later acknowledged that he had overestimated the support for his bill amongst congressional Republicans (Johnson and Broder, 1997, p.316). In some ways then the

Cooper plan had acted as something of a Trojan Horse, giving groups who were in truth quite happy to see no change to the existing system a berth in the reform camp from where they could denounce the HSA as an extremist response to problems which could be more moderately dealt with.

In the end, this cocktail of the vociferous resistance from groups such as the National Federation of Independent Business and the Health Insurance Association of America and the opposition of self-styled moderates who claimed to be offering bipartisan and more sober alternatives overwhelmed the sometimes ambivalent support, given to the Clinton plan by core pro-reform constituencies. The public responded to the message of the critics and by July 1994 polls showed that 'endorsement of the plan had dropped from 57 percent to 37 percent' (Yankelovich, 1995, p.11); and in terms of any possible legislative outcome this was crucial. Without a groundswell of popular support, Congress was not going to pass a bill with such powerful opponents. Thus the HSA never really came close to a floor vote in Congress and all the various other overhaul efforts died along with it.

Inasmuch as it possible to interpret the reasons for the shift in public opinion one primary factor seems to be that the terms of the debate mutated. There was genuine public concern about the plight of the already uninsured and many of the insured worried about the future of their coverage – and support for reform tapped into these sentiments. On the other hand, polls had always shown that the majority of people with insurance were happy with the actual health care they got. The strategy of the anti-Clinton plan forces was to persuade the public that they were more likely to see the quality of the medical care they received diminished and the cost of it increased by heavy-handed government intervention than by leaving things as they were.[6] That is, while there was authentic support for radical change, there was also a great scepticism that government could deliver this (Jacobs, 1994); and in the end it did not prove too difficult for the opponents of the HSA to maneuver enough of the public into concentrating more on their sceptism of government than their desire for reform. Ironically their task was helped by the improving economic situation. As fears about job insecurity eased so too did the related anxiety about losing insurance coverage. The uninsured were no better off, but the insured felt more comfortable and so the sense of a health care system in crisis diminished (Cloud, 1994; Rubin, 1994). Polls still showed much dissatisfaction with the existing arrangements, but as Julie Kosterlitz reflected, 'the public may be more tolerant of existing injustices than it would be of injustices that are perceived to be created by government' (1993, p.2938).

The depressing final result for the administration was that a flagship policy commitment put together in a fashion designed to be representative of its new paradigm approach to governing ended up ridiculed and derided as showing all that was worst about the Democratic Party. Managed competition had suggested itself as a means of achieving universal coverage and cost control without the direct government intervention which would have been necessary under the single-payer or play-or-pay models. The idea that managed competition could therefore be sold as an alternative to a Big Government approach was, however, completely confounded. Single-payer advocates saw the HSA as insufficiently interventionist, but this was a minority interpretation. In the end a bold effort at what would have constituted a radical social and economic reform which might have reshaped the political map to advantage of the Democrats had quite the opposite partisan consequence (Beland et al., 2002).

1995–96: Exploiting the health issue

After taking over Congress, the Republican leadership were keen to act on what they saw as their mandate *to downsize* the American welfare state. They were, however, unwilling at this stage to take on the biggest government-run program, Social Security, but thought that there was an opportunity to make fundamental changes to Medicare and Medicaid. Indeed if they were to hit their balanced budget targets, they had little choice but to propose serious cutbacks to projected spending on these programs; and it was through the budget process that the changes were to be made. That is, by bundling the cuts and restructuring into the budget reconciliation process, the moves would look less like a direct attack on public sector health care and more like measures necessary in the name of fiscal responsibility. Such claims were reinforced by the impending bankruptcy of the Medicare trust fund. This gave Gingrich the chance to insist that his party was determined to 'slow the rate of growth' of Medicare (as distinct from cutting spending) in order to save and preserve the program (Drew, 1997, pp.204–7).

The wider context of the 1995 budget battle was explained in Chapter 4, but it is worth re-emphasising how critical the struggle over Medicare and Medicaid was to the Gingrich revolution and to Clinton's political rehabilitation. With regard to the latter it is worth noting that Gingrich simply dismissed the President's capacity to fight and particularly his willingness to use the veto against his plans (Johnson and Broder, 1997, p.580); and at times throughout 1995 it appeared as if this might be an accurate analysis of the presidential backbone. According to Dick Morris, however, who was instrumental in devising Clinton's responses to Gingrich, the President was always aware of deep underlying differences between the two sides which were unlikely to be bridged. Morris relates how at first he was puzzled as to why a deal could not be struck over the scale of Medicare cuts. Conversations with Senator Trent Lott and then the President, however, made it clear that there was more at stake than just the budget numbers. That is, while Clinton had tried to find ways of reducing spending while minimising the damage to the programs, for the GOP the cuts to Medicare were only the start of an attack on middle-class entitlements (Morris, 1997, pp.172–4). Morris quotes Clinton as saying that the real intention of the Republicans was 'creaming off all the younger, richer, healthier elderly into private health insurance pools ... When they have only the sick and the old and the poor in traditional Medicare and everybody else is in private insurance ... Medicare will be a welfare program' (p.173).

This interpretation does rather conveniently portray triangulation as having a more principled basis than was always apparent. As it was, to the extent that a consistent modus operandi emerged from the White House through the budget imbroglio the strategy was to appear as the flexible party in the negotiations while drawing a line in the sand on certain matters. It turned out that this flexibility included a willingness to move this line as the incoming tide pushed Clinton back up the beach, but defending health care was one of the ideals he was willing and able to exploit; and, in the end the GOP made this quite easy by proposing enormous cuts. Their reconciliation bill proposed to cut $270 billion over seven years from projected Medicare spending. Medicaid was to be cut by less, $163 billion, but was to be fundamentally restructured with some of the existing entitlement elements of the program removed (see Weaver, 1996, pp.65–72). Faced with these proposals, Clinton was in a strong position to veto. The proposed Medicare cuts generated the most publicity, but if anything the changes to Medicaid would have been more serious. Indeed they would almost certainly have led to an *increase* in the number of uninsured in America. Thus, despite the fact that Clinton's own balanced budget proposals required cuts to spending growth rates in both programs, he consistently upped the rhetorical ante when condemning the GOP's health care proposals. This was demonstrated in early December 1995 when, flourishing the same pen that President Johnson had used to sign Medicare and Medicaid into law, Clinton vetoed the Republican budget, declaring, 'Today I am vetoing the biggest Medicare and Medicaid cuts in history' and concluded that 'With this veto, the extreme Republican effort to balance the budget through wrongheaded cuts and misplaced priorities is over' (Hager, 1995d, p.3721).

For this resistance Clinton won public approval. Indeed the perverse result of the Republican efforts to redesign the health care system was to renew popular enthusiasm for the original Clinton plan. A Harris poll one month before the 1996 election found that 54 percent of respondents thought that they would have been 'better off' if the HSA had become law. Over two-thirds of those polled wanted Clinton once again to put forward a package of 'major health care reforms' if re-elected (Peterson, 1998, p.208). Any such wishes, of course, were not fulfilled.

Incremental reform

Despite the failure of the Clinton and Gingrich grand designs, however, there were some changes to the nature of health care provision in the 1990s. The most significant of these were in fact market driven with the increasing domination of Health Maintenance Organizations (see Patel and Rushefsky, 1999, pp.304–38, for a discussion of the pros and cons of HMOs). There were, though, some public policy initiatives enacted which were heralded as steps in the direction of easing and improving access to care.

First, the Health Insurance Portability and Accountability Act, better known as the Kassebaum-Kennedy Act after its co-sponsors Senators Nancy Kassebaum and Ted Kennedy, passed in 1996. Its aim was to provide some protection to workers vulnerable to losing their existing coverage when changing, or worse simply losing, their job. The bill meant that such workers with a pre-existing medical condition could not then be denied access to insurance. When he signed it into law Clinton proclaimed that it represented 'a long step toward the kind of health care our nation needs' (Johnson and Broder, 1997, p.651). In reality, however, the bill was a much more limited accomplishment. Most obviously it did nothing for the uninsured, but even on its own terms it was not as significant as just about all sides in Washington subsequently liked to pretend. What the bill guarantees is that workers losing or changing jobs will have the right to continued coverage so long as they can pay for it. Skocpol rather pithily summarizes, 'many people who think they are going to be helped will be in for a rude surprise. At the very moment that their family's finances are under greatest stress, they will have to ante up huge sums for continuing coverage of marginal quality' (1997, p.194).

A second measure designed to expand coverage was part of the 1997 Balanced Budget Act. The Children's Health Insurance Program (CHIP) gave states $24 billion over five years to improve health coverage among children in low-income families. This reflected the fact that although there had been an increase in the number of children covered by Medicaid during the 1990s there were still at least 10 million uninsured children in the US in 1996 (Patel and Rushefsky, 1999, p.297). The broad aim of CHIP was to expand coverage to uninsured children in families with incomes above state Medicaid eligibility levels but below 200 percent of the poverty line. The estimates of how many children this might cover ranged from 2.5 million to 5 million children (The Kaiser Commission on Medicaid and the Uninsured, 2000, p.27). At the time Clinton left office it was still too early to pass a definitive judgement on the effectiveness of CHIP in helping its target constituency. Part of the problem is that like Medicaid, CHIP requires states to pay some of the costs and allows them to draw up some of the guidelines, which makes it difficult to come up with a national picture. Initial surveys suggested some, but slow, progress with variations across the states (Patel and Rushefsky, 1999, pp.303–4). Clinton himself was frustrated by the delays in enrolling potentially eligible children and made this point to the National Governors Association when he addressed them in the summer of 1999 (Pear, 1999).

Conclusion: little change

The story told in this chapter might suggest a stalemate on health care issues during the 1990s. Such a judgement, however, would be to underestimate the significance of the failure of the Clinton reform effort both in terms of health care policy and also, more broadly, in terms of how the memory of this failure downsized the ambition of the administration. Certainly on the health care front the situation at the end of 2000 was worse by some measures than when Clinton took office.

The extraordinary medical inflation of the start of the 1990s did ease somewhat in the mid-1990s, largely due to the spread of the HMOs and their managed care plans designed to cut back on 'unnecessary' treatments, but by late 2000 there were some signs that medical inflation was picking up again; and, as insurance premiums rose well beyond overall inflation, employers were once again faced with prospect of squeezing their employees, their customers or their profit margins (Verhovek, 2000). In addition state officials were beginning to complain again about the burden of Medicaid and also of CHIP's additional costs. In Ohio, for example, the state legislature had to authorize a $248 million bailout of Medicaid in December 2000 (Guiden, 2001).

Even more categorically, the data showed that the other overriding problem – that of the millions of uninsured people – had worsened. In 1999, 42.5 million people, representing 15.5 percent of the population, lacked insurance. The one crumb of comfort was that this figure did show a slight decline from the peak in 1998 of 44.3 million, amounting to 16.3 percent of the population, without coverage (US, 2000, p.14). Overall these statistics, especially in the light of low unemployment, the Kassebaum-Kennedy reform and the CHIP program, represented a very poor return to those who had vested such hope in the arrival of the Clinton administration. It is impossible to escape the conclusion that judged by the promises made in 1992 these numbers represent a failure to remedy one of the US's sorest social ills.

According to some critics, and not just conservative Republicans, this failure can be put down to the administration blowing its chance of enacting reform through its pursuit of too liberal a solution. For example, writing in the fall of 1995 Fred Siegel and Will Marshall, two leading voices of the New Democrat movement, reflected, 'The defeat of President Clinton's comprehensive health care reforms marked the end of a half-century effort to create a full-blown American version of the European welfare state. The question for Democrats now is what they should put in its place' (1995, p.8). The implication is that Clinton went too far – that maybe he should have gone with legislation resembling the Cooper plan which, if enacted, would have represented a significant advance. This, however, is a judgement based on the twenty-twenty vision of hindsight. Clinton would have come under immense fire if he had not delivered a plan promising universal coverage after the manner in which he had campaigned in 1992. Much, of course, ultimately depends on what the primary problems of the US health care system are deemed to be. During the 2000 election campaign, health issues did feature quite prominently, but in a select fashion. Incremental proposals were the order of the day with only Bill Bradley coming close to an embracing plan and this was ridiculed by Gore during the Democratic primaries as fiscally irresponsible. Revealingly, the debate also centred on those already insured. That is, there were two chief areas of contention; first, the question of a patients' bill of rights which had grown as a demand as a result of the perceived penny-pinching by HMOs; second, the question of paying for prescription drugs for seniors. These are without doubt matters of real consequence, but in 1992 the debate was addressed in a more fundamental fashion and Clinton was not out on a left-wing limb in calling for universal coverage within a tighter fiscal framework.

Furthermore, the evidence of the 1990s suggested that incremental reform, even when combined with the most favourable economic circumstances, will do little to resolve the underlying problems which prevent many people from getting access to insurance coverage. *The health care system will not heal itself.* If, therefore, lack of coverage *is* seen as a significant issue, it is difficult to discern how it can be comprehensively tackled except through government led action. The political dilemma is that the corporate voices will always be louder than the uninsured, particularly as those most likely to be uninsured are the poor or near poor – a weak political constituency – who are in fact often the people most in need of medical care (Wolfe, 1994). The administration may have been naïve in not appreciating the hostility that its proposals would arouse, but equally it is unrealistic to insist that some formula be found through which coverage can be expanded, costs contained, and all the players in the system left content. In this context, although it may have been far from ideal, the HSA was an attempt to balance and reconcile the various competing interests. It turned out that the potential losers were much more vociferous and well organized than those who would have benefited, but in their condemnation of the HSA New Democrats somewhat belied their talk of the need for tough choices and bold action; when Clinton actually followed this course through many of them looked askance. Theda Skocpol is particularly dismissive of the 'too liberal' thesis. She derided, 'Journalistic accounts that accuse the Clinton administration of devising a liberal, big-government approach to health care reform' as 'simply misrepresenting the most basic aspects of what happened from 1992 through 1994' because 'the Clinton Health Security plan was *a compromise* between market-oriented and government-centered reform ideas' (1997, p.15).

As it was, the health care wars of the first term, which were critical battles over the nature of the American welfare state, ended in defeat for both sides. Clinton's victory in 1992 seemed to point towards a major expansion of the government role in health care, but then scepticism of government got in the way. The 1994 results looked as though they might build on this scepticism and herald a dramatic withdrawal of the state, but Americans did not want this either. Thus, Clinton was able to win re-election in 1996 as a defender of social insurance programs, but this triumph was not a prelude to any more grand designs. In the much narrower, but highly emotive, area of means-tested welfare benefits to poor single parent families, however, there was to be dramatic action.

6
Reforming Welfare

The New Democrat objection to the health care reform attempt was not just that it was in itself too liberal, but that it came, in whatever form, before welfare reform. Given the complexity and significance of these two social policy issues, it was generally acknowledged that it would have been unreasonable to put them both before Congress at the same time. To New Democrats the decision to prioritize health care was a regrettable one as it gave the impression that the administration was more influenced by its liberal instincts than its centrist ones. Even while health care was still apparently a viable proposition, Will Marshall reflected on 'a questionable strategic judgement' which 'delayed action on welfare' but 'pressed ahead' with the 'plan to overhaul the nation's health care system' (1993, p.6). After the health care effort had disintegrated critics were more forthright. Indeed in the aftermath of the 1994 elections one commentator went as far as to claim, 'I don't think it is much of an exaggeration to say that if in 1994 Clinton had pushed for welfare reform instead of his health plan, we might now be talking about a Democratic realignment rather than a Republican realignment' (Kaus, 1995, p.xiv). Baer explains the New Democrat rationale behind these arguments, 'Welfare reform – and the theory of governance that undergirded it – was, quite simply, the most significant policy innovation that differentiated Clinton from liberal Democrats' (Baer, 2000, p.214). Simply put, welfare was widely perceived as the ultimate give-away program which served as an illustration of everything that was wrong with Big Government and the misguidedness of do-good liberalism. In a classic illustration of pre-emptive politics designed to combat the image of the Democrats as being the pro-welfare party, candidate Clinton had frequently promised 'to end welfare as we know it' and this message was vigorously pressed in potential swing states in the weeks leading to the 1992 election. In the place of welfare cheques Clinton proposed to substitute a work based social policy. This would require individual welfare recipients to take any available job or participate in a community work scheme in return for continued government assistance. To the DLC camp, quick delivery on this pledge would have been the best way of consolidating the New Democrat image and dispelling the idea that once in office Clinton would be beholden to the party's liberal wing.

In the end, unlike health care reform, radical welfare reform did duly arrive. The final passage of welfare reform has been interpreted by reference to John Kingdon's model of agenda setting in public policy and this does provide a valuable framework in aiding understanding of why welfare reform found a way through the congressional maze while the HSA did not (Kingdon, 1995; Camissa, 1998, pp.68–76; Weaver, 2000, pp.35–7). The purpose of this chapter, however, is not so much to look at the legislative mechanics of reform but at what the nature of the reform debate, the shape of the final legislation and Clinton's decision to sign it tell us about Clintonism as a political philosophy, particularly as, at the end of his presidency, Clinton and the New Democrats were eager to claim welfare reform as a successful example of their approach to government (Democratic Leadership Council, 2000). In fact the bill which Clinton signed into law in August 1996, titled the Personal Responsibility and Work Opportunity Reconciliation Act, was authored by Republicans, but the decision to actually sign it did represent a triumph for the New Democrats. There was bitter disagreement in the summer of 1996 over what to do when PRWORA arrived on the President's desk. Senior DLC figures urged him to sign it, but much of the cabinet and the liberal social policy community wanted a veto. The fact that Clinton took the former course was thus interpreted as a key New Democrat moment for him. For liberals it was perhaps the policy low point of the administration. What is sometimes overlooked in all of this is that Clinton did put forward a welfare reform proposal in the summer of 1994 which could be seen as a genuine effort at finding a Third Way path between liberal and conservative perspectives.

Welfare under fire

At the time of its passage all sides agreed that the PRWORA was a landmark in American social policy. It was, in the words of the Green Book, the bible of US social policy data, 'the first time that major welfare entitlement benefits have been repealed or substantially altered'

(US, 1996a, p.1328). The bill in fact had a number of objectives but its primary purpose was to end Aid to Families with Dependent Children which had been part of the 1935 Social Security Act. AFDC was a program which directed income support to poor, largely single parent, families with children under eighteen.[1] In 1994, when AFDC rolls were at their peak, the program provided benefits to a monthly average of just over 5 million families, adding up to just over 14.2 million recipients, and constituting 14.8 percent of American families with children under eighteen. The average monthly benefit per family was $376 (US, 1996a, p.386), although this figure hides large discrepancies between states which set their own level of benefit. The purpose of the new law was to shift these people off welfare, preferably by getting the mothers into work or into a stable relationship with another wage earner. The underlying theme of PRWORA was that AFDC had constituted a 'something for nothing' program which had undermined traditional American principles about the value of work and which, in doing so, had simultaneously created resentment among the majority, non-welfare, population and demeaned those on welfare by entrapping them in a cycle of dependency.[2]

The details of how PRWORA intended to end the so-called 'dependency culture' will be described in more detail later in the chapter. Before looking more closely at events in the 1990s, though, it is worth briefly recapping the development of welfare as a policy and political issue. In particular why had such hostility grown up to a program which predominantly served poor single parents and their children – clearly one of the most vulnerable family types in society?

In cost terms AFDC was a small program. In 1994 total expenditure was $23.4 billion of which the federal government paid just over half and the state governments the remainder (US, 1996a, p.386). This hardly put it in the same budget busting league as Social Security. The real point about AFDC was its resonance as a values issue. One of the reasons why Social Security enjoyed popular support was that it was assumed to be a benefit which its recipients, who could no longer be expected to work, had earned over their lifetime of working. The grounds of eligibility for AFDC, however, were not perceived to be similarly legitimate. Growing old is pretty well inevitable but the same cannot be said about being a poor, non-working, single parent. Thus, while popular understanding of the complexities of the American welfare system might have been limited, welfare as an issue encapsulated a clash of values about the importance of work in American life; and what was particularly at issue was the position of the long-term welfare dependent and the sense that they were not playing by the same rules as everyone else. Judith Shklar reflected that while the collection of American attitudes towards welfare 'is not perhaps a coherent ideology, ... it is certainly an intelligible one. Not to work is not to earn, and without one's earnings one is "nobody"' (1991, p.92). Polling evidence backed up this interpretation of popular feeling. Weaver et al. summarized their study of polls thus

> Welfare has come to connote dependence ... and the welfare system is perceived to have greater negative than positive effects ... majorities of the public are concerned that welfare benefits may be too high and that welfare encourages long-term dependence, and that too many welfare recipients do not want to work.... "Welfare," in short, is perceived as being at odds with the widely shared American values of individualism and the work ethic (1995, p.607).

This final point was further elaborated by Feldman and Zaller who maintained that most Americans have internalized the values of classical economic liberalism, particularly the emphasis on economic individualism and that it was thus actually supporters of welfare 'who are most beset by value conflict ... because they ... must somehow reconcile activist government with traditional principles of ... laissez faire' (1992, p.269). In the mid-1990s Urban Institute analyst Isabel Sawhill offered the following explanation of why policy was increasingly heading off in experimental directions which were not based on rigorous social science research.[3] Noting an October 1994 poll in which 89 percent favoured a 2 year welfare limit followed by work and 76 percent agreed that having another child while on welfare should not result in extra benefit, she reflected

> [R]esearch gives insufficient emphasis to the role of public morality in shaping the current welfare debate. It ignores the public's desire to align welfare rules with their own values. The public is not lacking in compassion, but it does believe that poor people should play by the same rules as the middle class. When you don't work, you don't get paid. And when you have another baby, you don't get a raise. The public may even be willing to risk doing some harm to children in order to instil more of this kind of discipline into the system (1995, p.8).

In short, there is an inherent suspicion of giving income benefits to those of working age; and this distrust was apparent even at the establishment of AFDC (then ADC) in 1935. ADC was always a secondary program in relation to the main contributory based social insurance old age and unemployment schemes set up for wage earners. ADC, for example, was the only benefit established by the 1935 Social Security Act which included a criteria of need. Furthermore, the benefit was intended only for single mothers who were deemed to be morally worthy – assumed to be widowers and some deserted mothers – which left claimants subject to investigation, with their fate in the hands of local caseworkers: and even if these criteria were satisfied the benefit level still reflected an ambivalence about substituting cash benefits for work. Thus, although the stated intention was to allow women to play the role of mother rather than worker, the benefit levels, which were set at state level, were often so low that the women could only survive by supplementing their benefit through working (Gordon, 1994, pp.294–301).

Nevertheless, by the latter half of the 1960s, AFDC had attained something approaching entitlement status for poor single parent families, especially after a series of Supreme Court decisions in the 1960s took away much of the effective discretion which had been exercised at state and local level about who was and who was not eligible for the benefit (Teles, 1996, pp.107–17). In the early 1960s only about 33 percent of families applying for welfare were successful. By 1971, however, around 90 percent were (Katz, 1989, p.106). The combination of these changes and the growing number of single parent families did lead to a significant jump in the number of families enrolled on AFDC in the decade. In 1950 the average monthly number of families receiving AFDC was 651,000. This had risen to 803,000 families by 1960, but jumped to just over 1.9 million by 1970 (US, 1998b, p.402). Not surprisingly this made the program more likely to catch the eye of both politicians and the public – and from 1969 "welfare reform" became a persistent refrain in American politics.

Through the 1970s various unsuccessful reform efforts contained both liberal and conservative strands (Moynihan, 1973; Leman, 1980; Waddan, 1998); but from the early 1980s the reform rhetoric took on a more distinctly conservative trajectory as Reagan railed against welfare dependency and invoked the stereotype image of the 'welfare queen'. In intellectual quarters Reagan's rhetorical bombast was matched by the work of Charles Murray and the near apocalyptic writings of George Gilder who predicted a descent into chaos if the welfare state and feminism were not rescinded forthwith (Gilder, 1981; Murray, 1984). Another strident proponent of these views is Robert Rector of the Heritage Foundation. Rector's attachment to such an influential right-wing think tank means that he is an important player in Washington politics and he has close ties to several of the Republican legislators who were at the centre of the 1996 reform (for indicative writing see, Rector, 1992; 1996). The primary contention of these writers is well-rehearsed and not that complex. In short the expansion of welfare programs, however well-intentioned, was a social disaster as it simply encouraged people to make choices which in the long-term deprived them of their dignity and their capacity to make a meaningful contribution to society. This in turn detached them from society and created a quasi-permanent underclass trapped into a culture of dependency. The necessary response was to be cruel to be kind and to end those programs which fuelled this deviant behavior.

While Murray and Rector have provided the most dramatic expression of anti-welfare sentiment, a subtler line of conservative thought has also emerged, championed most articulately by Lawrence Mead, which has had a greater impact on the development of non-conservative thought. In contrast to these writers Mead does not call for the withdrawal of the state and, indeed, his 'new paternalism' proposes measures which are highly interventionist (1997a). According to Mead by the late 1960s the declining work effort of the welfare poor had become a substantial problem which demanded a change of policy emphasis.

> Before 1960, poverty levels were much higher than now, but most poor adults were employed, and this tended over time to integrate them. Today, there is less poverty, but the separation of the poor from the economy makes integration more doubtful. Therefore, social programs must promote work, and even enforce it, assuming the function that the workplace did before (Mead, 1997b, p.229).

Mead's examination of the work levels of the non-poor and the welfare poor led him to conclude, 'High work levels for the general population sustain the citizenship rationale for the social insurance welfare state, but low work levels for the poor put that case in question for welfare and other antipoverty programs' (1997b, p.206). The crucial point for Mead is that the lack of work effort was not due to insurmountable structural barriers to steady employment, but to a failure by the welfare poor to hold down jobs which were available. The willingness to work, even for low wages in undesirable jobs, is an obligation which too many people had shirked by not taking jobs which were available and which they could do (1997c, pp.6–31).

For these conservative critiques to have a real impact it was important, however, that they enter the mainstream discourse in non-conservative circles. Thus one of the seminal books at the end of the 1980s was David Ellwood's *Poor Support* which recommended a clear time limit to relatively unconditional welfare receipt (1988). The book also discussed how government could provide a whole array of support services, including acting as an employer of last resort and making work a significantly more attractive financial option for welfare recipients; it was, however, the concept of time limits coming from a moderate Democrat which made his analysis politically compelling. Furthermore, the general tirades against dependency and cultures of poverty had gained greater credibility in the later 1980s when surveys illustrated that a greater proportion of welfare recipients than had previously been understood were long term clients. The traditional methods of data collection suggested that, while there was a lot of cycling on and off welfare, most welfare spells were relatively short-lived. Analysis, however, which did not look at the total number of welfare spells but at the welfare population at a given point in time showed that about half the recipients were in spells which would last eight years and more (Bane and Ellwood, 1994). This gave support to those who insisted that there was a chronic problem of long-term welfare dependence. Another critical change to the terms of the debate was the increase in female participation in the labour force. In 1960, less than 20 percent of mothers with children under six worked outside the home. In 1991, 58 percent did so – as indeed did 54 percent of mothers with a child less than three years old (Kamarck, 1992, p.13). The traditional perception of the mother's role as being one of nurturing her young was thus a less persuasive argument for not demanding work of welfare mothers.

Many liberals, however, while they agreed that AFDC was a poor program, worried that its unpopularity was based on more sinister factors than simple adherence to *laissez faire* principles. Their concern was that feelings about welfare were fuelled by racial stereotypes. For example, Gilens has argued that 'the symbolic power of welfare as a political issue stems in large measure from its racial undertones' (1996, p.602; see also, Gilens, 1999). Nevertheless, whatever the legitimacy of these misgivings about the motives of the reform agenda by the late 1980s, the conventional wisdom held that the welfare system was failing not only American society in the round, but especially the very recipients of AFDC benefits themselves. The evidence of the 1970s, however, was that welfare reform was a political quagmire, as the agreement that there should be change was not matched by any agreement on what form that change should actually take (Leman, 1980; Waddan, 1997). This apparent truism, though, was undermined when, after exhaustive negotiation, the Democratic Congress and the Reagan administration agreed on a compromise measure known as the Family Support Act of 1988. This gave a more formal structure to existing work requirements in US welfare law, but also instituted some supportive services. Its advocates championed the FSA as embracing a potentially productive carrot and stick approach – perhaps indeed a Third Way synthesis, although this was not a description used at the time.

The directives of the Act, however, were to be applied gradually and, before the changes had a chance to make a mark, the reform was over-taken by events as the welfare rolls grew rapidly after its passage. AFDC numbers had been relatively stable through the 1980s but between 1988 and 1992 the number of recipients rose from 10.9 million to 13.6 million (US 1994, p.325). This rather undercut those welfare experts who hoped that the FSA would draw a line under policy innovation, leaving the way open for concentration on implementation issues (Bane, 1992). By 1992, welfare reform was back high on the agenda, as many Americans, including many policymakers, had concluded that whatever the 'stick' element of the FSA too many of those on welfare were still not making a serious work effort and were therefore violating expectations of the American way – primarily to their own detriment. Conservatives had long tapped into anti-welfare sentiment. What was different about 1992 was that the Democratic candidate made the run-ning on the welfare issue, promising a bold, if not fully defined, over-haul.

To end welfare as known

To New Democrats then welfare was exactly the sort of area where liberalism's reflexive defence of existing government programs had for too long kept the party on wrong side of the issue, both in terms of good policy and good politics. Welfare was therefore a prime candidate for redrawing the relationship between individual and state in order to establish a new balance in the claims that each could make of the other. Welfare reform, in other words, would operationalize the 'new covenant' campaign rhetoric, and demonstrate that there was a path-way between the cruder conservative calls simply to cut benefits and liberalism's blinkered insistence on protecting the safety net whatever the broader, long-term, social cost. In *Mandate for Change*, the PPI's primer to the new President, Marshall and Kamarck emphasized the urgency of the issue. 'The new President must rekindle a sense of moral urgency and reciprocal obligation, and spell out the harmful consequences for all Americans of continued inaction' (1993, p.220). Clinton did in fact have a track record of action on welfare when as Governor of Arkansas he had been heavily involved in the development of the FSA. In *Putting People First* Clinton and Gore had explained their philosophy.

> It's time to honor and reward people who work hard and play by the rules. That means ending welfare as we know it – not by punishing the poor or preaching to them, but by empowering Americans to take care of their children and improve their lives. No one who works full-time and has children at home should be poor anymore. No one who can work should stay on welfare forever (1992, p.164).

Here then the subject of welfare was placed in a wider context and was associated with the plan to expand the EITC in order to make sure that work did pay. On the other hand, the 'ending welfare as we know it' commitment was also brandished indiscriminately in order to ensure that welfare could not be used as a wedge issue by President Bush's team. That is, however well Clinton understood the interdependence of welfare, access to health care, low-pay, and job insecurity, the dramatic campaign language focusing explicitly on welfare created a hostage to fortune which kicked in in 1996.

The Work and Responsibility Act

The fact that the administration did put forward a welfare reform plan of its own in the summer of 1994 has almost been relegated to a historical footnote, but the ideas behind what was known as the Work and Responsibility Act deserve some consideration. In a similar fashion to the HSA, the WRA did try to negotiate a path between competing prescriptions for change as it strived to strike a Third Way balance between the rights and responsibilities of government and welfare recipient. Perhaps predictably, this split the Democrats with the further unintended, though perhaps equally predictable, consequence of ultimately shifting the grounds of the debate further to the right.

The WRA was an extensive and detailed package, but the radical central plank was the proposal to limit the amount of time that people could stay on AFDC to two years. After this if recipients had not found a job in the private sector, they would be required to participate in community work schemes if they were to continue to receive financial assistance through a program called, simply enough, WORK. During their two years on AFDC, adults would have to engage with education and training schemes established by the FSA. If the 'adult' in the family was still of school-age then she would have to attend school, and single teenage mothers would also be required to live with their parents. If any eligible AFDC recipients refused to take part then, the whole family's money would be stopped. Other key provisions were the requirement on new single mothers to name the father in order to start receiving benefits, and plans to be more pro-active in chasing down so-called 'deadbeat dads' for child support. The administration compromised on the question of the 'family cap' by giving states the option of limiting AFDC benefit increases when additional children were born to a parent already on welfare.

A key part of the Clinton's presentation of his plan was that it would be deficit neutral, and funding was a real problem for the policy-makers in constructing an expansive program. The welfare policy community was agreed that serious implementation of welfare to work measures would mean spending more money than was paid out under the auspices of AFDC; but strict budgeting was still the overriding imperative in Washington in the summer of 1994 which meant that the WRA had to be self-financing. In turn this meant that the increased expenditures needed to pay for education, training, WORK and expanding child care facilities would either have to be paid for by new taxes or cutting spending elsewhere. The former was judged to be politically impossible, but relying on finding savings from other parts of the welfare system immediately meant that the money likely to be available was going to be very limited. In the end the net cost of the plan was estimated at $9.3 billion, with the administration forced to recoup this through a series of measures including tightening welfare eligibility for legal immigrants whose relatives were able to support them; capping emergency welfare programs run by the states, and limiting disability payments for drug and alcohol addiction.

One consequence of this limited budget was that it prevented a 'big bang' approach to the proposed implementation of reform. That is, the WRA would only have gradually phased in its work requirements to the extent that it was estimated that by 1999 less than five percent of the adult AFDC caseload would be at work in government sponsored jobs (Weaver, 2000, p.243). As Kent Weaver notes, this 'phase-in was both fiscally necessary and administratively prudent, but it did not constitute "ending welfare as we know it" – at least not in the short term' (1998, p.383).

As it was, the administration's efforts to reconcile demands for a more coercive workfare approach with continuing government support for the most vulnerable met with a mixed response. There had, in fact, already been considerable squabbling behind the scenes as the delay in the release of the WRA reflected not just its place behind health care in the social policy agenda but also some quite serious disagreements about its contents (Weaver, 2000, pp.232–5). According to David Ellwood, who had been drafted into the Department of Health and Human Services in order to work on the welfare bill, the most serious dispute was about how long people could stay in government sponsored jobs. The more DLC-oriented aides thought that this, like AFDC, should be time-limited. Others, like Ellwood, thought that it was enough that people were swapping a welfare cheque for a pay cheque and that they should therefore be allowed to stay on WORK as long as necessary. In the end the compromise was that no single WORK assignment could last for more than twelve months and that after two such assignments anyone still in need of a public job would have their case thoroughly reviewed, but there would be no cut-off point.[4] Once in the open, the bill split the Democrats in various ways. Despite the government agreeing to act as an employer of last resort, many liberals, and particularly those in the Congressional Black Caucus, just did not like the idea of time limits – and expressed dismay at the idea of depriving already desperate families of benefit.[5] At the other end of the party's ideological spectrum some conservative Democrats felt that the phasing-in of workfare was too gradual. Another concerned group were Hispanic Democrats who disliked the targeting of benefits to legal immigrants for cutbacks; and public sector unions worried that the subsidized jobs might displace people already in work, despite provisions in the Act designed to prevent this (Weaver, 1998, p.383).

New Democrats generally offered support even though their representatives in the internal deliberations had wanted something a little tougher. In an editorial, the DLC's magazine backed the plan while taking the opportunity for a spot of liberal bashing.

> President Clinton has it right: Welfare can't be reformed; it must be replaced by a work-based social policy.... To spurn time limits ... is to accept the welfare status quo with all its perversities and defects.
>
> ... Only by refusing to work could someone make themselves vulnerable to homelessness. If liberals believe society owes indefinite

financial support to those who flatly refuse to work, they should say so (*The New Democrat*, 1994, p.6).

Perhaps the best reception for the bill came from the press with a series of editorials offering praise to the administration for at least providing a good place to begin the process of reform, even as they noted that only a minority of welfare families would be immediately affected. The *New York Times* described the WRA as a 'measured attack on a social pathology' (1994); the *Los Angeles Times* reflected that that Clinton plan 'has the beginnings of a pretty good deal for both welfare mothers and taxpayers' (1994); the *Chicago Tribune* saw it as a 'good starting point' (1994), and the *Washington Post* gave its editorial the title 'A Solid Start on Welfare Reform' (1994). Republicans were not so complimentary. Representative James Talent from Missouri ridiculed the bill. 'It's like diagnosing a patient with a terminal disease and prescribing ... aspirin' (quoted in Kranish, 1994, p.3). Newt Gingrich chose another analogy to deride the plan. 'The President is brilliant at describing a Ferrari, but his staff continues to deliver a Yugo' (quoted in Marcus and Balz, 1994, p.A18).

In the end this discussion of the WRA was somewhat redundant inasmuch as the bill was introduced too near to the 1994 mid-term elections to make legislative headway, especially as health care was still formally on the decks, even if few any longer thought it had any chance of enactment. In fact, as it stood the WRA could not have proceeded without significant change as it was premised on the assumption of the HSA's passage thus taking the complicating question of continued Medicaid coverage for those leaving the welfare rolls out of the equation. Given the timing of the WRA's introduction, the presumption was that the administration had wanted to get something on record before the mid-term elections but that serious legislative activity would have to wait until 1995. This of course was premised on the Democrats retaining their congressional majorities. When Congress reconvened in January 1995 the dynamic of the welfare debate had significantly shifted. If the WRA was the starting point, then welfare reform had a long way to travel – in a distinctly rightwards direction.

The PRWORA

Welfare reform was one of the central promises of the Contract with America on which congressional Republicans, especially candidates for the House, campaigned in 1994. True to their word, the House leadership quickly introduced a bill which made it apparent that they wished to downsize even further the rights of citizens to call on the state for help. Although liberals were apprehensive about the manner in which the Clinton plan had redrawn the relationship between government and welfare recipient, it had at least maintained a sense of mutual obligation. That is, the WRA did acknowledge a role for government as an employer of last resort and, through a complex formula, allowed those who left welfare to move into work to buy back future welfare time. The Republican plans, though, firmly declared that no able-bodied, working-aged adult was entitled to cash assistance from the state either for herself or her children for more than a minimal period.

As it was, the Republicans also found that reforming welfare was not an easy legislative process, as they clashed about the specifics of their plan.[6] There was, however, a determination to force the issue to a head either to achieve a transformation of the welfare system or to force Clinton into a potentially damaging veto of reform legislation. Furthermore, when devising their proposals, the GOP had one distinct advantage over Clinton's welfare team inasmuch as they were not concerned to find extra revenues to fund the various training and job creation schemes envisaged under the WRA. Spending on welfare was to be reduced not just in the long-term but was to be part of the immediate deficit reduction effort.

In its final form, one of the key features of PRWORA was the devolution of responsibility for drawing up particular welfare to work programs down to the states.[7] The money which federal government had previously spent on AFDC was thus given to the states with no specific directives about how rolls should be reduced or work encouraged. On the other hand, this devolution came with considerable strings attached for the states in terms of how future federal money was tied to reaching work participation requirements and/or caseload reduction targets. More fundamentally, while the law included a variety of opt-in clauses which states could adopt or not at their own discretion, it set absolute time limits for how long welfare recipients could be paid benefits with federal money.

In brief, the PRWORA terminated AFDC and replaced it with a benefit named Temporary Assistance to Needy Families. The law stipulated that welfare recipients could receive TANF cash benefits for a maximum of two years before they were required to engage in some sort of work related activity – a time frame which could be shortened at state discretion. The law did allow that claimants could be engaged in government sponsored activities such as education, training or subsidized employment, at state discretion, for a further three years after their initial twenty-four months on welfare, but this marked the end of their assistance – and this five year limit was a *lifetime* limit on the receipt of TANF benefits (and again this five year limit was a maximum which could be shortened at state discretion).[8] Thus although the Act acknowledged that government had an *initial* duty to provide aid to those falling on hard times and perhaps also provide assistance in overcoming structural barriers to work, it stated that there does come a time when government no longer has an obligation to help those deemed not to be making a sufficient effort to help themselves and even, theoretically, those making a good faith effort to play by the rules but who do not have the resources to make it on their own. Furthermore, the clear expectation was that while in receipt of benefits, claimants would suffer financial sanctions if they did not comply with state rules about work effort. The regulations about and use of sanctions as an arm of policy varied considerably from state to state but all state programs utilised them in one form or another.

In addition to these workfare elements there were a series of other provisions contained in the legislation which drove liberals to despair. Legal immigrants already in the US became ineligible for Supplemental Security Income (SSI) and food stamps, with states having the option to deny them federal welfare money and Medicaid. New non-citizens would be ineligible for all of these programs. The Act also introduced new, stricter, criteria in determining whether children are disabled and thus eligible for SSI payments. At the time the Congressional Budget Office projected that this would have the effect of denying benefits to about 300,000 children who would have been eligible pre-PRWORA (Katz, 1996, p.2193). Furthermore, the Act also introduced work requirements for able-bodied recipients of food stamps aged between 18 and 50.

To sign or not to sign

Clinton did in fact twice veto Republican welfare reform. First, in December 1995, when it came to him as part of the much bigger reconciliation bill and then again in January 1996, when it was still accompanied by unpopular cuts in Food Stamps and School Lunch programs which provided enough political cover for a veto (Solomon, 1995; Weaver, 2000, p.320). In an election year the next question was whether the Republicans would call Clinton's bluff and send him a stand-alone welfare bill. In the early months of 1996 it was not clear that they would do this as Medicaid reform was tied in with welfare in a way that Clinton would clearly not accept. Much of the deliberation was less to do with the merits of welfare reform than about political strategy. Did Republican members of Congress want to be able to campaign on the accomplishment of welfare reform or did they want to give their presidential candidate an issue? In the end they chose the former course and in July the House and Senate passed their own versions of welfare reform. The next congressional obstacle was cleared when the conferees from the two chambers ironed out the differences and thus sent back PRWORA for the final floor votes. There was little doubt at this point that the bill would receive congressional approval, but many Democrats were in a quandary. In an election year they were unwilling to oppose a popular measure to no purpose. That is, if Clinton was going to sign the bill then they might as well follow his lead. If Clinton made it clear that he would veto the bill then there was a reason for resistance.

On 1 August Clinton called a White House meeting of senior advisers to discuss how he should respond. Lined up against PRWORA were some powerful voices including the Secretary of Health and Human Services Donna Shalala, the chief-of-staff Leon Panetta and most of the policy advisers present. Lobbying in favour were the political advisers and one senior domestic policy adviser Bruce Reed. DLCers present, such as Kamarck, urged him to say 'yes' (for accounts of this meeting see, Reich, 1998, pp.328–31; Stephanopoulos, 1999, pp.419–22). There were elements of the bill which the New Democrats did not like but they insisted that almost any change was better than none (Marshall, 1996). One person not at the August meeting but whose presence hung heavy over it was Dick Morris. According to his account, Clinton was deeply uneasy about PRWORA, particularly about the harshness to legal immigrants who did work and paid taxes. Morris, however, was clear about the possible impact of another veto now that the GOP had agreed to separate the welfare bill from Medicaid. 'I told him flatly that a welfare veto would cost him the election. Mark Penn had designed a polling model that indicated that a welfare veto by itself would transform a fifteen-point win into a three-point loss' (1997, p.300).

In the end, whether Clinton was more influenced by Morris's analysis or by his distaste for the existing welfare system, he announced he would sign the bill. With no political cover, uncertain congressional Democrats stampeded to the 'yes' camp. The final tallies showed House Democrats split exactly evenly, 98 votes to 98 votes, with 25 in

favour and 21 against in Senate. The opposition included the vast
majority of African-American, Hispanic and women members as well as
the senior Democrats in each chamber – Gephardt and Bonior in the
House and Tom Daschle in Senate. Of the Senate Democrats up for re-
election in 1996, however, only Paul Wellstone from Minnesota voted
against. Stephanopoulos, who was opposed to the bill, tries to explain
Clinton's rationale in the following manner. 'His heart urged a veto,
while his head calculated the risk. They were reconciled by his will – a
will to win that was barely distinguishable and basically inseparable
from the conviction that what was best for the poor was for him to be
president' (1999, p.421). Reich was much less sanguine. 'There's no
point to winning reelection if it has to be done this way' (1998, p.331).

Conclusion

Any classification of the various options for welfare reform being discussed in 1992 would have placed the ideas in PRWORA as being on
the far right of the spectrum. It is thus difficult to see how Clinton's
judgment that he should sign this bill can be regarded as a genuine
Third Way reconciliation of the differing perspectives on welfare
reform, yet this decision was widely identified as a key New Democrat
moment in his presidency. What is clear is how dramatically the
dynamic had shifted and how difficult it was, having joined in the setting up of a 'straw welfare queen', not to also join in knocking this
down. To E.J. Dionne this demonstrated the folly of not tackling welfare reform earlier, not just for the political reasons cited by some New
Democrats, but in order to ensure a good policy outcome. That is, it
was a measure of Clinton's impact that he had 'pulled large chunks of
the Democratic Party to a new posture toward the welfare state.' He and
the party, however, did not act when they controlled the agenda, at a
point when they 'might have occupied a sensible middle ground and
achieved substantial (and necessary) changes. Instead, they pushed the
debate to the right and opened the way for the Republicans' radical
departures' (1997b, p.173). In an interesting comment on the way the
issue developed Stephanopoulos reflected that his demand for a veto of
PRWORA was 'tempered by my complicity' (1999, p.420). That is, during 1992 he and the campaign team had been more than happy to promote the 'ending welfare' line 'even though I knew full well that it sent
a message far more powerful than, and somewhat contradictory to, the
fine print of our proposal in *Putting People First*, which had promised
more assistance to welfare recipients looking for work, not less' (p.421).

Critically, the WRA proved to be just a staging post on the journey to reform, yet to many liberals even this went too far in the direction of placing the burden of proof on welfare recipients. It is possible, however, to see the WRA as an attempt to balance the demand that welfare recipients take more personal responsibility for their fate with a continuing recognition of the state's responsibility to help struggling families if they were at least *trying* to help themselves – a justification for extended aid not apparent in PRWORA. Certainly there were enough differences between the WRA and the PRWORA that some of the chief designers of the former were outspoken in their condemnation of the latter (Ellwood, 1996; Bane, 1997; and see, Edelman, 1997, for a passionate critique from someone with close ties to the administration). Ironically, however, while the anger of those Democrats opposed to PRWORA was very real, most followed the administration's example and made the political calculation that the 1996 election was too important to risk too open a civil war over the issue. Thus Clinton signed a law which went well beyond anything anyone anticipated in 1992, yet took credit for doing so.[9]

It is important to note that by the time Clinton left office, the public debate about the merit of PRWORA was all but over as the welfare rolls had plummeted. Between August 1996 and September 1999 the number of families receiving welfare had dropped from 4.415 million to 2.453 million – a fall of 44 percent (Administration for Children and Families, 1999), with an increasing number of former welfare mothers active in the labour market to the extent that some needed advice on filling out tax forms (Mathews, 1999). Liberal think tanks continued to produce reports questioning the 'good news' interpretation of post-PRWORA events, and there is clearly reason to worry about what will happen in the event of recession, but these concerns remained on the inside rather than front pages (for preliminary evaluations of the effects of reform see; Parrott, 1998; Sherman et al., 1998; Primus et al., 1999; Rector and Youseff, 1999).

7
Clintonism and the Cultural Dimension in US Politics

As noted in Chapter 2 a key document in the evolution of New Democrat thinking was Galston and Kamarck's *The Politics of Evasion* (1989). Writing in the aftermath of the 1988 election, the authors were concerned by the manner in which Bush had been so easily able to caricature Dukakis as a 'bleeding heart' liberal out of touch with the values of mainstream America. In doing this Bush had successfully shifted the debate away from socio-economic issues and on to cultural type issues where, at least according to Galston and Kamarck, two decades of 'liberal fundamentalism' had made the Democrats politically vulnerable. The implicit separation of the political world into two, in some ways competing, dimensions contained in *The Politics of Evasion* was more thoroughly teased out by two academic scholars, Byron Shafer and William Claggett, in a book entitled *The Two Majorities* (1995). This argued that the American public had something of a split personality when popular attitudes across a range of issues were studied in terms of a standard liberal–conservative model. That is, while partisan activists on both sides of the ideological divide were consistently liberal or conservative across all issues, most of the public were not. Thus, all other things being equal, Shafer and Claggett found a majority liberal sentiment on economic and social welfare issues such as Medicare and Social Security (though not 'welfare' in the narrow sense discussed in the previous chapter) which favored the Democrats. On the other hand, the authors also discovered a presiding majority conservative sentiment on what they termed the cultural/national dimension – these might be identified as 'law and order' and foreign policy issues which can be exploited by the Republicans. Importantly, however, this is not the whole story. The authors go on to argue that the socio-economic dimension has a deeper-lying partisan base than the cultural/national dimension. In other words, again all things being equal, if it was possible to identify a single median voter then he or she would be moderately liberal on socio-economic questions and conservative on cultural ones, but the former factor would be more likely to affect voting behavior than the latter. The important qualification here is the stricture 'all things being equal' as, of course, they are often not. That is, while the issue contexts and the underlying preferences outlined by the 'two majorities' thesis do operate at a deep level, they can be disrupted by the fluctuations of political events. Thus, although the prevalence of socio-economic over cultural issues would suggest a natural advantage for the Democrats, this can be disturbed if there is a sustained period of emphasis on the latter type of issues. According to Shafer and Claggett, 'a two-dimensional portrayal of the political parties shows the powerful "organizing" role of economic/welfare concerns, and the potentially powerful "confusing" role of cultural/national matters' (1995, p.49).

It is important to understand that Shafer and Claggett were not examining American political attitudes with specific reference to the 1988 'L-word'. Their effort was to engage with a broad and historical scope, not simply to rebut the image created by a series of television advertisements. Thus, for example, they identify 'civil rights' as being part of the socio-economic dimension which has a mild liberal bias. This is clearly not quite the same as looking at race through the lens of the Willie Horton advertisements in 1988 and perceived angry white male resentment of affirmative action programs. The purpose of this chapter, however, is to use the 'two majorities' thesis as a framework for examining how a Democratic President dealt with the issue of crime, the complexities of racial politics and other elements of the L-word package which came to the fore in the 1990s. In particular, how did a self-professed New Democrat deal with the legacy of the New Politics and McGovernism? Would it be possible to reconcile the demands of the Democratic Party's liberal constituencies with their exaggerated ideological positioning on the cultural dimension, with the evidence that for many non-activist voters these are in fact cross-cutting issues which threaten to undermine *their* reasons for supporting the Democrats?

In terms of examining Clinton's pro-active agenda, the chapter will focus on two of the underlying themes arising from the use of the 'L-word' in 1988, that is crime policy and racial politics. The administration's substantive efforts in these areas, however, were framed by an immediate, unexpected, controversy over gay rights and accusations that some of its appointees did not reflect the values of mainstream America. If nothing else these incidents demonstrated that the 'L-word' factor was still a part of American political life, which put greater pressure on the administration's subsequent forays into the cultural dimension. On crime, the bold intention was to develop policy which would challenge this as an area of undisputed Republican supremacy by putting together a package which combined tough cures with sensible preventative measures – as with welfare reform, an example of combining the principles of the Third Way with the requirements of pre-emptive politics. On the pivotal question of racial politics, the trick was to blend a continued commitment to expanding opportunities for minorities while making sure that this did not appear to be at the expense of the majority.

From Dukakis to Clinton

The underlying message of *The Politics of Evasion* was that too many Democrats were violating the laws of 'two majorities' politics by spending too much time talking about issues where the party was, on the whole, in the minority and not enough time on matters where it did muster majority support. More than this, ideological purists were staking out positions on the social and cultural issues which were even more unpopular than they needed to be. That is, as Shafer and Claggett spell it out, the best strategy for Democrats is not only to emphasize socio-economic issues but, if they have to deal with cultural matters, to do so in a manner which is moderate enough to be sure that there is 'no incentive to defect' (1995, p.47). According to the New Democrat critique, however, liberals, particularly at the level of presidential politics, had perversely ignored this imperative and had chosen to flag up what might be termed their most unconventional views, with predictable electoral consequences. Then, in order to hide from the unpalatable truth that liberal views on cultural matters were quite simply unpopular, too many Democrats had indulged in a 'systematic denial of reality' in explaining away the series of defeats at presidential level (Galston and Kamarck, 1989, p.1). Central to this self-deception was the way in which liberals refused to recognize the part that their attitudes on social and cultural issues had played in the party's downfall. Noting that polls showed that many Americans believed that the nation 'had experienced a severe breakdown in moral standards over the past twenty years' the two authors insisted

> [F]or many Americans whose support is essential, Democrats are part of the problem, not the solution. In their eyes, Democrats have

become the party of individual rights but not individual responsibility; the party of self-expression but not self-discipline; the party of sociological explanation but not moral accountability (p.23).

Furthermore, Galston and Kamarck reject as a liberal cop-out the idea that Democrat vulnerability on social and cultural issues was simply a reflection of the GOP's willingness to play the race card in their discussion of these matters, especially when it came to crime. Many Democrats had been incensed by the Willie Horton advertisements in 1988, but the writers remarked, 'By concentrating on race alone, Democrats avoid confronting the fact that for years they have been perceived as the party that is weaker on crime and more concerned about criminals than about victims' (p.24).

Further criticism was aimed at those liberals who hoped that the party could avoid the logic of the two majorities and bring together a patchwork coalition of the various 'out' groups in American society to form an overall majority. This would mean that the Democrats could regain the ascendancy without having to win the white middle-class. This scenario was dismissed as the most wishful and unrealistic of thinking. Indeed, while Galston and Kamarck acknowledged the importance of the Democrats' commitment to minority groups, they argued that an important part of winning back lost, non-minority votes was that the party demonstrate that it was not behoven to these groups. In short the Democrats could not win if they did not compete for the votes of white working and middle class Americans. One explicit target of *The Politics of Evasion* was Jesse Jackson, who had run for the Democratic nomination in 1984 and 1988. Galston and Kamarck described these campaigns as representing 'the purest version of liberal fundamentalism' (p.5).[1] Overall the overriding message was that Democrats had to shut up about cultural issues, or even, and indeed preferably, talk about them in more conservative terms. Thus, the demand that Democrats place a greater emphasis on individual 'responsibility' rather than group identity. In other words people were not to be forgiven *their* sins because of membership of an ethnic, racial or social group, however much this had been collectively downtrodden over time.

Written as it was in 1989, Galston and Kamarck's thesis was of course heavily influenced by the events of 1988 when Dukakis, who was in fact quite moderate on the socio-economic dimension, was successfully portrayed as a remote liberal because of his views on cultural/national matters. According to Will Schneider, Dukakis was 'a brainy but bloodless

New Politics liberal, ... who turned out to be another McGovern. As in 1972, a lot of blue-collar Democrats deserted Dukakis in 1988 because of the 'values' issue' (1993b, p.2168). This is an oversimplification. Dukakis's overall political profile was not ultra-liberal, but the Republicans did run against him as if he were at least McGovern-lite by focusing on his cultural/crime track record as Governor rather than his economic one, and this did prove devastating. E.J. Dionne has written of the events in 1988 that, 'Michael Dukakis spoke contemptuously of the Republicans' campaign of "flags and furloughs." But flags and furloughs spoke precisely to the doubts that many Americans developed about liberalism from 1968 onward' (1992, p.79).

The question approaching the 1992 election was whether Bill Clinton would be able to dodge the 'L-word' bullet on cultural issues which had become such a standard part of the Republican armory. As it was, the immediate environment of the 1992 campaign meant that the public wanted the electoral combat to be fought on the socio-economic battleground because of dissatisfaction with the economy's performance on Bush's watch. This, of course, gave Clinton an enormous advantage which undid the assumptions of many pundits in early 1991 that Bush's perceived successful foreign policy leadership, reinforcing an area of traditional Republican strength, made him an impregnable incumbent. Certainly if the issue environment in 1992 had brought renewed concern about international matters, then Clinton would have been a flawed candidate; as it was, though, Bush's foreign policy interests may have worked against him as it intensified the impression that he was out of tune with pressing domestic worries. Clinton was clearly anxious not to allow this advantage to slip away as was manifested by his constant emphasis on those suffering as a result of the economic downturn, but it was also notable that, even if he did not do everything exactly according to the *Politics of Evasion* playbook, he minimized his vulnerability to accusations of 'L-wordism'.

The Clinton campaign: no more George McGovern

Ironically one of the most emotionally charged and symbolic of Dukakis's liberal positions – his opposition to the death penalty – was also one of the easiest to reverse. In his student days Clinton had argued against the death penalty (Walker, 1997, p.19), but had been converted by the time he ran for Attorney-General of Arkansas in 1976 albeit with some unease (Maraniss, 1996, p.434). The most noteworthy moment on the subject during the campaign came early in the primary season when Clinton, in his capacity as Governor, authorized the execution of Ricky Ray Rector. After being convicted of murdering a police officer, Rector had then shot himself in the head. He survived, but with little awareness of what was going on. Given these circumstances there was some question of whether Clinton would allow the execution to go ahead. When he did, critics accused him of playing politics with someone's life. As Stephanopoulos points out, however, Rector's case had twice gone before the Arkansas Clemency Review Board which had rejected his appeals, and Clinton had never overruled the decision of this Board (Stephanopoulos, 1999, pp.63–4). More generally on crime issues, Clinton emphasized the need for more community policing and for federal–state co-operation in developing effective policy solutions. He was certainly not about to repeat Hubert Humphrey's refrain that he too might throw a brick if he lived in the ghetto.

A potentially awkward issue for the Clinton campaign was how to respond to Jesse Jackson's overtures and demands. Stephanopolous reports on a meeting between Clinton and Jackson in November 1991 shortly after the latter had formally announced he would not be running for the nomination in 1992. This had created an opportunity for Clinton as it meant that the African-American vote was in play during the primaries, but it also posed a threat as it meant that Clinton had to negotiate a relationship with Jackson which paid tribute to his position as a spokesperson for the African-American community without acknowledging that he, and his brand of racial liberalism, was the representative voice of that community. Thus, according to Stephanopoulos

Dealing with Jackson was a delicate task....The only strategy ... was tough love. Clinton had to treat Jackson with the respect Jackson had earned ... but couldn't kow-tow to him or enter a no-win public negotiation for his endorsement that would only add to Jackson's power and cost us some white votes (1999, p.44).

Clinton's most public rebuttal of Jacksonism came in June 1992 when he spoke at a Rainbow Coalition gathering. Here he criticised another speaker, the black rap artist Sister Souljah, in a manner which was widely interpreted as a sign that he would not be entering into a bargaining process with Jackson in the run-up to the Democratic national convention.

On the other hand Clinton's campaign messages on race issues were not ones simply calculated for the best political effect. Thus, for example, he told both white and black audiences what he saw as both sides of the story and of the bargains which would have to be made. In a campaign visit to Michigan he went first to the Reagan Democrat turf of Macomb County. Here, talking to a white audience, he promised that he would introduce policies to reward their hard work, but he also urged them to accept that everyone should participate in future prosperity. In other words, he would help them get ahead, but they had to accept that black America would come on this journey as well. The following day, speaking to an African–American audience in Detroit, Clinton repeated this theme. This time, however, he emphasized that while he would ensure that race did not hold people back, it could not be used as an excuse for failure to take the opportunities on offer (Germond and Witcover, 1993c; Greenberg, 1995, pp.218–22). This was in many ways the classic Third Way message, stressing the need for inclusiveness but not special treatment, and the balance between opportunity and responsibility.

On the other potentially divisive cultural issues Clinton did tread carefully, but was known to be pro-choice on abortion, and he promised both ethnic and gender diversity in his cabinet selection. Where Clinton was fortunate was in the demise of foreign policy as a key issue, or at least one where it was easy to draw a line between stout Republican leadership and the timid Democrats. With no obvious 'bear in the woods' Clinton's personal history of opposition to the Vietnam War was less significant than it might have been, and he was helped by the fact that both he and Gore were among the limited number of senior Democrats who had always supported the use of force during the Gulf War (Baer, 2000, p.199).

The problem for Clinton was that, while the cultural dimension had played only a muted part in the campaign and while he had avoided creating further problems for himself beyond the controversies of his personal life, he was not going to be able to see out his presidency without having to deal more directly with at least some of the various issues which had proved so troublesome for Democrats: and it was inevitable that cultural issue incendiary devices would be thrown at him from both left and right of the political spectrum. One feature of the 1992 campaign was that Democrats of all stripes were so desperate to win back the White House that they were prepared to go in whatever direction Clinton took them – and of course he was canny enough to suggest several directions. Once he was in office, however, liberal interest groups were less likely to be tolerant of obfuscation and would demand that he deliver in their pet areas. Conservatives, on the other hand, had wheeled out the ghost of George McGovern every four years in order to haunt Democratic presidential candidates. This time the phantom had not scared off the voters, but Republicans were unlikely to pass up the opportunity for an extended spooking of the White House.

Reviving the L-word

For those New Democrats who felt liberated by Clinton's campaign and his apparent willingness to put some distance between himself and the party's liberals on the cultural dimension, there was an immediate reality check awaiting once Clinton actually got to the Oval Office. The L-word albatross would not so easily be shooed away. Everyone was surely aware that issues were bound to arise which would put Clinton under contrary pressures from different parts of the Democratic coalition, but the hope must have been that these would delayed for as long as possible. Questions of discrimination around sexual orientation were known to be potentially divisive but few could have anticipated that such a controversy, the issue of whether gays should be allowed to serve openly in the military, would at once put the President on the spot and would prove so disastrous for him politically. Furthermore, while Clinton's promise to choose 'a cabinet that looked like America' may have caused some qualms among New Democrat types worried by the implication that merit might be sacrificed for diversity, few would have guessed at the manner in which inadequate vetting of potential appointees would add to an impression of an administration that was too high-handed and out-of-touch.

In fact Clinton's second day in office saw him sign a series of executive orders related to the thorny issue of abortion, as he lifted various restrictions imposed by the Reagan and Bush administrations. These acts included easing restraints on first, the availability of counselling about abortions, second, the use of American funds by the United Nations on population programs that included advice about abortion, and third, the right of US military hospitals abroad to perform privately paid for abortions (Drew, 1994, p.42). This raft of measures, although on highly controversial ground, did not in themselves attract too much negative attention. A further proposal, however, to lift the ban on homosexuals and lesbians serving in the armed forces by executive order, set off a painful political crisis.

1. Gays in the military

Through the campaign, Clinton had developed a good relationship with the gay community and had consciously courted both gay money and votes. He had addressed a gay fund raising event in May 1992 in Los Angeles in which he spelled out that his vision of America included homosexuals and lesbians. This contrasted with the rhetoric of Pat Buchanan at the GOP's national convention in Houston. In return Clinton got several million dollars and 72 percent of the gay vote, with rest split evenly between Bush and Perot (Donovan, 1993, p.1815).[2] This obviously created an expectation that, if elected, Clinton would support efforts to broaden civil rights defences for gays, but the military issue was not specifically one at the top of the agenda. Indeed there is some evidence that gay groups were as caught out as the administration by the turn of events in Clinton's first week in office (Morrison, 1993).

The move to end the ban on gays in the military had in fact been an explicit campaign promise, but not one which had generated much publicity.[3] In hindsight it is slightly surprising that the Bush camp did not make more of this, though perhaps they were reeling from the intensity of the culture-war-conservatism demonstrated in Houston which had been so extreme that it overturned the laws of the two majorities and turned cultural issues into winning ones for the Democrats (Schneider, 1993c). It did, however, gain more prominence during the transition when, during an interview with NBC, Clinton answered a question on the subject by saying that he would try to fulfil this pledge in consultation with military chiefs. The way this subsequently came out, though, gave less attention to the prospect of consultation than of confrontation (Stephanopoulos, 1999, p.125). This set the stage for trouble which duly arrived as soon as Clinton took office.

Supporters of a repeal looked to the new President to exercise his authority quickly through an appropriate executive order ending a policy which had seen approximately 14,000 members of the armed forces dismissed since a Department of Defense directive in 1982 which stated 'homosexuality is incompatible with military service' (Lawrence, 1993, p.187). In reality, however, Clinton was in no position to flourish presidential power so decisively. Whatever Clinton's formal jurisdiction, there was vehement opposition from several quarters, which simply could not be overridden. In particular, a new President with no track record on defence and military issues to give him credibility, just could not steamroller the military chiefs – who, led by Colin Powell, made their fierce opposition quite public – and senior members of his own party in Congress, notably chair of the Senate Armed Services Committee, Sam Nunn – who also made his displeasure very evident. In an effort to buy time to reach an agreement, Clinton announced that there would be a six month interim period in which no one then serving in the armed forces could be dismissed for their sexuality although they could not be open about it, with a formal policy directive to be issued in July 1993. Unfortunately, rather than digging the President out of the hole this just meant that the affair gathered momentum, as advocates on both sides of the argument clearly saw that the manner in which this particular issue was resolved had wider implications for American society. Thus, for example, House Republican Tom DeLay from Texas, a vehement opponent of lifting the ban maintained, 'We feel very strongly that the homosexual movement is not asking for tolerance; they're asking for social endorsement' (quoted in Fessler, 1993, p.227). Reconciling DeLay's world view with that of gay activists was always going to be an impossible task, but even finding the 'sensible' middle ground was to prove elusive.

In the end when the July deadline for action came around, Clinton backed down from his starting position and settled for the so-called 'don't ask, don't tell' solution, which stipulated that the military would not pro-actively seek out homosexuals but which still left any evidence of homosexuality a cause for dismissal. Clinton somewhat lamely claimed that this both enhanced individual rights for gays and maintained military discipline. The plan was endorsed by the Joint Chiefs of Staff, but few others felt that it was an honourable conclusion. Stephanopoulos sums up the end result.

> The compromise satisfied no one, except Republican political strategists, who now had a killer issue for the 1994 midterm elections. The military resented the intrusion, Democrats were furious, the public was confused, and the gay community felt betrayed (1999, p.128).

In hindsight what is perhaps most surprising about the whole affair was the administration's naïveté in not seeing how potentially problematic the issue might turn out to be. Even though pressed to act, it would have been quite plausible for Clinton to send the matter off to a committee before making categorical commitments which were bound to offend some powerful constituencies and against which the President could be held to account. Ironically, it might have been better for the future President Clinton if then President Bush had picked up on the undertaking during the campaign and given the policy a political test drive.

2. The Zoe Baird and Lani Guinier affairs

Another unforeseen problem for the new administration arose when Clinton began to appoint officers to government. The decision to appoint a woman to the position of Attorney General can hardly be cast as an undue bowing to gender radicalism, but the agonies which preceded Janet Reno finally getting the job hurt the White House's credibility and, perhaps more damagingly, created an image of an administration disdainful of the rules when it came to dealing with its own. The initial choice for the Attorney General job was a corporate lawyer called Zoe Baird. When being interviewed for the post, she admitted that she and her husband had previously employed illegal immigrants as a nanny and chauffeur and had not paid social security taxes on them. At this point the Clinton transition team assured her that this was not an insurmountable problem and they pressed ahead. The confirmation hearings thus began before the Senate Judiciary Committee the day before Clinton's inauguration. It was quickly apparent that Baird was in trouble, however, and three leading New Democrat Senators, Bennett Johnston and John Breaux from Louisiana and David Boren from Oklahoma said that they could not support her confirmation (Drew, 1994, p.39). Eventually, when the new President realized the seriousness of the problem, he pulled the plug on Baird. Martin Walker neatly sums up why this matter had a resonance beyond its immediate bearing which touched on the raw nerves of the cultural dimension. 'Zoe Baird and her husband were not members of that "forgotten middle class who work hard and play the rules," to whom the Clinton campaign had appealed. They were the overpaid yuppie and ubiquitous lawyers whom American voters had come to resent' (1997, pp.179–80).[4]

There was, however, a further and more serious problem through April and May 1993 when Clinton nominated Lani Guinier, both a family friend and prominent civil rights lawyer, as Assistant Attorney General for Civil Rights. The difficulty was that Guinier, in an academic guise, had written articles about the need to expand the influence of minorities in terms of both their voting rights and also granting an effective power of veto over legislation in certain fields. These views were not mainstream. At first, even when warnings about how these views might prove problematic in Senate were passed on, the White House pressed ahead on the basis that Guinier was not being nominated for a policy-making position. As it became increasingly evident, however, that Guinier had little chance of surviving the Senate confirmation procedure, the pressure to withdraw her nomination increased, with the New Democrat Bureaux, once again, a leading figure urging Clinton to withdraw her nomination (Idelson, 1993). The awkwardness of the situation was exacerbated by Guinier's determination to see the process through and Clinton's unwillingness to confront her directly (Drew, 1994, pp.204–10). Eventually on 3 June Clinton did withdraw her nomination. He declared that he had not read her academic writings prior to proposing her for the post, and that had he done so he would not have nominated her, as he could not reconcile her views with his own. This was not a universally welcomed decision. Kweisi Mfume, chair of the Congressional Black Caucus, accused Clinton of giving up in the face of 'a whispering campaign by a few faceless and spineless Senators who masquerade as Democrats' (quoted in Walker, 1997, p.312).

On the other hand, for New Democrats, Clinton's retreat on Guinier as on the question of gays in the military was so delayed that much damage had already been done. According to the DLC's senior figures, Al From and Will Marshall, it had been Clinton's 'unequivocal embrace' of core values such as 'family and community' which 'More than anything else … helped him to define himself as a "different kind of Democrat."' They added that these 'values were not always front and center' in the administration's first weeks in power. They argued that Clinton had unfortunately failed always to explain his policies in the appropriate terms. Thus, although his pro-choice preferences and his support for the right of gays to participate in the military were clear campaign promises, their implementation had created a political firestorm. This was because the President had failed 'to put the issues in the context of values for which he stands. As a result, the issues seemed to reflect the strident demands of activists and constituency groups rather than the President's own more balanced discussion of rights and responsibilities' (From and Marshall, 1993b, p.6). According to Baer, the Guinier affair, combined with the gays in the military business, 'continued to send an Old Democratic, culturally liberal message to the public' (2000, p.213); and the issue of gays in the military in particular was cited as an explanation for the dramatic initial drops in Clinton's approval ratings (Drew, 1994, p.48; Baer, 2000, p.212).

The wider problems that these early controversies created for the administration was illustrated by an article in *The New Republic* by John Judis. This argued that while Clinton's positions on abortion and gays were 'morally justifiable' they 'showed the degree to which Clinton gave priority to cultural and social rather than economic issues' (1993, p.19). This, in turn, had quickly alienated New Democrats in

Congress and middle-class voters whose support was vital if Clinton was to 'reform the economy' and 'turn the country around' (p.21). Where this analysis seems unfair is in the assertion that the administration wanted to tackle the cultural dimension before the economic. This certainly had not been the message of either the campaign or the transition period, and Clinton was firmly aware that his own re-election chances rested on demonstrable economic progress. After this initial flirtation with cultural matters it was the economy in the shape of the budget, NAFTA and healthcare which dominated the agenda in 1993 (even if it is argued that the health care plan was part of a too liberal agenda, it was an issue very firmly in the socio-economic dimension). Furthermore, when Clinton next turned to a cultural type issue it was one where he wished firmly to lay down a New Democrat marker. On the fulcrum political issue of crime, which had been so thoroughly appropriated for the Republicans by Richard Nixon, Clinton set out to show that the Democrats too had hitched themselves to the law and order bandwagon.

Finding the Third Way on the cultural dimension

1. Crime policy

Rather like education, crime policy is in fact an area where much of the detail, and hence much of the operational effectiveness, is determined at state and local rather than federal level. Nevertheless, 'The subject routinely appears at or near the top of every public opinion survey of *national* problems' which means that politicians for national office must have a crime policy to hand (Kilgore, 1997, p.111, emphasis added). The potential for crime to play big as a national issue was realised in the presidential election campaign of 1988 when perhaps one of the most effective lines of attack in presidential politics was unleashed by George Bush when he hammered away at Michael Dukakis as someone who was simply out-of-touch with popular sentiment on crime and, perhaps more pertinently, the desire for categorical punishment. Dukakis, of course, did not help himself with his wooden answer when asked about his opposition to capital punishment during a television debate between the two candidates, nor did his campaign team ever come up with an effective retort to the Willie Horton advertisements. Furthermore, his membership of the American Civil Liberties Union won few converts to his cause, likely confirming the belief of many that the Democrats were more interested in protecting the rights of criminals than their victims. Indeed, as Shafer and Claggett point out, many natural Democrats, when judged against socio-economic markers, find themselves strongly cross-pressured by their more conservative inclinations when civil liberties issues are to the fore (1995).

Not surprisingly, therefore, New Democrats saw it as a requirement to banish the perception that their party was 'soft on crime'. In the campaign this had been achieved through the selection of a candidate who favored the death penalty, and more generally the Democrats were helped by the fact that crime did take a relative backseat in voters' priorities through 1992. As, however, Anne Chih Lin points out, crime turned out to be 'the stealth issue of the Clinton administration.' While in January 1993 only 9 percent of respondents cited crime as one of the country's most important problems, a year later 37 percent did so. This rose to 49 percent after Clinton's endorsement of 'three strikes and you're out' in his State of the Union address. Lin adds that the political imperative to act in response to these findings was heightened by mayoral elections in New York and Los Angeles and a gubernatorial contest in New Jersey which focused heavily on crime (Lin, 1998, p.312).

The administration's efforts both to ease public concerns and simultaneously to redefine the Democrats' problematic relationship with the crime issue centred on what eventually became law as the Violent Crime Control and Law Enforcement Act in August 1994. In brief this, expanded the list of federal crimes for which the death penalty could be prescribed, mandated life imprisonment for federal criminals found guilty of a third violent offence, banned the future manufacture and possession of 19 types of assault weapons, authorized spending $8.8 billion over six years to hire an extra 100,000 police officers, authorized $7.9 billion in grants to states to build prisons and boot camps, and $6.9 billion for preventative programs – including $1.6 billion to enforce the Violence Against Women Act (Masci, 1994b; DiIulio, 1999, p.334). In total the bill set aside $30.2 billion to be spent between fiscal 1995 and fiscal 2000. In late summer of 1994 the administration was desperate for a legislative achievement as it became clear that health care was not going to happen, and so there was much relief when the bill finally went through. On the other hand, the tortured process which preceded passage revealed all sorts of continuing tensions within Democratic ranks and also illustrated that the Republicans were not going to give up one of *their* issues lightly.

In short, the bill divided Democrats over gun control and the death penalty and, while enough Republicans were won over finally to secure passage, others, particularly in Senate, attacked it as containing too much pork-barrel spending in the guise of crime prevention. On gun control questions, while the norm is that Democrats are more likely to support greater regulation, there are still many who are opposed to restrictive measures. This was particularly significant in the 1994 negotiations as the House Judiciary Committee chair, Jack Brooks from Texas, was one such Democrat and he invested considerable effort into trying to remove or at least dilute the assault weapons stipulations (Idelson, 1994a).[5]

Liberal Democrats, and in particular the Congressional Black Caucus, wanted included in the bill a Racial Justice Act (RJA). This would have allowed statistical evidence regarding the racial profile of people sentenced to death to be taken into account when deciding what punishment to enforce in individual cases. The basic complaint of the CBC was that a disproportionate number of blacks convicted of capital offences were sentenced to death, especially when the victim was white. Not surprisingly, the bringing together of race issues and the death penalty so explicitly raised the political temperature (Masci, 1994a). The problem for the CBC in pressing its case with the administration was that, whatever the merits of the proposal, it did not have majority support in either chamber. Linda Faye Williams argues that, although the CBC thought that it had the support of the White House in its call for the RJA, in truth the administration was busy lobbying other black interest groups, notably the big-city black Mayors who wanted the extra funding in the overall bill, in order to put pressure on CBC members to vote for the bill regardless of the status of the RJA (Williams, 1998, pp.430–2).

The other source of opposition was more predictable inasmuch as the Republicans were always unlikely to be willing to give Clinton an easy victory, especially in an election year. Predictably enough the GOP line of attack was that the bill was not sufficiently tough and that it spent too much on preventative social programs and an inadequate amount on prison building. Bob Dole, for instance, labelled it 'an overhyped, multibillion-dollar boondoggle that emphasized social theory over law enforcement' (quoted in Idelson, 1994b, p.2342).

All this added up to a tortured process. At one point, after an agonized House-Senate conference had thrashed out a bill which included the weapons ban but not the RJA, it still looked as if a combination of Republican opposition, disgruntled members of the CBC and anti-gun control Democrats was going to kill the bill when defeat on a procedural motion in the House halted further action. Finally at the end of August, after a little more tinkering to reduce preventative spending, a number of moderate Republicans came onboard to see the bill home by margins of 235 to 195 in the House and 61 to 38 in Senate. In the House, the Republican support was crucial, as there was still a residue of opposition from the CBC with nearly 50 anti-gun control Democrats prepared to continue their opposition (Idelson and Sammon, 1994; Masci, 1994b).[6] At the conclusion of all of this it was possible, as Dionne points out, to see the bill as 'in many ways, the classic Clinton-style New Democratic compromise' combining harsher sentencing and gun control, prison building and community programs (1997, p.143). Furthermore, polls showed that most of the measures in themselves were popular (p.145). Yet, at best, it was a limited triumph for the administration which sent out a confusing message. As Lin sums up, Clinton had delivered on his promise to fund more police officers, yet the amount allocated for this, which in fact constituted an unprecedented sum for federal government to earmark for such a purpose, was derided as too little. In addition, the negotiations over the bill had revealed a passionately divided congressional Democratic Party unable to reconcile in order to deliver for its President. Moreover

> A bill that was intended to show that Democrats were ready to challenge Republicans for the "law-and-order" mantle had succeeded, but only after attempts to paint it as a bill full of failed Great Society programs had succeeded as well (Lin, 1998, p.322).

On the other hand, Baer's conclusion that 'although it was a New Democratic piece of legislation, the crime bill became bogged down and defined by liberal Democratic politics' is too simple (2000, p.218). Liberals were not likely to acquiesce to the harsher elements of the bill without demanding something in return and in terms of sheer numbers it was the *NRA Democrats* rather than the bleeding hearts who constituted the biggest hurdle. Moreover, the GOP leadership's tactic of labeling all the non-punitive spending as 'pork' was clearly simply political and ignored some evidence of success for programs such as 'midnight basketball'. In these circumstances, and with the benefit of hindsight admittedly not available to those involved in the political melee of the summer of 1994, it seems sensible to regard the bill as a legislative achievement rather than rue the fact that it did not come easier.

Briefly, in 1995 it looked as if even this might be a short-lived triumph which would be undone in both political and policy terms as the House Republicans got to work on their own crime bill. Their proposal would have given state and local authorities more flexibility in the delivery of the programs just passed in the 1994 bill, but would have cut overall spending by $4 billion – in effect foreclosing many of the preventative measures before they had even got started. Fortunately for Clinton, the Senate never really seriously embarked on similar legislation, which spared him the prospect of either killing projects which had kept much of his party onboard during 1994 or vetoing a tough Republican crime bill. Either choice would have had demoralising political consequences (Lin, 1998, 324–5). When a much more limited bill finally did emerge from the Republican Congress in the spring of 1996, Clinton had little compunction about signing into law new limits on death row appeals. Bizarrely, this bill, which had started out in the aftermath of the Oklahoma bombing, did not contain a number of provisions such as allowing the military to aid civilian law enforcement agencies in terrorist cases and extending federal wiretapping authority which Clinton wanted, because of objections from conservative members of the House concerned about federal government infringement of civil liberties.

2. Racial politics

According to the respected journalist and commentator Thomas Edsall, 'Race pervades almost every aspect of American politics' (Edsall, 1997, p.137). As clearly demonstrated by the discussion of the crime bill and as also evident in the debate over welfare reform, race issues arise in many different forms in American politics, attaching themselves to policy debates that need not, a priori, be race conscious ones (that is, crime and welfare could be discussed in societies with no racial divisions). In addition there are what might be described as 'stand alone' racial issues such as affirmative action. This combination of implicit and explicit racial topics has had a demonstrable effect on national politics. That is, while in the heyday of the civil rights era in the mid-1960s 'the issue of race empowered liberalism and the Democratic Party' since then 'race has been a major source of power for conservatism and the Republican Party' (Edsall, 1997, p.138). In crude electoral terms, blacks have become the loyalest of Democrat voters but no Democratic presidential candidate since Lyndon Johnson has won a clear majority of the white vote.

The question of whether there is a causal, as distinct from contiguous, relationship between the Democrats fully emerging as the party of racial liberalism and the white migration from the party is an immensely complex one which is beyond the scope of this book. What is evident, however, is that racial politics has been enormously divisive for the

Democratic Party with many liberals and blacks adamant that the civil rights quest did not end in the 1960s and that further government action is needed to remedy continuing instituionalized inequalities. Further, they argue that issues such as crime do need to be seen through a race conscious lens (witness the call for the RJA). New Democrats, on the other hand, while acknowledging the existence of serious inequalities, maintain that the best way of improving the overall situation of minorities is through policies which will advance all groups in society simultaneously. They also assert that the Democratic Party's association with programs offering selected groups preferential treatment has been damaging, not as a result of white racism but because such programs offend against the central American value of distributing rewards according to merit. In other words, New Democrats want the party to move away from race conscious policies on both policy and political grounds.

In the 1992 campaign, Clinton established his New Democrat credentials on racial politics when he deliberately distinguished himself from Jesse Jackson and also when he emphasized the importance of individual responsibilities rather than group rights. On the other hand, whatever his message, he consciously appealed to the African-American community, regularly visiting black neighbourhoods and churches, and, by the end of his period in office, it had become something of a cliché that Clinton enjoyed a special relationship with the African-American community. This was particularly evident through the impeachment crisis with, ironically, Jesse Jackson emerging as one of the President's foremost defenders. Given the tough, explicitly New Democrat rhetoric and actions on crime and welfare reform on exactly those race coded issues which might have been expected to undermine Clinton's appeal to black America, this might appear somewhat surprising. Certainly, during the debates on these issues in 1994 and 1996, Clinton adopted positions which were opposed by both the CBC and the leading voices of the black community outside Congress. Some have thus attributed black support for Clinton and his party as being largely due to the lack of an alternative (Williams, 1998, pp.452–3), but this may be a little harsh. While it would be difficult to pinpoint a host of substantive reasons, particularly definite legislative achievements, to explain Clinton's popularity amongst blacks, the following quotation from Stephanopoulos offers a more positive interpretation of it than simply seeing Clinton as the lesser of two evils.

From his Little Rock announcement speech, in which he had promised to stop the Republicans from stealing another presidential election by playing the race card; to his sermons in Memphis and Macomb County, in which he had appealed to black and white audiences alike without pandering to their prejudices; to his meditative campaign interview with Bill Moyers, in which he had vowed that race was the one issue that he would never compromise for political gain, Bill Clinton inspired me most when he spoke about race (1999, p.362).

The real test of this commitment came in 1995 when the administration was effectively forced to take a stance on affirmative action. The complex politics of affirmative action and the chaos it threatened within Democratic ranks suggest that it was an issue the administration would probably have preferred to avoid altogether, but rumblings of Republican presidential politics with Senators Gramm and Dole seemingly seeking to outflank each other to the right on the topic, placed it squarely on the agenda (Drew, 1997, p.290). Thus, when Clinton announced in February 1995 that he was ordering a review of federal affirmative action programs, there was a sense of foreboding in liberal quarters. The spin explaining the 1994 mid-term elections was about the revolt of the 'angry white male' (AWM) and it appeared that renouncing affirmative action might be the method chosen to avoid giving the GOP a wedge issue to exploit in 1996. That is, while crime and welfare had obvious racial connotations, affirmative action was the most up-front of racial issues and was widely regarded as a potential political timebomb; yet, on this, Clinton decided, if not exactly to pick up the baton of racial liberalism and run with it, at least not to turn back to the starting line.

The debate in the White House went on for five months after Clinton announced the review of existing programs. There were various political calculations made about who would be alienated most by whatever action was taken. How significant were the AWMs and would revoking affirmative action spur an independent Jackson candidacy? According to Dick Morris, however, Clinton 'ended up disregarding politics altogether. He grew up in the south and saw racism every day of his life. This is what made him determined to hold fast on affirmative action' (1997, p.214). The idea that Clinton's decision had no political rationale may be a little too hard to swallow, but his eventual statement of a 'mend, don't end' policy did stray somewhat from what had become, and continued to be, the New Democrat construction of pursuing colour-blind racial policy and politics. As it was Clinton's 19 July address outlining his preferred policy could be read in different ways. He acknowledged that there were 'legitimate questions about the way affirmative action works', and he was clear that he did not support quotas or any business employing a less well qualified candidate in order to meet a racial target. Much of the speech was, however, an attempt to explain why there was still a need for federal government to set aside some of its contracts for minorities. He expressed resolution that this need would not continue indefinitely, but declared 'the evidence suggests, indeed, screams' that the time to end all programs had not yet arrived (Clinton, 1995). Overall, whatever the qualifications made in the speech the media led with the line 'Affirmative action has been good for America' (Drew, 1997, p.295).

At this point Clinton's actions still looked like a gamble. A week after the speech, Dole released details of a plan he was to introduce in Senate which would abolish federal affirmative action programs (Wells with Langdon, 1995). This was primarily to make sure that no contenders for the Republican nomination would get to the right of him on the subject, but showed that he thought that Clinton's intervention had far from finished the matter (Woodward, 1996, pp.225–6). In California the brouhaha surrounding the emergence of Proposition 209 enhanced the issue's reputation as one to excite conservatives. It turned out, however, that Clinton had successfully defused the controversy, at least in terms of presidential politics. Race did not play in the national 1996 election contest despite various race related matters at state level. According to Morris, Clinton's approach had been the right one, as a poll he conducted just after Clinton's July 1995 speech 'found that over three quarters of blacks *and* three quarters of whites felt that Clinton did not favor one race over the other' (1997, p.215). Reflecting his own overriding concern, Morris's emphasis is on the findings of this poll with regard to white opinion; it could be seen as equally significant, however, after the Reagan-Bush era that blacks felt that they were likely to get a fair deal from the President.

Overall then, from an electoral perspective, Clinton's balancing act on racial politics was a successful one. Twice he campaigned as a New Democrat who was not going to be beholden to minority groups, which helped prevent potentially disastrous white flight, yet at the same time he managed to improve his standing with the black community. This is not to say that the Democratic Party is now free from racial tension but that, at the level of presidential politics in an improving economic environment for all, Clinton was able to find a settlement which did not alienate either blacks or white swing voters. Unfortunately for the Democrats there are important qualifications here.

In particular there is still the prospect that, in a less happy economic environment, blacks and whites will once again see themselves as being in competition with each other which will likely push affirmative action and associated stereotypes more damagingly to the fore. Furthermore, while Clinton's accommodation was one which worked at national level there are still consistently evident discomforting cross pressures on congressional Democrats torn between different voting blocks. Indeed there were a few signs of this in the aftermath of the 2000 election – with black congressional Democrats at the forefront of the protests demanding a recount, but with some of their more conservative southern colleagues nervous about how to reconcile the wishes of a group of their white constituents, who had voted Democrat at congressional level but who had also voted for Bush, with the hopes of their steadfastly pro-Gore African–American voters. The dilemma for these Democrats on the conservative wing of the party, the so-called 'Blue Dogs', was that they needed to retain the support of both sets of these voters for their own electoral security (Edsall, 2000).

V-chips and school uniforms: downsizing the values debate

Clinton's principled stand on affirmative action was one of few risky liberal moments on cultural issues after his initial bumpy ride. Bearing in mind the lasting scars caused by the gays in the military episode, it was not too surprising that the administration took a more cautious line on the other more unanticipated cultural issues which it came across. In particular in preparation for 1996, Clinton concentrated on a series of micro-initiatives to make sure that he was on the right side in the 'family values' debate. Thus, for example, he announced his support for the V-chip, a device by which parents could control their children's ability to access violence on television. He also urged school authorities to insist on school uniforms (Drew, 1997, p.379).

More substantively, when the issue of gay rights was revisited in the summer of 1996, Clinton was not to repeat his 'mistake' of 1993 and hand the Republicans a topic to run with. The Defense of Marriage Act, which Clinton signed into law in September, stated that federal government would only recognize heterosexual marriages.[7] This legislation was in fact introduced into Senate in May 1996 by Bob Dole in one of his last moves before resigning to concentrate on his presidential bid. To liberal-left commentators this laid bare its attempt to exploit homophobia as a political issue (Stacey, 1998), but as a strategy it rather failed. Even though gay groups were disappointed with Clinton, there was a recognition of his dilemma and, given Dole's direct association with the measure, Clinton was still the clearly preferred candidate of gay rights organizations in 1996 (Carney, 1996).

Another largely symbolic move came when Clinton's desire to preach racial harmony found an outlet in June 1997 when he set in motion what he called a 'national dialogue on race'. This resulted in numerous conferences, 'town hall' style gatherings and finally a report which somewhat piously recommended, among other things, major investments in improving minority educational attainment, an increase in the minimum wage, and a more positive portrayal of minorities on television (Wright, 2000, p.226). This, however, remained a wish list rather than an agenda for presidential action and, overall, there were few signs that the effort ever captured widespread attention or resulted in any substantive improvement in race relations. On the other hand, it probably caused little offence.

Polls showed that there is room for a limited liberal politics on abortion and gun control issues, but these remain controversial, with opponents of choice and of gun regulation more likely to be highly motivated than supporters of these issues. In October 1997, Clinton did veto a bill banning so-called 'partial-birth' abortions. This was controversial – the veto was very nearly overridden with the necessary two-thirds majority being achieved in the House and falling short by only three votes in Senate.

Conclusion: messy outcomes

Overall, objectively assessing the merits of Clinton's actions on the cultural dimension is almost impossible as there is no real means of defining success. There are no productivity charts to look at, no poverty rates to measure and no median income levels to compare. Some things do stand out; for example, the gays in the military affair was a political disaster which did little to improve the lot of gays in the armed services as rates of dismissal for reasons of sexual orientation in fact increased after 1993 (Jost, 2000, p.174). It would thus be difficult to fit this in with any definition of success, but more generally the nature of 'values' issues is that they are just that, without identifiable right and wrong answers. Examining the record from a more instrumental perspective – that is, did Clinton manage to hold together the Democratic coalition from the centre to the left while ridding the party of the 'L-word' tag? – is also a difficult task as there are various contradictory pieces of evidence.

According to many New Democrats, things went off on a seriously unplanned liberal track at first before finally beginning to right themselves; though not before a high political cost had been paid, as this initial cultural liberalism tainted the overall perception of what Clinton was trying to achieve and made it easier for the Republicans to deride all aspects of Clintonism as warmed over old style liberalism. Thus, as Baer describes it, the gays in the military and Guinier episodes constituted reversions to the old Democracy, though of a New Politics rather than New Deal grain, which were more damaging in the whole than would be suggested by a simple sum of their parts. That is, because 'this combination of early priorities and highly charged symbols painted Clinton in liberal hues and undermined his claim to be a New Democrat...it became easier for Republicans to portray any of Clinton's initiatives as traditional Democratic policies' (2000, p.213). Indeed it is possible to extend this argument to say that long-term political damage was caused by the early examples of liberalism on the cultural dimension as this initial 'L-wordism' carried over to hurt the Democrats hugely in 1994, which in turn restricted the whole Clintonism project thereafter. For example, Baer laments that the dominant early liberal image, along with the vociferousness of CBC, was crucial in filtering perceptions of the anti-crime bill of 1994 and thus undermining its central New Democrat message that the party had moved away from bleeding heart angst towards a tougher approach which combined punishment and prevention in a realistic and hard-nosed fashion (2000, pp.217–8).

This, however, is too one-dimensional an approach to the manner in which short-term political events interact with more long-standing underlying factors. Indeed the crime issue illustrates well the difficulties of Third Way politics and the sometimes no-win situation the White House found itself in even when legislation it championed was enacted. From the start, the administration's efforts on crime were likely to be hindered by two underlying political realities which could not be easily bypassed by either reason or force. First, attempting to build a new consensus on a complex issue which brought into play matters such as race, capital punishment and gun control, each of which brought to the table a series of entrenched and passionately held beliefs, was always going to be enormously difficult. That is, however ideologically balanced the overall package might be, different groups of legislators were inevitably going to alight on particular elements of the bill which they could not accept, but which in turn were necessary components if the sense of balance was to be maintained.

Second, in crude partisan terms, making crime into a *Democratic* issue was always likely to be near impossible. The Republican leadership was never going to hand Clinton one of its best wedge issues without some attempt to demean his efforts.

The point is that whatever position Clinton took on cultural matters in order to distance himself from the 'L-word' he was never going to get to the right of the GOP as they would always be willing to take a step further; but outdoing the GOP was not a requirement of the two majorities logic. It sufficed simply to defuse the issues, which on crime and race Clinton did, perhaps as much as it was possible to do, without completely alienating the Democratic base. In the end, however disappointed various minority groups were by specific actions of the administration, they remained loyal parts of the Clinton and then Gore coalitions. On the other hand, the Democrats' own polling showed that the GOP was still more trusted on family values when these are described as 'knowing right from wrong', 'personal responsibility' and 'discipline' (Greenberg and Greenberg, 2000); and here it may be that Clinton did hurt his party through his own behavior. The V-chip is of little use when parents have to explain to their children what news broadcasters mean by 'oral sex' and why it does not actually count. More fundamentally, if downsizing the cultural dimension was seen as the way to win back the white male vote for the Democrats, then Clintonism failed. Gore surely did not lose because of an outburst of liberal fundamentalism on the cultural dimension, yet *The New York Times* exit polls show that Gore won only 36 percent of the white male vote – indeed even the gender gap disappears if the African-American vote is taken out.[8] At this, liberals might allow themselves a wry smile and suggest that at times New Democrats became so obsessed with the cultural dimension that they forgot about appealing to whites on the economic one (Teixeira and Rogers, 2000).

Conclusion: A New Paradigm?

One of the themes emphasized in the introduction which has constantly underpinned subsequent discussion was that despite all the hoopla which inevitably greeted Clinton's 1992 triumph, his presidency actually commenced in a restrictive political environment – well described by Skowronek's reference to pre-emptive politics. In short, Clinton's was a limited mandate and any attempt to act expansively was likely to produce a wrenching reaction. The Perot vote in particular made it clear that the 1992 result was as much an expression of disaffection with politics as it was a positive endorsement of Clinton. Indeed in some ways Clinton's campaign had paid tribute to both the general disillusion and also the fact that the Democrats had been so resoundingly rejected through the 1980s in presidential elections. That is, the promise to introduce a different type of politics which would reinvigorate the dialogue on national issues by moving debate beyond the existing, tired, ideological framework aimed both to reassure voters that while Clinton was not going to revisit the Great Society he still did have exciting answers to America's pressing problems. This was articulated as the philosophy of the New Democracy and the Third Way. One difficulty he was always going to face, however, was that, although his success illustrated that he had captured the head of his own party, much of the rest of the body still acted as if it had a mind of its own. Furthermore, there was little evidence that the Republicans were at all willing to engage meaningfully with the Clinton experiment.[1] On the other hand, whatever the constraining political factors, it was inevitable that the Clinton presidency would be seen as a test of the New Democrat project. As Byron Shafer has reflected, 'Because he was elected and, especially, reelected using precisely these [New Democrat] campaign thematics, his fortunes put the issue of the existence, content, and consequence of a New Democracy at the center of any Clinton legacy in partisan affairs' (2000, p.2).

The good news as the Clinton era drew to a close was that according to the President and the DLC this test had been resoundingly passed. Indeed the leaders of the New Democrat movement asserted that the Clinton experience had served as a model for the centre-left beyond the US, as the Third Way approach had been crucial to reviving the electoral fortunes of parties previously hamstrung by clinging to the rhetoric of the political settlement of the post war period. Thus, in a speech to DLC officeholders in July 1999 Al From, declared, 'you are part of the most significant political story of the 1990s – the resurgence of center-left, progressive centrist parties all around the globe, beginning right here in the United States' (1999). A year earlier Clinton had elaborated on the benefits the Third Way had brought to the US as he told a similar gathering of New Democrats, 'We have called our approach "the third way" – with a government that is more active, more effective, less expensive; one that can bring us together and move us forward, not drive us apart and set us back.' He also referred back to the anti-government rhetoric prevalent at the start of the 1990s when, whatever the problem, government was assumed not to be part of the solution. He noted that this style of anti-government invective had become more marginalized because his administration, guided by DLC ideas, had shown that government could work. The results he pointed to included the lowest crime rate in 25 years, the lowest welfare rolls in 27 years, the lowest rate of inflation in 32 years, the first balanced budget and surplus in 29 years, and the highest rate of home ownership in history (Clinton, 1998).

This is an impressive list of achievements, but does not in itself answer the question of whether Clinton's Third Way will have a life-span beyond his term in office. This book has examined Clintonism's manifestation across a range of key policy areas in order to get to grips with this question and it is worth briefly recapping these discussions before drawing some final conclusions on the totality of the Clinton project and its likely longevity.

Clintonomics

The potential conflict exhibited during Clinton's 1992 campaign over fiscal policy, either to spend in order to boost the economy or to cut the deficit was quickly resolved in favour of the latter. This was in fact something of a false choice as some juggling of the budget was possible, but the clear prioritization of deficit reduction resulted from the administration's perception of the fiscal and political imperatives in the early 1990s.

First, though it was hardly news to the Clinton team when it took office, it has to be said that the deficit numbers did look bad. Of perhaps even more significance than the raw figures was the way in which the new President and his economic team bought into the idea that the key to economic success was to have lower long-term interest rates, as this would increase both market and consumer confidence. Paul Pierson notes how this argument took increasing hold over the White House. 'Over time, an interest rate strategy virtually supplanted the administration's earlier investment strategy for economic growth. Success of this interest rate strategy hinged on serious deficit reduction' (Pierson, 1998, p.141).

Second, the deficit agenda had crowded in during the 1992 campaign in the form of Ross Perot's persistent refrains on the topic and, whether or not people understood why the deficit was damaging, they saw it as bad book-keeping and a sign of government incompetence; if anything, this was particularly problematic for a Democratic President. Reagan had done little seriously to try to control the deficit and Bush had not acted until 1990 but, as Republicans and conservatives, they were still somehow credited as wanting to balance the budget. Democrats, however, were more associated with wanting to spend regardless of the consequences. However much these stereotypes ran contrary to the actual evidence, they put extra pressure on Clinton. He could not prove he was serious about deficit reduction simply by talking a good fight – he indeed had to deliver. Furthermore, these factors combined to produce a mood in Congress which emphasized deficit reduction over stimulus spending. This was particularly the case for freshmen Democrats who 'had run in a policy environment shaped as much by Perot as by Clinton' (Shafer, 1997, p.164). The irony is that Clinton's own effort to deal seriously with the deficit in 1993 resulted in both the downsizing of his domestic ambitions and political rebuke, while the much more artful politicking of 1995 received popular applause.

A second major commitment of Clintonomics was trade liberalization and the argument over NAFTA was thus crucial to the Third Way project, as it set the tone in welcoming increasing global competition rather than trying to limit its impact. While, however, Clinton continued to oversee an increased pace of globalization, he was unable either to cajole or bully his party into lining up behind him. From the perspective of the future development of the Democratic Party and its attitude on trade matters, this became more critical with Al Gore's defeat. That is, the free trade project within the party was a top down one from the White House. Without a President leading this charge, the foremost Democrat voices will be more sceptical ones.

There were some compensations for those in the party disappointed by the diminished investment program and the emphasis on free trade. In the clearest break from the policies of the 1980s, there was a deliberate effort to get more cash to low income working families. The EITC expansion and the top tax rate rise in the first budget were only mild measures of redistribution but at least they reversed the impetus of Reaganomics. Nevertheless liberals remained critical of administration for not doing enough to tackle inequality (Mishel and Schmitt, 1995). Critics pointed out that the administration did little to reverse the ideological and institutional shifts apparent from the 1970s which had fundamentally altered the balance of power between capital and labor; for example, while the decline in union membership from 24 percent of the workforce in 1979 to 13.9 percent in 1998 was not explicit government policy, it did reflect an institutional context which had encouraged deregulation and discouraged collective bargaining (Howell, 2000). By 2000 the background noise of a low unemployment and low inflation economy dimmed sensitivity to these complaints but it is hard not to agree with Clinton's own assessment, as reported by Woodward, when in April 1993 he stormed to his staff, 'We're Eisenhower Republicans here, and we are fighting the Reagan Republicans. We stand for lower deficits and free trade and the bond market' (1994, p.165). Thus while Clintonomics does satisfy one of the tests of Third Wayism inasmuch as it combined policies in a fashion which fitted neither Republican nor traditional Democratic preconceptions, there was little that constituted a 'radical departure' in this program, with the voices of the conventional wisdom, pro-deficit reduction, pro-free trade and indifferent to expanded investment, to the fore.

Social policy

Clinton came to office with a complex social policy agenda illustrated by the manner in which the two most significant policy proposals, fundamental reform of the health care and welfare systems, appealed to quite distinct elements of the Democratic coalition. Clinton in fact embarked on his reform agenda simply enough by signing the Family Medical Leave Act into law within his first month. This measure, which had twice been vetoed by President Bush, allowed an employee to take twelve weeks of unpaid leave in order to look after a new baby or ill family member (Zuckman, 1993b).[2] Such harmony between Congress and White House was not, however, repeated when the HSA was revealed.

Following the 1994 mid-term disaster for the Democrats, the dominant interpretation was that the attempt at health care reform had constituted a reckless piece of old fashioned liberalism which had undone Clinton's New Democrat image and left the party vulnerable to the charge of being addicted to Big Government. In short, Clinton was deemed to have acted in a fashion inconsistent with his limited mandate, of which a principal feature was the commitment to limited government. In this context Skowronek provides an interesting interpretation of what he labels a 'signature issue' – an effort by Clinton to reach beyond the confines of the pre-emptive framework. That is, pre-emptive leaders spend most of their time 'accommodating their party to prevailing norms' but they are also keen 'to put down a marker that will serve to establish the distinctiveness of their course' (1997, p.456). The problem is that these signature issues tend to backfire because of the 'underlying resilience of the older political categories and associations which these presidents were at such pains to submerge in their initial rise to power' (p.457). In hindsight this is a persuasive analysis, but it needs to be emphasized that the administration assumed that it did have authority to act decisively in the health care arena because of the high profile of the topic during the early 1990s. Furthermore, having decided to pursue major reform, the administration did so in a fashion designed, as far as was possible, to accommodate the prevailing interests. Unfortunately it turned out that corporate interests had not been accommodated enough; but to imply, as many New Democrats subsequently did, that the administration should not have acted on health care or should have gone for a scaled down program would seem to narrow significantly the horizons of the Third Way. Certainly if the rhetoric about taking bold action when needed is to have credibility, then health care would seem to be a case in point where bold action could be and needed to be taken. Clinton's proposal would have led to a dramatic improvement in the security of the millions of Americans without health coverage.

An issue where Clinton did explicitly choose to emphasize his 'different kind of Democrat' credentials was that of welfare reform; the plan which emerged in the summer of 1994 can indeed be seen as an exemplar of Third Way thinking. Unconditional welfare receipt was to be time-limited with a stronger emphasis on welfare to work and sanctions for those who failed to comply; but there was also a guarantee that government would act as an employer of last resort for those who demonstrated that they were willing to fend for themselves but were unable to do so successfully in the private sector. After November 1994, however, the environment for the welfare reform project changed significantly. While the Clinton plan had redrawn the relationship between government and welfare recipient, it had maintained a sense of mutual obligation. The final Republican proposals very firmly declared that, in the long-term, individuals are responsible for their own fate, and that no able-bodied, working-aged adult is entitled to cash assistance from the state either for herself or her children.

The critical political question for Clinton was whether to sign the Congressional welfare bill. There was great unease among some senior staff, but key New Democrat advisers pushed for his signature and the decision to sign the welfare bill has come to be seen as a key 'New Democrat' moment for Clinton; once he let it be known what he had decided, the large margins in Congress in favour of PRWORA suggest something of a rout of liberal forces on the issue. Moreover, the subsequent decline in the welfare rolls has further marginalized those liberals still protesting against the measure. If, however, the bill is representative of the Third Way then the pendulum marking the balance between government activism and government retreat has swung strongly in the latter direction. Some states have responded to the challenge of welfare reform by providing a host of supportive services to ease the path from welfare to work, but others have not, and as an expression of Clinton's 'new covenant' the PRWORA's emphasis is very much on the 'Personal Responsibility' element rather than the 'Work Opportunity' aspect.

Overall in social policy then, there was neither a clear and consistent articulation of a policy framework nor a decisive pattern of success either by accident or design. This is not to say that there was not an attempt to develop some sort of Third Way social policy agenda, and in the first two years it is possible to identify a distinctively emerging welfare state discourse (Beland et al., 2002); it is fair to say, however, that this was not fulfilled and was, to all intents and purposes, abandoned after 1994 when the White House primarily reacted to initiatives from Congress either conceding ground or making play of its defence of the status quo. In political terms this was quite a successful strategy, but at the end of Clinton's presidency there was little that was discernible as a Clintonite social policy template.

Indeed, as Clinton left office, there were some social policy issues pending which illustrated that there was little consensus over quite where the Third Way should go next. The DLC had consistently advocated reform of the major entitlement programs but had not pressed this too strongly during the first term, except in the case of AFDC which reflected the political weakness of the welfare population.[3] Indeed one of the ironies of the second half of Clinton's first term, so lauded by New Democrats, was that he rebuilt his political base by defending Medicaid and Medicare, two of the biggest government programs, from GOP attack. He was also quick to stave off the Republican leadership's call for a tax cut to celebrate the surplus, by asserting the need to buttress the Social Security system. As the administration moved into its second term, however, there was an emerging debate about the long-term financial viability of Social Security, the biggest American welfare state program. As it was, both Clinton and then Gore decided to use Social Security as a political tool by talking about how Republican plans threatened the integrity of the program. Beneath this, however, there was a nascent controversy brewing within party ranks as the DLC began to circulate policy documents suggesting partial privatization style reforms of both Social Security and Medicare which were an anathema to many Democrats (Shapiro, 1997; Kendall, 1997).

The rationale for these proposals was that they would protect the long-term fiscal integrity of these programs and maintain the government's safety net obligations. Others, however, see this type of suggestion as evidence that the New Democrat movement has gone beyond its initial, and valid, remit of getting the party to focus on peoples' everyday concerns, and has now started 'veering off course' (Skocpol and Greenberg, 1997, p.10). These two influential writers argue that the DLC/PPI have developed a reflex desire to downsize government even when government is doing a good job, by advocating 'changes that resonate much more with the ideas of Wall Street than with the needs and values of average Americans' (p.11).[4] This debate about how best to administer social assistance such as pensions and health care for the elderly suggests that the Third Way is approaching an important cross-roads in its attitudes towards government-run social programs. Should policy makers automatically look to lessen the direct burden on government of providing such services by encouraging greater use of a regulated private sector or do some collective problems still demand collective solutions? The DLC has consistently moved towards calling for the state to offload its responsibilities onto the market, suggesting that its version of the Third Way sees the downsizing of the government's part in the government–market mix as an end in itself. This is despite the evidence from the 1990s on, for example, access to health care – with more people uninsured in 2000 than in 1993 – which suggests that the private sector has an agenda which is not necessarily compatible with the public good.

Cultural issues

While cultural issues had been pushed to the back burner somewhat during 1992 by the concentration on economic concerns, there remained several matters which could not be long postponed; as President Clinton quickly discovered, these issues had real potential to disrupt the equilibrium which he was trying to restore to the broad based Democratic coalition. According to the New Democrat analysis, Clinton did not help himself by responding too willingly to the party's liberal constituencies as highlighted by the gays in the military and Guinier episodes. The problem was that people, disconcerted by these displays of cultural liberalism, were more likely to be sympathetic to Republican jibes that the first budget was just old-fashioned tax and spend, when it palpably was not. In this vein John White reflected that the combination of gays in the military, the Brady Bill and the health care effort 'reminded voters why they disliked the Democratic party in the first place. Instead of Bill Clinton, many suspected that they had elected George McGovern' (1998, pp.251–2).

On the other hand, it is unclear that this scenario could have been as easily avoided as is implied by some of the New Democrat critiques of the first two years. Clinton had managed to get through the election campaign largely avoiding cultural dimension controversies but this in itself did not mean that the Democratic Party had changed its spots, simply that all its factions were desperate not to lose again. The pressures were inevitably going to change when Clinton reached office and, with the Republican sharks circling ready to pounce on any scent of a bleeding heart, there was always a likelihood that there would be at least some exposure of the party's McGovernite wing; and in fact on crime and race and other potential cultural dimension time bombs Clinton, at least by the end of his presidency, had largely defused the 'L-word' device inasmuch as George W. Bush was not in a position to run a campaign akin to that of his father in 1988.[5]

Clintonism in the round: a new paradigm?

Studying these various elements of the Clinton project in isolation does not, however, answer the question of what they aggregate when considered in the round. In particular, is there a discernible Clintonian legacy which gives rise to a new understanding of politics?

There is indeed a case to be made to answer this positively. Across a range of issue areas there was evidence of a distinctive Third Way thinking as Clinton tried to put together a different political mix. For example, his first budget tried to marry together deficit cutting, a tax hike and some investment initiatives. In its support for free trade, the administration angered organized labor but it was serious about trying to make low-paid work pay better by expanding the EITC and pushing for the minimum wage increase. The initial effort at health care reform tried to produce a liberal outcome through a market oriented approach and the administration's own welfare reform proposals can be seen as trying to marry together the rhetoric of responsibility while still maintaining a government commitment to ensure opportunity. Furthermore, the anti-crime bill packaged together both punitive and preventative measures.

In addition to this, the DLC could point to their influence in pulling the presidential party back from the brink of self-indulgent self-destruction in the 1980s. This is not to say that liberals had jumped onboard the New Democrat wagon, but they had at least accepted that there was little purpose to parading opinions which the public regarded negatively (Teixera, 1995, p.63). A big moment for the DLC came in the 1996 State of the Union address when Clinton declared 'The era of big government is over'. In his detailed study of the New Democrat movement Baer notes that this declaration produced an 'ecstatic' reaction at DLC headquarters (2000, p.241).

In the end, though, the Clinton era was too full of ambiguities to be seen as having established a sustained and coherent new philosophy of governance. One of the interesting features about the Third Way is the manner in which its self-proclaimed leaders such as Clinton, Blair and Schröder have conducted various seminars and conferences in a conscious effort to add intellectual credibility to their political cocktail. To a degree this may seem to be putting the cart before the horse (that is, declaring allegiance to an idea and then deciding what that idea actually is) and reflects a confusion about whether the Third Way should be guided by principles which lead to policies, by the bottom-up maxim of 'what is best is what works', or by some sort of hybrid of principles and pragmatism; if looked at as a practical manifestation of the Third Way, the course of the Clinton administration, and the reactions it has provoked, seem to reflect this confusion. Too often Clinton's actions – and, possibly even more so, the DLC's response to his fortunes – were too much about finding the median voter and establishing quite where the balance of power lay to be properly seen as establishing a series of fundamental principles.

The conventional wisdom about the Clinton presidency is that the first two years saw a phase of Big Government liberalism followed by a period of New Democracy; this is an analysis with which the New Democrats appear to agree. At a DLC convention just after the 1996 election, the then DLC chair, Senator Joseph Lieberman, enthused, 'We at the DLC welcome you home' (Broder, 1996a). This was an interesting choice of words, for two years earlier, following the 1994 mid-term disaster, Clinton's presence had not been so courted. Then chair Dave McCurdy, who had just lost in his bid for an Oklahoma Senate seat, denounced the direction of the Clinton presidency. He maintained that the administration had failed to fulfil its promise to pursue mainstream values and labeled Clinton a 'transitional figure' who had the 'mind of a New Democrat' but the 'heart of an old Democrat' (Cook, 1994).

Furthermore, according to DLC pollster Mark Penn, Clinton owed his re-election to his espousal of New Democrat policies in 1995 and 1996, while Congressional Democrats failed to recapture either chamber because too many still advertised their old Democrat beliefs (1997). If, however, the New Democrats and their version of the Third Way are to be judged by the Clinton administration's actions after 1995, then there is little evidence of the 'radical' and 'dynamic' centrism to which the movement claims to aspire. It is clear that one of the administration's problems during the first two years was its failure 'to move the public on behalf of its programs' (Edwards, 2000, p.53). The lesson learned from this was to generate ever more poll data in order to gauge where the White House could best position itself (Harris, 2000). Thus, the influence of Dick Morris and the strategy of triangulation – a classic statement of pre-emptive politics – was at its most blatant during the budget negotiations in 1995 and 1997. This proved successful for the President but it is difficult to see how it can be interpreted as a form of higher politics in pursuit of a grand design (Burns and Sorensen, 1999).

As it was, the administration was more adroit in its dealings with the Republican Congresses than it had been when the Democrats were in the majority through 1993 and 1994. Sometimes Clinton conceded ground and at others he managed to push through elements of his own agenda, while most of the time winning the public relations battle with Republican leaders. The problem was that artful opportunism became the end in itself with the administration satisfied to push for a series of micro-initiatives as Clinton effectively shied away from the type of bold proposals which would have left a distinctive 'Clinton' imprint on the 1990s. Of course Republican control of Congress meant that any ambitious new schemes would likely be dead even before arrival, but it perhaps says much about the New Democracy that Clinton found it so much easier to express what it stood for when reacting to external stimuli than when having to set out a pro-active agenda of his own. That is, from 1995 onwards Clinton was able to operationalize a successful defensive strategy which opposed the changes being advocated by Gingrich. When he had the opportunity, however, to play offence in 1993 and 1994 he found that the complexities of designing what almost had to be two-tier policies, asking the various vested interests to accept an outcome which was less than their preferred optimum but which might constitute a positive sum result overall, were overwhelming. That is, Clinton's major initiatives relied on striking complex political bargains between both contending ideas and competing political actors. Thus deficit reduction *and* investments; free trade *and* retraining; removing the guarantee of welfare *but* providing help moving into work; tougher sentencing *and* preventative programs to reduce crime; mend *but* do not end affirmative action, with the HSA attempting to broker a whole series of deals to ensure universal coverage *and* cost control. Looking back it is possible to see that there was action on a number of these fronts, but the whole bargain was rarely struck.

Moving right

One consistent consequence of this failure to persuade people of the virtues of the whole of the Third Way agenda was that even when elements of it were fulfilled they did not reflect the political balance implicit in the initial rhetoric. Sometimes the compromise result was simply feeble, notably the 'don't ask, don't tell' policy with respect to gays in the military, but the general tendency was for the conservative aspects of the package to emerge relatively intact while the more liberal ones fell by the wayside. For example; deficit reduction triumphed over spending initiatives; trade agreements were designed to satisfy capital rather than labor; health care reform was effectively abandoned; welfare reform took a significant lurch to the right, and the anti-crime bill found its preventative spending trimmed in order to win over vital Republican votes. This policy evolution was also reflected in the make-up of Clinton's advisers and cabinet. In particular at the end of the first term some of the more liberal hands such as Reich and Stephanopoulos left and were replaced by more moderate ones such as the new chief-of-staff, Erskine Bowles (Broder, 1996b).

A related phenomenon was the manner in which the DLC and the New Democrats kept moving to the right. That is, even as many old style Democrats accepted that they had to adjust and at least market themselves differently, so the New Democrats edged further across the political spectrum – almost as if in an effort to maintain the ideological differential between themselves and those liberals who had, even if reluctantly, dragged themselves across the political spectrum. The continuing divisions within party ranks were fully exposed in the aftermath of the 2000 election as Gore proved unable to win in what was in the end a highly partisan election (Broder, 2000).

The 2000 presidential election in fact provides a neat summary of how the Clinton years had changed the Democratic Party and yet also how much had remained the same. The battle for the Democratic nomination in 2000 suggested that the party had traveled some distance since 1988. Al Gore had long been a favourite son of the DLC and, at least during the primaries, he ran as an unmistakable New Democrat. This was reflected in comments made by Elaine Kamarck, a senior Gore advisor, when discussing his election strategy early in 2000. She noted that Gore's campaign would look much like Clinton's on the basis that, 'We have won twice. We have won twice on the general thrust of the 'Politics of Evasion" (quoted in Confessore, 2000, p.24). Just as revealing as Gore's ties to the DLC, however, was the fact that the only competition came from the former Senator from New Jersey, Bill Bradley. What was particularly significant was the absence of Gephardt from the race. During 1997, as the battles over fast track and the balanced budget agreement were taking place, it had appeared that Gephardt was positioning himself to challenge Gore by offering a populist economic message (Broder, 1997b). In Gephardt's absence, Bradley was portrayed as challenging Gore from the liberal-left, but to see him in such a way was to ignore the substance of his political record. In reality the records of the two men showed them to be ideologically like-minded. In the eight years the two served together in Senate, from 1985 to 1993, they voted the same centrist path the vast majority of the time. During the 2000 campaign there was some focus on Bradley's more liberal track record on welfare. He had voted against the FSA in 1988 while Gore had voted in favor, and Bradley opposed the 1996 reform while Gore was one of those urging Clinton to sign PRWORA. On the other hand, if anything, Bradley had proved himself even more of a deficit hawk than Gore (Foerstel with Willis, 2000). Thus, while

Bradley's concentration on issues such as child poverty and gun control did win over some liberals (Coniff, 1999; Kuttner, 1999), the fact that he was perceived to be the tribune of liberalism illustrated just how subdued the party's liberal wing had become in the face of the ascendant centrism.

Furthermore Gore's choice of Senator Joseph Lieberman from Connecticut as his Vice Presidential running-mate showed that he felt no need to balance the national ticket by opting for a more liberal candidate. Lieberman's selection was perhaps primarily a reflection of his forthright criticism of Clinton's behaviour over the Lewinsky scandal, but his status as a leading DLCer very much reinforced the New Democrat message (Victor et al., 2000). He certainly was not chosen to pacify liberals. One profile described him as someone who had 'triangulated the triangulator' by 'parting company with Clinton ... in favor of the Republican position on a range of economic issues' (Meyerson, 2000, p.28).

On the other hand, Gore had clearly not won over all of the party's base. As late as the party's national convention he had to spend valuable campaigning time convincing traditional Democratic groups to mobilize on his behalf and not to defect to Ralph Nader (Pierce, 2000). The ironic upshot of this was that after all the post-election shenanigans had died down, the post-defeat post-mortem conducted by the DLC attacked Gore for running too far to the left. According to Al From 'Gore chose a populist rather than New Democrat message. As a result, voters viewed him as too liberal and identified him as an advocate of big government' (From, 2001). Will Marshall chimed in that 'the Gore campaign often looked and sounded like a throwback to the doomed Democratic campaigns of the 1980s, replete with vintage class warfare themes, and narrowly tailored appeals to constituency groups' (Marshall, 2001). This type of analysis, however, was contradicted by liberals who maintained that until he asserted his more populist themes, Gore was heading for a heavy defeat (Babington, 2001; Broder, 2001). Indeed some of the DLC's logic is a little tortured. DLC pollster Mark Penn's polls showed that Gore clearly won on the socio-economic dimension issues such as the economy, health care, and preserving the social security and Medicare systems. Penn, however, then turns this into a negative by asserting that Gore's concentration on these subjects made him appear to be a Big Government liberal so that he actually 'lost on the philosophy' of these issues (Penn, 2001). It might be, however, that the DLC and the New Democrats need to revisit the 1992 and 1996 elections to be reminded that Clinton never received a majority of the popular vote.

Overall the Clinton experience suggests that the Third Way's ambitions of creating a new paradigm which bypasses existing political and ideological conflict is not likely to materialize. Many voters are not ideologically consistent along a left-right axis, but this does not make it easy for politicians to adapt a pick and mix approach in their choice of policies. First, voters' opinions are often not just ideologically inconsistent but are fundamentally so, and no amount of triangulation can reconcile incompatible desires. In short what the public wants may well not be 'what works'. Second, and in contrast to the public and the Third Way, many political actors do remain ideologues in a traditional sense, and the problem for Clinton was that he had to build new coalitions on each issue. Sometimes he was able to do this, as demonstrated by the budget and NAFTA votes in 1993. The downside of this was that even though he won on a case by case basis, he was dependent on a shifting rather than resilient political base to support the fundamentals of his program. In short, however much Clinton himself knew what he wanted to do, there were not enough others who shared the whole of this vision for it to be enacted in an integrated and coherent fashion.

Notes

1 Introduction

1. Clinton became chair of the DLC in March 1990 at a time when he was already thinking about his chances of making a presidential bid in 1992. As Shafer notes, 'The DLC chairmanship would provide him not only with a pre-packaged program but with organizational connections around the country' (2000, p.13).
2. Al From, president of the Democratic Leadership Council, made the following reflections after a policy seminar in November 1997 which brought together government officials and policy analysts representing the New Democrats and New Labour. 'The similarities between our movements are striking. Both were born out of frustration with repeated losses in national elections due to our parties' far-left policies. Both aimed to build a majority coalition composed of those who are in the middle class and struggling to stay there, and those who aspire to get there. Both led our parties out of the political wilderness by offering voters new, progressive ideas that rejected our parties' recent excesses but remained true to our parties' first principles' (1997a, p.35).
3. See Kuttner and Dionne, 2000 for a discussion of the merits of the Clinton presidency.

2 Redefining the Democrats

1. It is important to be aware of potential terminological confusion here. The terms neo-conservative and also neo-liberal were commonly used in US political debate in the late 1970s and early 1980s to describe a breed of politician and political commentator who, for want of a better description, were 'nearly' conservative or 'nearly' liberal. For a fuller explanation of 'neo-' in this sense see Steinfels, 1979; Kondracke, 1982; Rothenberg, 1984; Dolbeare and Medcalf, 1988. What is important is not to confuse the labels when being used in this context with the neo-conservative and neo-liberal wings of New Right thought and ideology.
2. Carter had used the concept of the misery index to attack president Ford in the 1976 election. It was the aggregate of the unemployment rate and the inflation rate.
3. Towards the end of the 1988 presidential campaign in a desperate effort to revitalize his bid for the White House, Michael Dukakis changed his response to the taunt of Vice President Bush that he was a 'liberal'. Rather than ignoring or denying the label, Dukakis protested that he was a liberal, but one in the mold of Presidents Roosevelt, Truman and Kennedy (Toner, 1988). This was an explicit attempt to associate himself with memories of the New Deal and the great names of the Democratic past while dissociating himself from the more recent New Politics tribunes of liberalism.

4. The 1984 Democratic primary had seen a clash over the nature of economic policy with Mondale cast as the New Dealer and Gary Hart as the champion of the 'Atari' economy.
5. Hale quotes DLC executive director Alvin From as saying of the organization's early efforts through to 1988, 'We were fine until the presidential nominating process got going in earnest, but then that process defines the party' (Hale, 1995, p.218).
6. The Republicans of course followed the Democrats in introducing a binding primary system and they too have had some bitter campaigns. Notably, in 1992 and 1996, Pat Buchanan ruffled the feathers of Bush and Robert Dole.
7. An editorial in *The New Republic* commenting after Cuomo finally announced that he would not be running stated, 'all Democrats – at least those who want to regain the White House – should realize that Cuomo's non-candidacy is the best news they've had in years' (*The New Republic*, 1992a, p.7). The same piece did reflect, however, that Cuomo might have helped Clinton steer his centrist ship.

> ironically, a Cuomo candidacy might have helped Clinton define himself against the old dogma of the Democratic party. With Cuomo out of the race, Clinton will be more tempted to usurp the middle ground, and appease the party's left wing. Luckily, he still has Tom Harkin whose constituency is substantially the same as Cuomo's. Defeating it in 1992, whether a Democrat regains the White House or not, is not just a prerequisite for the Democratic Party's renewal, but for the country's as well (p.8).

8. See Baer, 2000, pp.194–7, on the help the DLC provided to the Clinton campaign.
9. The nomination campaign, of course, was about more than just ideology, as various events from Clinton's past threatened to derail his bid. For the story of the primary battle and how Clinton survived early scares see Baker, 1993.
10. Party platform reprinted in *Congressional Quarterly Weekly Report*, 18 July 1992, p.2107.

3   Clintonomics I

1. One problem was that $500 billion was too easily an identifiable figure to back away from without losing credibility especially after a public intervention by Alan Greenspan who reflected, 'If the markets perceive that we are backing off the size of the commitment... I think that they will react appropriately negatively... The $500 billion program is probably about the right size' (quoted in Hager and Cloud, 1993c, p.1939).
2. Clinton had in fact asked that 85 percent of benefits be taxed, rather than 50 percent, for recipients with an income of over $25,000 for individuals and $32,000 for couples. Congress raised these income levels to $34,000 for individuals and $44,000 for couples.
3. Times–Mirror and Gallup polls featured in 'Opinion Outlook' in *National Journal*, 21 August 1993, p.2102.
4. This dispute over whether to use budget projections from the CBO or the OMB was something of an absurdity. In truth neither could be relied upon.

For example, the final deficit for fiscal 1996, which ended on 30 September 1996, was $107 billion; yet in March the OMB projected a deficit of $154 billion and in May the CBO one of $144 billion. Even in July and August when revised estimates were issued both still missed the figure by over 10 percent (Hager, 1997a).

5. 20 percent of respondents blamed both President and Congress. Polls in 'Opinion Outlook' in *National Journal*, 20 January 1996, p.142.

6. In exasperation Bush at one point during the campaign said that Clinton must be developing 'straddle sores' (Cloud, 1992, p.3711).

7. A Gallup poll in September 1993 showed respondents opposed to NAFTA by 41 percent to 35 percent. Asked whether they thought it would lead to more or less jobs in the US respondents overwhelmingly replied that it would result in job losses, by 67 to 22 percent ('Opinion Outlook' in *National Journal*, 25 September 1993, p.2334). Another Gallup poll showed that while 59 percent thought that NAFTA would be good for US corporations and 55 percent for US consumers, 57 percent felt that it would damaging to US workers ('Opinion Outlook' in *National Journal*, 23 October 1993, p.2560).

8. According to Bob Woodward's account, Treasury Secretary Lloyd Bentsen was worried for a short while that Clinton was going to abandon the NAFTA ship because of labor's opposition. Thus in 'a table-pounding' speech Bentsen insisted that 'it was absolutely imperative that [Clinton] show he was a strong leader, willing to fight.... to take on an interest group in his own party.' Howard Paster, the White House's congressional liaison officer is also reputed to have told the President, 'If you abandon NAFTA, Mr. President, there goes New Democrat' (Woodward, 1994, p.318).

9. This would in fact have been difficult on NAFTA where Clinton effectively inherited a done deal.

4   Clintonomics II

1. The $16 billion figure stayed within the overall budget cap for discretionary spending in fiscal year 1993 imposed by the 1990 balanced budget act. The shortfall in appropriations was actually in defence and foreign aid spending, and in order to transfer the money to a domestic area, without having to get a supermajority in congress, Clinton declared the matter an economic emergency.

2. In May 1993 a *U.S. News and World Report* poll found that 36 percent of respondents thought that the job creation proposals were the most important part of Clinton's plan against 34 percent who thought that deficit reduction was (poll cited in 'Opinion Outlook' in *National Journal*, 26th June 1993, p.1670). In April an NBC–Wall Street Journal poll found that 44 percent believed unemployment to be the most important economic issue facing the country compared with 28 percent who nominated the deficit. By September these numbers read 40 percent and 26 percent (polls in 'Opinion Outlook' in *National Journal*, 25th September 1993, p.2334). More specifically, a Yankelovich poll for CNN–Time magazine asked, 'Which do you think is more important – cutting the federal budget deficit, even if that does not improve the economy in the next year or two, or creating jobs and

improving the economy, even if the budget deficit is not cut?' In response 25 percent called for deficit reduction, while 68 percent favored an immediate boost for jobs and the economy (in 'Opinion Outlook' in *National Journal*, 24th July 1993, p.1891). For details of Gallup polls reinforcing this data see Weatherford and McDonnell, 1996, p.424.

3. Reich recounts how Stanley Greenberg had assembled a focus group to monitor reactions to Clinton's 1994 State of the Union address. After the speech Greenberg told Reich of the highly favorable reaction to the sections about investment in education and training, 'In fact, when the President said he wanted to move from an *un*employment insurance system to a *re*-employment system, the meter went ballistic' (1998, p.150).

4. The main point here is that the EITC surpassed the much reviled Aid to Families with Dependent Children (see Chapter 6). The overall, that is non means-tested, program removing the most Americans from poverty remained Social Security.

5. In June 1989 President Bush vetoed a minimum wage increase passed by Congress and some New Democrats expressed support for his stand. Will Marshall said, 'There's no constituency any more for this kind of policy' (quoted in Rauch, 1989, p.1746).

6. It should be noted that not all those previously taxed at the 31 percent marginal rate would be subject to the 36 percent rate, as the level at which the top rate kicked in on a single income rose from $89,150 to $115,000 (Novak and Starobin, 1993).

7. All attempts to make sense of the federal tax code come with a health warning. Due to the various itemized deductions, credits and allowances, people within the same income bracket can pay quite different sums in tax (Aaron et al., 1999).

5 The politics of health care

1. Some Republican strategists were always acutely conscious of the possibility that successful health care reform might inspire a middle class embrace of the federal government. Johnson and Broder quote a memorandum from the influential strategist William Kristol, a former Chief of Staff to Vice President Dan Quayle. The memo, distributed to leading Republicans in early December 1993, urged that the Clinton plan be 'killed' rather than modified. Kristol's concern was that any reform 'will re-legitimize middle-class dependence for 'security' on government spending and regulation. It will revive the reputation of the party that spends and regulates, the Democrats, as the generous protector of middle-class interests. And it will at the same time strike a punishing blow against Republican claims to defend the middle class by restraining government' (1997, p.234).

2. It might be argued that there was in fact a fourth version of reform manifesting itself through the 1990s as HMOs increasingly came to dominate to the health insurance market. The changes wrought by this were quite profound, but were driven by private sector considerations rather than public policy legislation. On the other hand, popular resentment about the practices of HMOs did trigger debate on whether there was a need for a 'Patient's Bill of Rights'.

3. In 1992, 220 million Americans had some health insurance. Of these 148.3 million had employment related insurance (US, 1996b, Table 173, p.120).
4. Many people would in fact carry more than one type of insurance.
5. The figures about the number of uninsured are familiar ones to even casual students of American social policy, but the human drama behind the numbers is often less well explained. For an insight into the types of problems endured by those without insurance see Patel and Rushefsky, 1999, pp.142–44 and Johnson and Broder, 1997, pp.247–53.
6. The issue of increased costs for some of those who already had insurance quickly hit the headlines when Health and Human Services Secretary Donna Shalala testified before the Senate Finance Committee that 'a few' such people would end up paying more for their care under the Clinton plan. An aide then said that this in fact meant 40 percent. The administration quickly revised its figures down to 30 percent and then Hillary Clinton claimed that only '6 percent of all Americans will pay more for the same benefits' (Kosterlitz, 1993, p.2938). An *ABC/Washington Post* poll, however, found that 60 percent of respondents believed that they would be paying more than they already were for similar levels of coverage (p.2939).

6   Reforming welfare

1. In 1996, 4,553,000 families received AFDC. Of these only 302,000 were covered by the so-called AFDCB–UP program where needy two parent families could claim benefit if the principal wage earner was unemployed but had a recent work history (US, 1998b, p.402).
2. AFDC was not an absolutely unqualified entitlement, as the Work Incentive Program (WIN) amendments which came into force in 1971 and the Family Support Act of 1988 had attached work requirements to the benefit, but these had only ever been applied to a minority of recipients (see Berkowitz, 1991, pp.133–6 on WIN and King, 1991, on the FSA).
3. In contrast the FSA had reflected the thoughts of much of the social science community (Baum, 1991; Haskins, 1991; Wiseman, 1991).
4. Overall Ellwood described himself as very satisfied with the final product. Interview with author, April 1999.
5. Some did take a position out of line with their normal ideological station. Senator Tom Harkin, for example, who had run to the left of Clinton in the 1992 Democratic primaries said that he was disappointed that the WRA would not force more people off the welfare rolls before two years (Suskind, 1994, p.A2).
6. See Weaver, 2000, pp.252–315 for a detailed discussion of how the final version of the PRWORA was arrived at.
7. The devolution of welfare administration reflected the lobbying of the National Governors Association as well as the fact that many states were already experimenting within their own borders under so-called 'waivers' schemes (for surveys of what had been happening under the waivers see, Friedlander and Burtless, 1995; Norris and Thompson, 1995).
8. The states can in fact exempt 20 percent of their welfare caseload from the five year limit. This figure was not based on any social science research but

was a compromise political number. The PRWORA does not stop the states from continuing to provide aid to recipients beyond five years at their own expense.
9. It should be said that Clinton did have some success in reversing elements of the bill which targeted legal immigrants.

7   Clintonism and the cultural dimension

1. Indeed it appears that Jackson was invited to a DLC conference in March 1989 in order to challenge him with the Galston-Kamarck thesis. The intention was that this would lead to public confrontation which in turn would allow the DLC to claim distance from Jackson (Baer, 2000, pp.132–3).
2. Exit polls showed that the gay vote constituted 2 percent of the total, although both pollsters and gay activists said that this was probably an underestimate. Gay activists pointed to the election tallies in Georgia in 1992 as evidence of their potential to swing results. Clinton narrowly won the state with the support of the gay community but Democratic Senator Wyche Fowler lost to Republican Paul Coverdell who talked of his previous efforts to tackle discrimination in the Peace Corps (Donovan, 1993, p.1815).
3. *Putting People First* referred to the intention to 'issue executive orders to repeal the ban on gays and lesbians from military or foreign service' (Clinton and Gore, 1992, p.64).
4. Bizarrely, Baird's enforced withdrawal was not the end of the embarrassment, as the next in line Kimba Wood was found to have used an illegal alien as a baby-sitter. Wood's offence was considerably less substantive than Baird's but this time the White House quickly backtracked.
5. Brooks did in the end vote for the bill. He also lost his seat in 1994.
6. After the defeat on the procedural motion, there was debate about how to resurrect the bill. The House Democrat leadership urged Clinton to drop the assault weapons ban as this would guarantee the votes, get people like Brooks off the hook and unite the congressional party. Clinton, however, decided that this would look too unprincipled and so sought moderate Republicans through cuts to the prevention programs (Sinclair, 2000, pp.82–3).
7. In practical terms this meant that even if a gay couple claimed to be married this would not be recognized for matters of federal taxation and benefits, including survivor's benefits.
8. The gender gap here refers to Democrats winning among women. There was still a large discrepancy between white women, who split evenly between Gore and Bush, and white men who voted overwhelmingly for Bush.

Conclusion

1. There were some tentative efforts, involving figures such as Mickey Kaus and James Pinkerton, to develop cross-party links around the language of a 'new paradigm' but these remained cerebral rather than practical in their manifestation (Stoesz, 1996, pp.18–19).

2. The FMLA was in fact more limited than was sometimes appreciated as it only applied to workers in businesses with more than fifty employees.
3. Writing in 1992, for example, the PPI's Robert Shapiro had argued that entitlement reform 'could and should be…a basic plank in a new covenant of rights and responsibilities, governing the way Americans secure basic goods' (1992, p.16).
4. Greenberg's position is a particularly interesting one as his polling had been instrumental in the early Clinton years.
5. There is a complicating factor here related to Clinton's personal behavior. Indeed for many Republicans the *Clintons* epitomized everything they thought had gone wrong with America since the 1960s.

Bibliography

Aaron, H.J., Gale, W. and Sly, J. (1999), 'The Rocky Road to Tax Reform' in H.J. Aaron and R. Reischauer eds, *Setting National Priorities: the 2000 Election and Beyond* (Washington DC: Brookings Institution Press), pp.211–68

Administration for Children and Families (1999), 'Change in TANF Caseloads Since the Enactment of New Welfare Law' (Washington DC:US Department of Health and Human Services)

Akard, P. (1998), 'Where Are All the Democrats? The Limits of Economic Policy Reform' in C.Y.H. Lo and M. Schwartz eds, *Social Policy and the Conservative Agenda* (Oxford: Blackwell Publishers) pp.227–44

Anderson, M. (1988), *Revolution* (New York: Harcourt Brace)

Angle, M. (1994), 'The Clinton Budget: Agony and Angst', *Congressional Quarterly Weekly Report*, 5 February 1994, p.278

Arden, C. (1988), *Getting the Donkey Out of the Ditch: the Democratic Party in Search of Itself* (Westport, Connecticut: Greenwood Press)

Avery, W.P. (1998), 'Domestic Interests in NAFTA Bargaining', *Political Science Quarterly*, Vol. 113, No. 2, pp.281–305

Babington, C. (2000), 'Clinton Opens Push for School Proposals', *The Washington Post*, 4 May 2000, p.A08

Babington, C. (2001), 'Democratic Soul Searching Begins', *The Washington Post*, 24 January 2001, http://www.washingtonpost.com/ac2/wp-dyn/A40624-2001Jan24

Baer, K.S. (2000), *Reinventing Democrats: the politics of liberalism from Reagan to Clinton* (Lawrence: University of Kansas Press)

Baker, R.K. (1993), 'Sorting Out and Suiting Up: The Presidential Nominations', in G. Pomper ed., *The Election of 1992: Reports and Interpretations* (New Jersey: Chatham House)

Bane, M.J. (1992), 'Welfare Policy After Welfare Reform' in J.A. Pechman and M.S. McPherson eds, *Fulfilling America's Promise: Social Policies for the 1990s* (New York: Cornell University Press), pp.109–28

Bane, M.J. (1997), 'Welfare As We Might Know It', *The American Prospect*, No. 30, pp.47–55

Bane, M.J. and Ellwood, D. (1994), *Welfare Realities: From Rhetoric to Reform* (Cambridge, Massachussetts: Harvard University Press)

Barnes, J.A. (1992), 'Tainted Triumph', *National Journal*, 7 November 1992, pp.2537–41

Baum, E.B. (1991), 'When the Witch Doctors Agree: The Family Support Act and Social Science Research', *Journal of Policy Analysis and Management*, Vol. 10, No. 4, 603–15

Beland, D., Vergniolle de Chantal, F. and Waddan, A. (2002), 'Third Way Social Policy: Clinton's Legacy?' *Policy and Politics*, forthcoming

Benenson, B. (1994a), 'With Health Care Receding GATT Pact Gains Urgency', *Congressional Quarterly Weekly Report*, 24 September 1994, pp.2661–6

Benenson, B. (1994b), 'Free Trade Carries the Day As GATT Easily Passes', *Congressional Quarterly Weekly Report*, 3 December 1994, pp.3446–50

Bennett, W.L. (1995), 'The Cueless Public: Bill Clinton Meets the New American Voter in Campaign' 92', in S. Renshon ed., *Campaiging, Governing and the Psychology of Leadership* (Boulder, Colorado: Westview Press), pp.91–112

Berkowitz, E.D. (1991), *America's Welfare State: from Roosevelt to Reagan* (Baltimore: John Hopkins University Press)

Box-Steffensmeier, J.M., Arnold, L.W., and Zorn, C.J.W. (1997), 'The Strategic Timing of Position Taking in Congress: A Study of the North American Free Trade Agreement' in *American Political Science Review*, Vol. 92, No. 2, 324–38

Brinkley, A. (1997), 'The Economy, the Community, and the Public Sector', in S.B. Greenberg and T. Skocpol eds, *The New Majority: Toward a Popular Progressive Politics* (New Haven: Yale University Press), pp.42–56

Broder, D. (1996a), 'Turnabout', *The Washington Post*, 15 December 1996, p.C07

Broder, D. (1996b), 'What's Left of the Left?', *The Washington Post*, 18 December 1996, p.A23

Broder, D. (1997a), 'The Politics of Minimalism', *The Washington Post*, 14 May 1997, p.A21

Broder, D. (1997b), 'Gore v. Gephardt: The Good Fight', in *The Washington Post*, 4 June 1997, p.A23

Broder, D. (2000), 'Voters' Views Sharply Divided', *The Washington Post*, 8 November 2000, p.A01

Broder, D. (2001), 'Party's Fault Lines Likely to Surface', *The Washington Post*, 21 January 2001, p.A22

Broder, J.M. (1999), 'Clinton Begins Tour of Hard-Pressed Areas With Pledge to the Needy', New York Times, 6 July 1999, http://www.nytimes.com/library/politics/070699clinton-poverty.html

Brown, P. (1991), 'Minority Party', *The New Democrat*, September 1991, pp.4–7

Brownstein, R. (1997), 'Balanced-Budget Deal May Tip Scales Toward a New Kind of Washington', *Los Angeles Times*, 12 May 1997, p.A5

Burnham, W.D. (1970), *Critical Elections and the Mainsprings of American Elections* (New York: Norton)

Burnham, W.D. (1995), 'American Politics in the 1990s', in R. Kuttner ed., *The American Prospect Reader in American Politics*, New Jersey: Chatham House, pp.1–14

Burns, J.M. and Sorensen, G.J., Gerber, R. and Webster S.W. (1999), *Dead Center: Clinton-Gore Leadership and the Perils of Moderation* (New York: Simon and Schuster)

Burtless, G. (1999), 'Growing American Inequality: Sources and Remedies', in H.J. Aaron and R. Reischauer eds, *Setting National Priorities: the 2000 Election and Beyond* (Washington DC: Brookings Institution Press), pp.137–66

Camissa, A.M. (1998), *From Rhetoric to Reform: Welfare Policy in American Politics* (Westview Press)

Carmines, E.G. and Stimson, J.A. (1989), *Issue Evolution: Race and the Transformation of American Politics*, (Princeton University Press)

Carney, D. (1996), 'GOP Bill Restricting Gay Unions Clears – But Does Not Yield Political Dividends', *Congressional Quarterly Weekly Report*, 14 September 1996, pp.2598–9

The Chicago Tribune (1994), 'Clinton Takes on the Welfare Machine', *The Chicago Tribune*, 16 June, 1994, p.30

Clinton, W.J. (1992), 'Nominee Clinton Describes Vision of New Covenant', *Congressional Quarterly Weekly Report*, 18 July 1992, pp.2128–30

Clinton, W.J. (1994), *Economic Report of the President* (U.S. Government Printing Office)

Clinton, W.J. (1995), 'Mend, Don't End, Affirmative Action', Presidential address reprinted in *Congressional Quarterly Weekly Report*, 22 July 1995, pp.2208–09

Clinton, W. (1998), 'Remarks by the President to DLC National Conversation', The White House, Office of the Press Secretary, 4 June 1998

Clinton, W.J. (2000), *Economic Report of the President* (U.S. Government Printing Office)

Clinton, W.J. and Gore, A. (1992), *Putting People first: A Strategy For Change* (New York: Times Books)

Cloud, D. (1992), 'Warning Bells on NAFTA Sound for Clinton', *Congressional Quarterly Weekly Report*, 28 November 1992, pp.3710–13

Cloud, D. (1993a), 'It's Democrats vs. Democrats As Conference Nears', *Congressional Quarterly Weekly Report*, 10 July 1993, pp.1799–801

Cloud, D. (1993b), '"Undecideds" Are Final Target In Battle Over Trade Pact', *Congressional Quarterly Weekly Report*, special report, 6 November 1993, pp.3011–22

Cloud, D. (1993c), 'Decisive Vote Brings Down Trade Walls With Mexico', *Congressional Quarterly Weekly Report*, 20 November 1993, pp.3174–9

Cloud, D. (1994), 'Health Care: Clinton's Quandary', *Congressional Quarterly Weekly Report special supplement*, 10 October 1994, pp.17–20

Cook, R. (1991), 'Cuomo says "No" to Candidacy At Last Possible Moment', *Congressional Quarterly Weekly Report*, 21 December 1991, pp.3734–6

Cook, R. (1992a), 'Republicans Suffer a Knockout That Leaves Clinton Standing', *Congressional Quarterly Weekly Report*, 12 December 1992, pp.3810–3

Cook, R. (1992b), 'Arkansan Travels well Nationally As Campaign Heads for Test', *Congressional Quarterly Weekly Report*, 11 January 1992, pp.58–65

Cook, R. (1994), 'President Defends Record, Concedes Mistakes', *Congressional Quarterly Weekly Report*, 10 December, p.3516

Confessore, N. (2000), 'The Odd Couple', *The American Prospect*, Vol. 11, No. 11, 24 April, pp.23–5

Conniff, R. (1999), 'A Flash of Hope', IntellectualCapital.com, http://www.intellectualcapital.com/issues/issue294/item6401.asp

Council of Economic Advisers (1994), *Annual Report of the Council of Economic Advisers* (Washington DC: U.S. Government printing Office)

Council of Economic Advisers (1999), *Annual Report of the Council of Economic Advisers* (Washington DC: U.S. Government printing Office)

Council of Economic Advisers (2000), *Annual Report of the Council of Economic Advisers* (Washington DC: U.S. Government printing Office)

Crotty, W. (1978), *Decision for the Democrats: Reforming the Party Structure* (Baltimore: John Hopkins University Press)

Danziger, S. and Gottschalk, P. (1995), *America Unequal* (New York: Russell Sage Foundation)

Davies, G. (1996), *From Opportunity to Entitlement: The Transformation and Decline of Great Society Liberalism* (Lawrence: University of Kansas Press)

Democratic Leadership Council (1990), *The New Orleans Declaration: A Democratic Agenda for the 1990s* (Washington DC: Democratic Leadership Council)

Democratic Leadership Council (1991), *The New American Choice: Opportunity, Responsibility, Community* (Washington DC: Democratic Leadership Council)

Democratic Leadership Council (2000), 'A Final High Note on Welfare Reform', dlcppi.org, New Democrats online, 21 December 2000

DeParle, J. (1999), 'Clinton's Poverty Tour Draws Skepticism and Indifference', *New York Times*, 9 July 1999, p.A1

Destler, I.M. (1992), *American Trade Politics* (New York: Institute for International Economics with the Twentieth Century Fund), 2nd edition

Destler, I.M. (1999), 'Trade Policy at a Crossroads' in H.J. Aaron and R. Reischauer eds, *Setting National Priorities: the 2000 Election and Beyond* (Washington DC: Brookings Institution Press), pp.73–96

DiIulio, J. (1999), 'Federal Crime Policy: Declare a Moratorium' in H.J. Aaron, R. Reischauer eds, *Setting National Priorities: the 2000 Election and Beyond* (Washington DC: Brookings Institution Press), pp.333–58

Dionne, E.J. (1992), *Why Americans Hate Politics* (New York: Simon and Schuster)

Dionne, E.J. (1997a), 'Why the Democrats Bolted', *The Washington Post*, 14 November 1997, p.A27

Dionne, E.J. (1997b), *They Only Look Dead: Why Progressives Will Dominate the Next Political Era*, Touchstone edition (New York: Simon and Schuster)

Dionne, E.J. (2000), 'Why Americans Hate Politics: A Reprise', *The Brookings Review*, Vol. 18, No. 1, Winter, pp.8–11

Dolbeare, K. and Medcalf, L.J. (1988), *American Ideologies Today: from neopolitics to new ideas* (New York: Random House)

Donovan, B. (1993), 'Cash, Votes Ride on Ban Decision', *Congressional Quarterly Weekly Report*, 10 July 1993, pp.1814–16

Drew, E. (1994), *On the Edge: the Clinton Presidency* (New York: Simon and Schuster)

Drew, E. (1997), *Showdown: The Struggle Between the Gingrich Congress and the Clinton White House*, Touchstone edition (New York: Simon and Schuster)

Dutton, F.G. (1970), *Changing Sources of Power: American Politics in the 1970s*, (New York: McGraw Hill)

Edelman, P. (1997), 'The Worst Thing Bill Clinton Has Done', *Atlantic Monthly*, March 1997, pp.43–58

Edsall, T.B. (1984), *The New Politics of Inequality* (New York: W.W. Norton and Company)

Edsall, T.B. (1988), 'Polls Show GOP Attacks Worked Against Dukakis', *The Washington Post*, 16 November 1988, p.A12

Edsall, T.B. (1997), 'The Cultural Revolution of 1994: Newt Gingrich, the Republican Party, and the Third Great Awakening', in B. Shafer ed., *Present Discontents: American Politics in the Very Late Twentieth Century* (New Jersey: Chatham House), pp.135–46

Edsall, T.B. (2000), 'Voting Conflict Reopens Racial Split Among Democrats', *The Washington Post*, 29 November 2000, p.A29

Edsall, T.B. and Edsall, M.D. (1991), *Chain Reaction: the Impact of Race, Rights and Taxes on American Politics* (New York: W.W. Norton and Company)

Edwards, G.C. (2000), 'Building Coalitions', Presidential Studies Quarterly, Vol. 30, No. 1, March, pp.47–61

Ellwood, D. (1988), *Poor Support: Poverty in the American Family* (New York: Basic Books)

Ellwood, D. (1996), 'Welfare Reform As I Knew It', *The American Prospect*, No. 26, pp.22–29

Elthstain, J. (1993), 'Issues and Themes: Spiral of Delegitimation or New Social Covenant', in M. Nelson ed. *The Elections of 1992* (Washington DC: Congressional Quarterly Press), pp.109–24

Elving, R.D. (1992), 'Clinton Sets Out to Recast Personal, Party Images', *Congressional Quarterly Weekly Report*, 18 July1992, pp.2075–7

Elving, R.D. and Taylor, A. (1997), 'A Balanced-Budget Deal Done, A Defining Issue Lost', *Congressional Quarterly Weekly Report* , 2 August 1997, pp.1831–6

Faux, J. (1993), 'The Myth of the New Democrat', *The American Prospect*, No. 15, pp.20–29

Faux, J. (1995), 'Preface', in L. Mishel and J. Schmitt eds, *Beware the U.S. Model: Jobs and Wages in a Deregulated Economy* (Washington DC: Economic Policy Institute) pp.ix–xiii

Faux, J. (1999), 'Lost on the Third Way', *Dissent*, Spring 1999, pp.65–74

Feldman, S. and Zaller, J. (1992), 'The Political Culture of Ambivalence: Ideological Responses to the Welfare State', *American Journal of Political Science*, Vol. 36, February, pp.268–307

Ferejohn, J. (1998), 'A Tale of Two Congresses: Social Policy in the Clinton Years', in M. Weir ed., *The Social Divide: Political Parties and the Future of Activist Government* (Washington DC: The Brookings Institution), pp.49–82

Ferguson, T. and Rogers, J. (1986), *Right Turn: the Decline of the Democrats and the Future of American Politics* (New York: Hill and Wang)

Fessler, P. (1993), 'Evolution of an Explosive Issue', *Congressional Quarterly Weekly Report*, 30 January 1993, p.227

Foerstel, K. (2000), 'Unions and Pro-Trade Democrats: Estrangement But No Divorce', *Congressional Quarterly Weekly Report*, 27 May 2000, p.1251

Foerstel, K. and Willis, D. (2000), 'Letting the Record Speak for Gore and Bradley', *Congressional Quarterly Weekly Report*, 8 January 2000, pp.48–9

Foley, M. (1999), 'Clinton and Congress', in P.S. Herrnson and D.M. Hill eds, *The Clinton Presidency: The First Term* (Basingstoke: Macmillan Press – now Palgrave)

Frank, R.H. and Cook, P.J. (1995), *The Winner Take-All Society* (New York: The Free Press)

Franklin, G.A. and Ripley, R.B. (1984), *C.E.T.A.: Politics and Policy, 1973–1982* (Knoxville: University of Tennessee Press)

French, M. (1997), *US Economic History Since 1945* (Manchester: Manchester University Press)

Friedlander, D. and Burtless, G. (1995), *Five Years After: The Long-Term Effects of Welfare-to-Work Programs* (New York: Russell Sage Foundation)

From, A. (1993a), 'The Ruling Class', *The New Democrat*, July–August 1993, pp.2–3

From, A. (1993b), 'The Mother Lode: Clinton Must Hold the Middle Class, but not With New Entitlements', *The New Democrat*, December 1993, pp.21–2

From, A. (1997a), 'Securing Our Gains: New Democrats and New Labour Must Now Win the Battle of Ideas', *The New Democrat*, November–December 1997, pp.35–6

From, A. (1997b), 'Statement by Al From, President, Democratic Leadership Council', http://www.dlcppi.org/press/statements/altrade.htm, 17 October 1997

From, A. (1999), 'The Third Way: Reshaping Politics Throughout the World', New Democrats online http://www.dlc.org/nc/1999/alspeech.htm

From, A. (2001), 'Building a New Progressive Majority: How Democrats Can Learn From the Failed 2000 Campaign', *Blueprint Magazine*, 24 January 2001, http://www.ndol.org/print.cfm?contentid=2919

From, A. and Marshall, W. (1993a), 'Preface', in W. Marshall, and M. Schram eds, *Mandate For Change* (New York: Berkley Books/the Progressive Policy Institute) pp.xv–xviii

From, A. and Marshall, W. (1993b), 'The First 100 Days' in *The New Democrat*, May, pp.4–7

From, A. and Marshall, W. (1997), 'From Big Government to Big Ideas', in W. Marshall ed., *Building the Bridge: 10 Big Ideas to Transform America* (Lanham, Maryland: Rowman and Littlefield/Progressive Policy Institute)

Galbraith, J.K. (1996), 'The Surrender of Economic Policy', in R. Kuttner ed., *Ticking Time Bombs* (The New Press), pp.102–12

Galston, W. and Kamarck, E. (1989), *The Politics of Evasion: Democrats and the Presidency* (Washington DC: Progressive Policy Institute)

Germond, J. and Witcover, J. (1993a), *Mad As Hell: Revolt at the Ballot Box, 1992* (Warner Books)

Germond, J. and Witcover, G. (1993b), ' Gephardt Support Critical on NAFTA', *National Journal*, 31 July 1993, p.1938

Germond, J. and Witcover, J. (1993c), 'A Promise that Could Haunt Clinton', *National Journal*, 9 January 1993, p.94

Gilder, G. (1981), *Wealth and Poverty* (New York: Basic Books)

Gilens, M. (1996), 'Race Coding and White Opposition to Welfare', *American Political Science Review*, Vol. 90, No. 3, pp.593–604

Gilens, M. (1999), *Why Americans Hate Welfare: Race, Media and the Politics of Antipoverty Policy* (The University of Chicago Press)

Glassman, J.K. (1997), 'A Victory for the Flat-Earth Caucus', *The Washington Post*, 11 November 1997, p.A19

Gordon, L. (1994), *Pitied But Not Entitled: Single Mothers and the History of Welfare* (New York: The Free Press)

Greenberg, S. (1995), *Middle Class Dreams: The Politics and Power of the New American Majority* (Yale University Press)

Greenberg, A. and Greenberg, S. (2000), 'Adding Values', *The American Prospect*, Vol. 11, No. 19, 28 August 2000, pp.28–31

Greenfield, J. and Newfield, J. (1972), *A Populist Manifesto: The Making of a New Majority* (New York: Praeger)

Guiden, M. (2001), 'State Medicaid Budgets Start To Squeeze', *Stateline.org*, 4 January 2001, http://www.stateline.org/story.cfm?storyid=107874

Hacker, J.S. (1997), *The Road to Nowhere: The Genesis of President Clinton's Plan for Health Security* (Princeton: Princeton University Press)

Hager, G. (1993), President Throws Down Gauntlet', *Congressional Quarterly Weekly Report*, 20 February 1993, pp.355–9

Hager, G. (1995a), 'Clinton's Message to Congress: Seek No Cover Here', *Congressional Quarterly Weekly Report*, 11 February 1995, pp.403–8

Hager, G. (1995b), 'Trials Ahead Are Taking Shape As GOP Maps Path to 2002', *Congressional Quarterly Weekly Report*, 22 April 1995, pp.1111–15

Hager, G. (1995c), 'Clinton Shifts Tactics, Proposes Erasing Deficit in 10 Years', *Congressional Quarterly Weekly Report*, 17 June 1995, pp.1715–20

Hager, G. (1995d), 'Harsh Rhetoric on Budget Spells a Dismal Outlook', *Congressional Quarterly Weekly Report*, 9 December 1995, pp.3721–5

Hager, G. (1997a), *Congressional Quarterly Weekly Report*, 29 March 1997, p.735

Hager, G. (1997b), 'As Each Side Moves to Center, Plan Is Almost a "Done Deal"', *Congressional Quarterly Weekly Report*, 24 May 1997, pp.1179–81

Hager, G. and Cloud, D. (1993a), 'Test For Divided Democrats: Forge a Budget Deal', *Congressional Quarterly Weekly Report*, 26 June 1993, pp.1631–5

Hager, G. and Cloud, D. (1993b), 'Democrats Seek Wiggle Room As Conference Begins', *Congressional Quarterly Weekly Report*, 17 July 1993, pp.1853–5

Hager, G. and Cloud, D. (1993c), 'Negociators Begin to Shape Deficit-Reduction Deal', *Congressional Quarterly Weekly Report*, 24 July 1993, pp.1935–9

Hager, G. and Cloud, D. (1993d), 'Democrats Tie Their Fate to Clinton's Budget Bill', *Congressional Quarterly Weekly Report*, 7 August 1993, pp.2122–9

Hager, G. and Rubin, A. (1995a), 'Last-Minute Maneuvers Forge A Conference Agreement', *Congressional Quarterly Weekly Report*, 24 June 1995, pp.814–19

Hager, G. and Rubin, A. (1995b), 'Fight Over Interim Measures Previews a Bigger Battle', *Congressional Quarterly Weekly Report*, 11 November 1995, pp.3439–44

Hale, J. (1995), 'The Making of the New Democrats', in *Political Science Quarterly*, Vol. 110, No. 2, pp.207–32

Harris, J.F. (1997), 'President Takes Blame For Fast Track Delay', *The Washington Post*, 11 November 1997, p.A01

Harris, J.F. (2000), 'A Clouded Mirror: Bill Clinton, Polls and the Politics of Survival', in S. Schier ed., *The Postmodern Presidency: Bill Clinton's Legacy in US Politics* (University of Pittsburgh Press)

Haskins, R. (1991), 'Congress Writes A Law: Research and Welfare Reform', *Journal of Policy Analysis and Management*, Vol. 10, No. 4, pp.616–32

Healey, J. (1993a), 'Stimulus Plan Emphasizes Quick Creation of Jobs', *Congressional Quarterly Weekly Report*, 6 March 1993, pp.501–3

Healey, J. (1993b), 'Clinton Now Must Sell Urgency of Stimulus Bill's Jobs', *Congressional Quarterly Weekly Report*, 10 April 1993, pp.907–9

Healey, J. and Moore, T. (1993), 'Clinton Forms New Coalition To Win NAFTA's Approval', *Congressional Quarterly Weekly Report*, 20 November 1993, pp.3181–5

Hershey, M.J. (1997), 'The Congressional Elections', in G. Pomper ed., *The Elections of 1996: Reports and Interpretations* (New Jersey: Chatham House), pp.205–40

Hook, J. (1997), 'Is Budget Deal Coming Unglued Over Tax Cut', *Los Angeles Times*, 9 May 1997, p.A1

Howell, D. (2000), 'Skills and the Wage Collapse', *The American Prospect*, Vol. 11, No. 15, June19–July 3, pp.74–7

Idelson, H. (1993), 'Withdrawing the Guinier Nomination a No-Win Situation for Clinton', *Congressional Quarterly Weekly Report*, 5 June 1993, pp.1425–7

Idelson, H. (1994a), 'Democrats' Disagreements Delay, Imperil Crime Bill', *Congressional Quarterly Weekly Report*, 23 July 1994, pp.2048–9

Idelson, H. (1994b) 'Clinton, Democrats Scramble to Save Anti-Crime Bill', *Congressional Quarterly Weekly Report*, August 13 1994, pp.2340–3

Idelson, H. and Sammon, R. (1994), 'Marathon Talks Produce New Anti-Crime Bill', *Congressional Quarterly Weekly Report*, 20 August 1994, pp.2449–54

Jacobs, L.R. (1994), 'The Politics of American Ambivalence toward Government', in J.A. Morone and G.S. Belkin eds, *The Politics of Health Care Reform: Lessons From the Past, Prospects for the Future* (Durham and London: Duke University Press)

Jacobson, G. (1993), 'Congress, Unusual Year, Unusual Election', in M. Nelson ed., *The Elections of 1992* (Washington DC: Congressional Quarterly Press), pp.153–82

Johnson, L.B. (1964), *My Hope for America* (New York: Random House)

Johnson, H. and Broder, D. (1997), *The System: The American Way of Politics at Breaking Point* (Boston: Little, Brown and Company)

Jost, K. (2000), 'Gay Rights', in *Issues in Social Policy: Selections from the CQ Researcher* (Washington DC: Congressional Quarterly Press), pp.171–88

Judis, J. (1993), 'The Old Democrat', *The New Republic*, 22 February 1993, pp.18–21

Judis, J. (1995), 'Abandoned Surgery: Business and the Failure of Health Reform', *The American Prospect*, No. 21, Spring, pp.65–73

The Kaiser Commission on Meidicaid and the Uninsured (2000), *Uninsured in America: a chart book* (Washington DC: The Henry J. Kaiser Family Foundation)

Kamarck, E.C. (1992), 'The Welfare Wars', *The New Democrat*, July 1992, pp.12–15

Katz, J.L. (1996), 'After 60 Years, Most Control is Passing to the States', *Congressional Quarterly Weekly Report*, 3 August 1996, pp.2190–6

Katz, M. (1989), *The Undeserving Poor: From War on Poverty to War on Welfare* (New York: Pantheon Books)

Kaus, M. (1995), *The End of Equality* (New York: Basic Books)

Kellam, S. (1994), 'More Jobless Aid Focus of Plan', *Congressional Quarterly Weekly Report*, 12 March 1994, p.611

Kendall, D. (1997), 'Modernizing Medicare and Medicaid: The First Step Toward Universal Health Care', in W. Marshall ed., *Building the Bridge: 10 Big Ideas to Transform America* (Washington DC: Progressive Policy Institute), pp.57–74

Kessler, G. (2000), 'Score One for the Legacy', *The Washington Post*, 20 September 2000, p.E01

Key, V.O. (1955), 'A Theory of Critical Elections', *Journal of Politics*, February 1955, pp.3–18

Kilgore, E. (1997), 'Community Self-Defense: A New Strategy for Preventing Crime and Restoring Public Order', in W. Marshall ed., *Building the Bridge: 10 Big Ideas to Transform America* (Washington DC: Progressive Policy Institute), pp.111–28

King, D. (1991), 'Citizenship as Obligation in the United States: Title II of the Family Support Act of 1988', in U. Vogel and M. Moran eds, *The Frontiers of Citizenship* (London: Macmillan – now Palgrave), pp.1–31

Kingdon, J. (1995) *Agendas, Alternatives and Public Policies*, 2nd edition (New York: Harper Collins)

Kirchnoff, S. (1998), 'Head Start is Growing, But Is It Improving?', *Congressional Quarterly Weekly Report*, 27 June 1998, pp.1743–6

Kirkpatrick, J. (1975), 'Representation in the American national Convention, 1972', *British Journal of Political Science*, Vol. 5, pp.265–325

Klotkin, J. (1993), 'Forhet Moderation', *The New Democrat*, December 1993, pp.25–6

Kondracke, M. (1982), 'Liberalism's Brave Neo World', *Public Opinion*, Vol. 5, No. 2, April/May 1982, pp.2–5

Kosterlitz, J. (1990), 'What's Fair', *National Journal*, 8 December 1990, pp.2956–61

Kosterlitz, J. (1993), 'Winners and Losers', *National Journal*, 11 December 1993, pp.2938–41

Koszczuk, J. (1997a), 'Lawmakers React to Package With Grudging Acceptance' *Congressional Quarterly Weekly Report*, 10 May 1997, pp.1051–2

Koszczuk, J. (1997b), 'Gephardt's Opposition', *Congressional Quarterly Weekly Report*, 24 May 1997, p.1180

Kranish, R. (1994), 'Clinton Unveils Welfare Reform Proposal', *Boston Globe*, 15 June 1994, p.1

Krugman, P. (1994), *The Age of Diminished Expectations: US Economic Policy in the 1990s*, 3rd edition (Washington DC: The Washington Post Company)

Kuttner, R. (1988), *The Life of the Party: Democratic Prospects in 1988 and Beyond* (New York: Penguin Group)

Kuttner, R. (1996), 'Introduction', in R. Kuttner ed., *Ticking Time Bombs* (The New Press) pp.ix–xviii

Kuttner, R. (1999), 'Is Bradley for Real?', *The American Prospect*, Vol. 11, No. 2, 6 December, pp.4–5

Kuttner, R. and Dionne, E.J. (2000), 'Did Clinton Succeed or Fail', *The American Prospect*, Vol. 11, No. 19, 28 August 2000, pp.42–6

Laham, N. (1996), *A Lost Cause: Bill Clinton's Campaign for National Health Insurance* (Westport, Connecticut: Praeger)

Lawrence, C.C. (1993), 'Ban on Homosexuals to End in Two Steps, Frank Says', *Congressional Quarterly Weekly Report*, 23 January 1993, p.187

Leman, C. (1980), *The Collapse of Welfare Reform: Political Institutions, Policy, and the Poor in Canada and the United States* (Cambridge, Massachusetts: M.I.T. Press)

Lengle, J. (1981), *Representation and Presidential Primaries: the Democratic Party in the Post-Reform Era* (Westport, Connecticut: Greenwood Press)

Leuchtenberg, W. (1963), *Franklin D. Roosevelt and the New Deal* (New York: Harper and Row)

Levitan, S., Gallo, G. and Shapiro, I. (1993), *Working But Poor: America's Contradiction* (Baltimore: John Hopkins University Press)

Lin, A.C. (1998), 'The Troubled Success of Crime Policy', in M. Weir ed., *The Social Divide: Political Parties and the Future of Activist Government* (Washington DC: The Brookings Institution), pp.312–60

Livingston, C.D. and Wink, K.A. (1997), 'The Passage of the North American Free Trade Agreement in the U.S. House of Representatives: Presidential Leadership or Presidential Luck?', *Presidential Studies Quarterly*, Vol. 27, No. 1, pp.52–70

Los Angeles Times (1994), 'A Good Place to Begin the Welfare Debate', *Los Angeles Times*, 19 June 1994, p.M4

Maraniss, D. (1996), *First in His Class: The Biography of Bill Clinton*, Touchstone edition (New York: Simon and Schuster)

Marcus, R. and Balz, D. (1994), 'Clinton Outlines Plan to Break Welfare Cycle', *The Washington Post*, 15 June 1994, p.A1 and p.A18

Marshall, W. (1993), 'Under Indictment: Americans Want to Change, But Not Demolish, the Welfare System', *The New Democrat*, December 1993, pp.6–9

Marshall, W. (1994), 'Friend or Faux?', *The American Prospect*, No. 16, Winter 1994, pp.10–15

Marshall, W. (1996), 'Mr. Clinton Keeps His Welfare Promise', *Wall Street Journal*, 1 August 1996

Marshall, W. (2001), 'Revitalizing the Party of Ideas', *Blueprint Magazine*, 23 January 2001, http://www.ndol.org/print.cfm?contentid = 2920

Marshall, W. and Kamarck, E.C. (1993), 'Replacing Welfare with Work', in W. Marshall and M. Schram eds, *Mandate For Change* (New York: Berkley Books), pp.217–36

Marshall, W., From, A., Galston, W. and Ross, D. (1996), *The New Progressive Declaration: A Political Philosophy for the Information Age* (Washington DC: The Progressive Foundation)

Masci, D. (1994a), 'Controversial Racial Justice Proposal ... An Explosive Issue for Lawmakers', *Congressional Quarterly Weekly Report*, 18 June 1994, pp.1626–7

Masci, D. (1994b), '$30 Billion Anti-Crime Bill Heads to Clinton's Desk', *Congressional Quarterly Weekly Report*, 27 August 1994, pp.2488–93

Mathews, J. (1999), 'Off Welfare, new workers seek tax help', *The Baltimore Sun*, 15 April 1999, p.1A

Matusow, A.J. (1984), *The Unraveling of America: a History of Liberalism in the 1960s* (New York: Harper and Row)

Mayer, W.G. (1996), *The Divided Democrats: Ideological Unity, Party Reform, and Presidential Elections* (Boulder, Colorado: Westview Press)

McCutcheon, C. and Nitschke, L. (1999), 'Clinton Will Have to Fight For Democratic Backing in Votes on China, Members Say', *Congressional Quarterly Weekly Report*, 20 November 1999, p.2795

McIntyre (2000), 'The Taxonomist', *The American Prospect*, Vol. 11, No. 19, 28 August 2000, p.11

McGrory, M. (1997), 'Shades of Awful', *The Washington Post*, 11 May 1997, p.C01

McWilliams, W.C. (2000), *Beyond the Politics of Disappointment: American Elections 1980–1998* (New York: Seven Bridges Press)

Mead, L. (1997a), *The New Paternalism* (Washington DC: Brookings Books)

Mead, L. (1997b), 'Citizenship and Social Policy: T.H. Marshall and Poverty', in E.F. Paul, F.D. Miller and J. Paul eds, *The Welfare State* (Cambridge University Press), pp.197–230

Mead, L. (1997c), 'From Welfare to Work: Lessons From America', in A. Deacon ed., *From Welfare to Work: Lessons From America* (London: Institute of Economic Affairs)

Meyerson, H. (2000), 'Gore's Mating Ritual', *The American Prospect*, Vol. 11, No. 17, 31 July, pp.25–28

Mishel, L. and Bernstein, J. (1993), *The State of Working America, 1992–93* (Armonk, New York: M.E. Sharpe)

Mishel, L., Bernstein, J. and Schmitt, J. (1999), *The State of Working America, 1998–99* (New York: Cornell University Press)

Mishel, L. and Schmitt, J. eds (1995), *Beware the U.S. Model: Jobs and Wages in a Deregulated Economy* (Washington DC: Economic Policy Institute)

Morgan, I.W. (1994), *Beyond the Liberal Consensus: a Political History of the United States Since 1965* (London: Hurst and Company)

Morris, D. (1997), *Behind the Oval Office: Winning the Presidency in the Nineties* (New York: Random House)

Morrison, D.C. (1993), 'Gay Groups Were Left in the Dark', *National Journal*, 6 February 1993, pp.343–4

Moynihan, D.P. (1973), *The Politics of a Guaranteed Income: Community Action in the War on Poverty* (New York: Random House)

Mucciaroni, G. (1990), *The Political Failure of Employment Policy, 1945–1982* (Pittsburgh: University of Pittsburgh Press)

Murray, C. (1984), *Losing Ground: American Social Policy, 1950–1980* (New York: Basic Books)

Neal, T. (1997), 'Business Leaders Gear Up Lobbying and Ad Campaign for "Fast-Track" Bill', *The Washington Post*, 19 September 1997, p.A04

Nelson, M. (1993), 'The Presidency: Clinton and the Cycle of Politics and Policy', in M. Nelson ed., *The Elections of 1992* (Washington DC: Congressional Quarterly Press) pp.125–52

The New Democrat (1994), 'Status Quo Plus: Some Would Save Welfare as We Know It', *The New Democrat*, August–September 1994, p.6

The New Republic (1992a), 'Unsupermario', *The New Republic*, 20 January 1992, pp.7–8

The New Republic (1992b), 'Notebook', *The New Republic*, 29 June 1992, p.8

The New York Times (1994), 'Message to Teen-Age Mothers', *The New York Times*, 15 June 1994, p.A24

Nitschke, L. (1999), 'Trade Winds From Seattle Will Soon Sweep Over Capitol Hill', *Congressional Quarterly Weekly Report*, 11 December 1999, pp.2983–4

Nitschke, L. (2000), 'After the China Bill: Fresh Start For the Trade Expansion Debate', *Congressional Quarterly Weekly Report*, 23 September 2000, pp.223–6

Nitschke, L. and Tully, M. (2000), 'Big Victory For China Trade Needs Senate Blessing', *Congressional Quarterly Weekly Report*, 27 May 2000, pp.1244–52

Norris, D. and Thompson, L. eds (1995), *The Politics of Welfare Reform* (Thousand Oaks: Sage Publications)

Novak, V. (1993a), 'Spending Spree', *National Journal*, 27 February 1993, pp. 509–11

Novak, V. (1993b), 'To Tell the Truth ...', *National Journal*, 24 July 1993, p.1893

Novak, V. (1994), 'The Long Brawl', *National Journal*, 8 Jan. 1994, pp. 58–62

Novak, V. and Starobin, P. (1993), 'Spreading the Money', *National Journal*, 14 August, pp.2016–23

Parks, D.J. (2000), 'A Legacy of Budget Surpluses And Thriving Markets', *Congressional Quarterly Weekly*, 5 February 2000, pp.228–33

Parrot, S. (1998), *Welfare Recipients Who Find Jobs: What Do We Know About Their Employment and Earnings?* (Washington DC: Center on Budget and Policy Priorities)

Patel, K. and Rushefsky, M.E. (1998), *Politics, Power and Policy Making: The Case of Health Care Reform in the 1990s* (Armonk, New York: M.E. Sharpe)

Patel, K. and Rushefsky, M.E. (1999), *Health Care Politics and Policy in America*, second edition (Armonk, New York: M.E. Sharpe)

Pear, R. (1999), 'Clinton Chides States for Failing to Cover Children', *New York Times*, 8 August 1999, http://www.nytimes.com/library/politics/080899 clinton-kids-medicaid.html

Penn, M. (1997), 'Seizing the Center: Clinton's Keys to Victory', in W. Marshall ed., *Building the Bridge: 10 Big Ideas to Transform America* (Lanham, Maryland: Rowman and Littlefield/Progressive Policy Institute), pp.9–16

Penn, M. (2001), 'Turning a Win Into a Draw', *Blueprint*, Winter 2001, http://www. ndol.org/blueprint/winter2001_special/penn.1

Peterson, M.A. (1998), 'The Politics of Health Care Policy: Overreaching in an Age of Polarization', in M. Weir ed., *The Social Divide: Political Parties and the Future of Activist Government* (Washington DC; The Brookings Institution), pp.181–229

Peterson, M.A. (2000), 'Clinton and Organized Interests: Splitting Friends, Unifying Enemies', in C. Campbell and B. Rockman eds, *The Clinton Legacy* (New York: Chatham House)

Phillips, K. (1969), *The Emerging Republican Majority* (New York: Doubleday)

Phillips, K. (1990), *The Politics of Rich and Poor: Wealth and the American Electorate in the Reagan Aftermath* (New York: Random House)

Phillips, K. (1994), *Boiling Point: Democrats, Republicans and the Decline of Middle Class Prosperity* (Harper Perennial edition)

Pierce, E. (2000), 'Holding the Center', *Congressional Quarterly Weekly special report*, 12 August 2000, pp.21–4

Pierson, P. (1994), *Dismantling the Welfare State?* (New York: Cambridge University Press)

Pierson, P. (1998), 'The Deficit and the Politics of Domestic Reform', in M. Weir ed., *The Social Divide: Political Parties and the Future of Activist Government* (Washington DC: The Brookings Institution), pp.126–78

Podhoretz, N. (1981), 'The New American Majority', *Commentary*, Vol. 1, No. 1, January 1981, pp.19–28

Polsby, N. (1983), *Consequences of Party Reform* (New York: Oxford University Press)

Primus, W., Rawlings, L., Larin, K. and Porter, K. (1999), *The Initial Impacts of Welfare Reform on the Incomes of Single-Mother Families* (Washington DC: Center on Budget and Policy Priorities)

Quirk, P. and Cunion, W. (2000), 'Clinton's Domestic Policy: The Lessons of a New Democrat', in C. Campbell and B. Rockman eds, *The Clinton Legacy* (New York: Chatham House), pp.200–25

Quirk, P. and Dalager, J. (1993), 'The Election: A "New Democrat" and a New Kind of Presidential Campaign', in M. Nelson ed., *The Elections of 1992* (Washington DC: Congressional Quarterly Press), pp.57–88

Radosh, R. (1996), *Divided They Fell: The Demise of the Democratic Party, 1964–1996* (New York: The Free Press)

Rae, N. (2000), 'Clinton and the Democrats', in S. Schier, ed. *The Postmodern Presidency: Bill Clinton's Legacy in US Politics* (University of Pittsburgh Press), pp.167–82

Rauch, J. (1989), 'Paycheck Politics', *National Journal*, 8 July 1989, pp.1746–9

Ravitch, D. (1998), 'Is Head Start Smart?', *The New Democrat*, July–August 1998, pp.8–9

Ravitch, D. (1999), 'The National Agenda in Elementary and Secondary Education', in H.J. Aaron and R. Reischauer, eds, *Setting National Priorities: the 2000 Election and Beyond* (Washington DC: Brookings Institution Press), pp.269–302

Rector, R. (1992), 'Requiem for the War on Poverty: Rethinking Welfare After the Los Angeles Riots', *Policy Review*, Summer 1992, pp.40–46

Rector, R. (1996), 'God and the Underclass', *National Review*, 15 July, pp.30–33

Rector, R. and Youseff, S. (1999), *Welfare Reform and Caseload Decline* (Washington DC: Heritage Foundation)

Reich, R.B. (1998), *Locked in the Cabinet* (New York: Vintage Books edition)

Reich, R.B. (1999), 'We Are All Third Wayers Now', *The American Prospect*, No. 43, March–April, pp.46–51

Reischaur, R. (1999), 'The Dawning of a New Era', in H.J. Aaron and R. Reischaur eds, *Setting National Priorities: the 2000 Election and Beyond* (Washington DC: Brookings Institution Press) pp.1–34

Renshon, S. (1995), 'The Psychological Context of the Clinton Presidency: A Framework for Analysis', in S. Renshon ed., *Campaigning, Governing and the Psychology of Leadership* (Boulder, Colorado: Westview Press), pp.1–8

Riley, R.W. and Reich, R.B. (1996), '*Implementation of the School-To-Work Opportunities Act of 1994: Report to Congress*' (Washington DC: U.S. Department of Education and U.S. Department of Labor)

Rosner, J.D. (1993), 'A Progressive Plan for Affordable, Universal Health Care', in W. Marshall and M. Schram eds, *Mandate For Change* (New York: Berkley Books), pp.107–28

Rothenberg, R. (1984), *The Neo-Liberals: Creating the New American Politics* (New York: Simon and Schuster)

Rothstein, R. (1998), 'Charter Conundrum', *The American Prospect*, No. 39, July–August 1998, pp.46–60

Rubin, A. (1994), 'A Salvage Operation', *Congressional Quarterly Weekly Report*, special supplement, 10 September 1994, pp.11–16

Rubin, A. (1995a), President's Tax Cuts Draw Fire, Reopen Rifts Within GOP', *Congressional Quarterly Weekly Report*, 11 February 1995, pp.409–10

Rubin, A. (1995b), 'GOP Walking into a "Hornet's Nest" As It Takes Aim at Health Programs', *Congressional Quarterly Weekly Report*, 22 April 1995, pp.1112–13

Rubin, A. (1996), 'Congress Clears wage Increase with Tax Breaks for Business', *Congressional Quarterly Weekly Report*, 3 August 1996, pp.2175–7

Sawhill, I. (1995), 'Distinguished Lecture on Economics in Government; The Economist vs. Madmen in Authority', *Journal of Economic Perspectives*, Vol. 9, No. 3, summer, pp.3–13

Scammon, R. and Wattenberg, B. (1970), *The Real Majority* (New York: Coward McCann)

Schneider, W. (1988), 'An Insider's View of the Election', *The Atlantic Monthly*, July 1988, pp.29–57

Schneider, W. (1993a), 'A Fatal Flaw in Clinton's Health Plan', *National Journal*, 6 November 1993, p.2696

Schneider, W. (1993b), 'How Gays in Service Became a Hot Issue', *National Journal*, 6 February 1993, p.374

Schneider, W. (1993c), 'Scars of '68 Still Aren't All Healed', *National Journal*, 4 September 1993, p.2168

Schwarz, J. (1997), *Illusions of Opportunity: The American Dream in Question* (New York: W.W. Norton and Company)

Shafer, B. (1983), *The Quiet Revolution: The Struggle for the Democratic Party and the Shaping of Post-Reform Politics* (New York: Russell Sage Foundation)

Shafer, B. (1997), '"We Are All Southern Democrats Now"', in B. Shafer ed., *Present Discontents: American Politics in the Very Late Twentieth Century* (New Jersey: Chatham House), pp.147–76

Shafer, B. (2000), 'The Partisan Legacy: Are there any New Democrats? (And by the way, was there a Republican Revolution?)', in C. Campbell and B. Rockman eds, *The Clinton Legacy* (New York: Chatham House), pp.1–32

Shafer, B. and Claggett, W. (1995), *The Two Majorities: the Issue Context of Modern American Politics* (Baltimore: the John Hopkins University Press)

Shapiro, R. (1992), 'The End of Entitlement', *The New Democrat*, July 1992, pp.16–19

Shapiro, R. (1993), 'The First Test', *The New Democrat*, May 1993, pp.8–11

Shapiro, R. (1997), 'A New Deal on Social Security', in W. Marshall ed., *Building the Bridge: 10 Big Ideas to Transform America* (Lanham, Maryland: Rowman and Littlefield/Progressive Policy Institute), pp.39–57

Shear, J. (1995), 'Hey, What's Happened to the Budget?', *National Journal*, 11 February 1995, pp.357–9

Sherman, A., Amey, C., Duffield, B., Ebb. N. and Weinstein, D. (1998), *Welfare to What: Early Findings on family Hardship and Well-Being* (Washington DC: Children's Defense Fund/National Coalition for the Homeless)

Shklar, J. (1991), *American Citizenship: the Quest for Inclusion* (Cambridge, Massachussetts: Harvard University Press)

Siegel, F. and Marshall, W. (1995), 'Liberalism's Lost Tradition', *The New Democrat*, September–October 1995, pp.8–13

Sinclair, B. (2000), 'The President as Legislative Leader', in C. Campbell and B. Rockman eds, *The Clinton Legacy* (New York: Chatham House), pp.70–95

Skocpol, T. (1995a), 'The Rise and Resounding Demise of the Clinton Plan', *Health Affairs*, Vol. 15, Spring, pp.66–85

Skocpol, T. (1995b), *Social Policy in the United States: Future Possibilities in Historical Perspective* (Princeton: Princeton University Press)

Skocpol, T. (1997), *Boomerang: Health Care Reform and the Turn Against Government* (New York: W.W. Norton and Company)

Skocpol, T. and Greenberg, S. (1997), 'A Politics for Our Time', in S. Greenberg and T. Skocpol eds, *The New Majority: Toward a Popular Progressive Politics* (Yale University Press)

Skowronek, S. (1997), *The Politics Presidents Make: Leadership From John Adams to Bill Clinton*, second edition (Cambridge, Massachusetts: Harvard University Press)

Solomon, B. (1995), 'Clinton as a Profile in Courage? Sorry, Not on Welfare Reform', *National Journal*, 30 September 1995, pp.2434–5

Stacey, J. (1998), 'The Right Family Values', in C.Y.H. Lo and M. Schwartz eds, *Social Policy and the Conservative Agenda* (Oxford: Blackwell Publishers), pp.267–89

Stanfield, R. (1994), 'A New Course for Schools?', *National Journal*, 4 June 1994, pp.1303–4

Starobin, P. (1992), 'Time to Get Real', *National Journal*, 19 December 1992, pp.2878–82

Starobin, P. (1993), 'A Clinton–Greenspan Duet?', *National Journal*, 30 January 1993, p.310

Starr, P. (1994), *The Logic of Health Care Reform: Why and How the President's Plan Will Work*, revised edition (New York: Penguin Books)

Starr, P. (1995), 'What Happened to Health Care Reform?', *The American Prospect*, No. 20, Winter, pp.20–31

Steinfels, P. (1979), *The Neoconservatives* (New York: Simon and Schuster)

Stephanopoulos, G. (1999), *All Too Human: A Political Education* (Boston: Little, Brown and Company)

Stoesz, D. (1996), *Small Change: Domestic Policy Under the Clinton Presidency* (New York: Longman Publishers)

Stokes, B. (1993), 'A Hard Sell', *National Journal*, 16 October, pp.2472–6

Suskind, R. (1994), 'Clinton Unveils Welfare-Reform Plan That is Limited By Budget Austerity', *Wall Street Journal*, 15 June 1994, pp.A2 and A8

Tatalovich, R. and Frendreis, J. (2000), 'Clinton, Class and Economic Policy', in S. Schier ed., *The Postmodern Presidency: Bill Clinton's Legacy in US Politics* (University of Pittsburgh Press), pp.41–59

Taylor, A. (1997), 'Internal Divisions, White House Frustrate GOP's Tax Agenda', *Congressional Quarterly Weekly Report*,19 July 1997, pp.1681–5

Teixeira, R. (1995), 'Intellectual Challenges Facing the Democratic Party', in J.K. White and J.C. Gren eds, *The Politics of Ideas: Intellectual Challenges to the Party after 1992* (Maryland: Rowman and Littlefield)

Teixeira, R. (2000), 'Beyond the Third Way', *The American Prospect*, Vol. 11, No. 19, 28 August, pp.56–8

Teixeira, R. and Rogers, J. (2000), *America's Forgotten Majority: Why the White Working Class Still Matters* (New York: Basic Books)

Teles, S. (1996), *Whose Welfare: AFDC and Elite Politics* (Lawrence: University of Kansas Press)

Thompson, G. (1994), 'From Long Boom to Recession and Stagnation? The Post War American Economy', in G. Thompson ed., *The United States in the Twentieth Century: Markets* (London; Hodder and Stoughton in association with The Open University Press), pp.99–134

Toner, R. (1988), 'Dukakis Asserts that He is a Liberal, But in the Old Tradition of His Party, *New York Times*, 31 October 1988, p.A1

U.S. (1994), Committee on Ways and Means, US House of Representatives, *1994 Green Book: Background Material and Data on Programs within the Jurisdiction of the Committee on Ways and Means* (Washington DC: US Government Printing Office)

U.S. (1996a), Committee on Ways and Means, US House of Representatives, *1996 Green Book: Background Material and Data on Programs within the Jurisdiction of the Committee on Ways and Means* (Washington DC: US Government Printing Office)

U.S. (1996b), *Statistical Abstract of the United States: 1996*, 116th edition (Washington DC: Bureau of the Census)

U.S. (1996c), *Current Population Reports: Health Insurance Coverage: 1995* (Washington DC: Bureau of the Census), pp.60–195

U.S. (1998a), *Statistical Abstract of the United States: 1998*, 118th edition (Washington DC: Bureau of the Census)

U.S. (1998b) Committee on Ways and Means, US House of Representatives, *1998 Green Book: Background Material and Data on Programs within the Jurisdiction of the Committee on Ways and Means* (Washington DC: US Government Printing Office)

U.S. Department of Education (1998), *Goals 2000: Reforming Education to Improve Student Achievement* (Washington DC: U.S. Department of Education)

U.S. Department of Education (2000), Brief on Educational Progress, 1992–2000, http://www.whitehouse.gov/media/pdf/edprogress.pdf

Verhovek, S.H. (2000), 'Frustration Grows With Cost of Health Insurance', *New York Times*, 18 September 2000, http://www.nytimes.com/2000/09/18/national/18INSU.html

Victor, K. (1994), 'Friend or Enemy', *National Journal*, 5 November 1994, pp.2575–8

Victor, K., Cohen, R.E. and Baumann, D. (2000), 'Liebermann: Pros and Cons', *National Journal*, 12 August 2000, pp.2590–3

Waddan, A. (1997), *The Politics of Social Welfare: the Collapse of the Centre and the Rise of the Right* (Cheltenham: Edward Elgar)

Waddan, A. (1998), 'A Liberal in Wolf's Clothing: Nixon's Family Assistance Plan in the Light of 1990s Welfare Reform', *Journal of American Studies*, Vol. 32, No. 2. pp.203–218

Walker, M. (1997), *Clinton: the President They Deserve* (London: Vintage)

The Washington Post (1994), 'A Solid Start on Welfare Reform', *The Washington Post*, 16 June 1994, p.A24

Wattenberg, M. (1991), 'The Republican Presidential Advantage in the Age of Party Disunity', in G. Cox and S. Kernell eds, *The Politics of Divided Government* (Boulder, Colorado: Westview), pp.39–55

Weatherford, M.S. and McDonnell, L.M. (1996), 'Clinton and the Economy: The Paradox of Policy Success and Policy Mishap', *Political Science Quarterly*, Vol. 111, No. 3, pp.403–36

Weaver, R.K. (1996), 'Deficits and Devolution in the 104th Congress', *Publius: The Journal of Federalism*, Vol. 26, No. 3, Summer, pp.45–86

Weaver, R.K. (1998), 'Ending Welfare As We Know It', in M. Weir ed., *The Social Divide: Political Parties and the Future of Activist Government* (Washington DC: The Brookings Institution), pp.361–416

Weaver, R.K. (2000), *Ending Welfare As We Know It* (Washington DC: Brookings Institution Press)

Weaver, R.K., Shapiro, R.Y. and Jacobs, L.R. (1995), 'The Polls-Trends: Welfare', *Public Opinion Quarterly*, No. 59, pp.606–627

Weir, M. (1998), 'Wages and Jobs: What is the Public Role', in M. Weir ed., *The Social Divide: Political Parties and the Future of Activist Government* (Washington DC: Brookings Institution Press), pp.268–311

Wells, R.M. (1994), 'Ways and Means Subcommittee OKs Job Training Bill', *Congressional Quarterly Weekly Report*, 23 July 1994, p.2058

Wells, R.M. and Langdon, S. (1995), 'Dole, Canady Propose Rollback of Affirmative Action' in *Congressional Quarterly Weekly Report*, 29 July 1995, p.2279

White, J.K. (1998), *The New Politics of Old Values*, 3rd edition (Lanham, Maryland: University Press of America)

Williams, L.F. (1998), 'Race and the Politics of Social Policy' in M. Weir ed., *The Social Divide: Political Parties and the Future of Activist Government* (Washington DC: The Brookings Institution), pp.417–63

Wiseman, M. (1991), 'Research and Policy: An Afterword for the Symposium on the Family Support Act of 1988', *Journal of Policy Analysis and Management*, Vol. 10, No. 4, pp.657–66

Wolfe, B.L. (1994), 'Reform of Health Care for the Nonelderly Poor', in S.H. Danziger, G. Sandefur and D.H. Weinberg eds, *Confronting Poverty: Prescriptions for Change* (Cambridge, Massachusetts: Harvard University Press)

Woodward, B. (1994), *The Agenda: Inside the Clinton White House* (New York: Simon and Schuster)

Woodward, B. (1996), *The Choice: How Clinton Won* (New York: Simon and Schuster)

Wright, S. (2000), 'Clinton and Racial Politics' in S. Schier ed., *The Postmodern Presidency: Bill Clinton's Legacy in US Politics* (University of Pittsburgh Press), pp.223–37

Yankelovich, D. (1994), 'The Debate That Wasn't: The Public and the Clinton Plan', *Health Affairs*, Vol. 15, Spring, pp.7–23

Zelman, W.A. (1994), 'The Rationale Behind the Clinton Health Reform Plan', *Health Affairs*, Vol. 14, Spring, pp.9–29

Zuckman, J. (1993a), 'Senate Clears National Service Despite GOP's Objections', *Congressional Quarterly Weekly Report*, 11 September 1993, p.2397

Zuckman, J. (1993b), 'As Family Leave is Enacted Some See End to Logjam', *Congressional Quarterly Weekly Report*, 6 February 1993, pp.267–9

Index

abortion, 19, 149
  Clinton's views on, 134
  lifting restrictions on, 135
affirmative action, 144, 148
  angry white males, 129
  Clinton's review of, 146–7
  and Republican presidential
    politics, 146, 147
anti-crime bill of 1994, 14, 99, 150,
  160
  Democratic divisions over, 141–2,
    143
  gun control, 141, 142, 143
  New Democrat response to, 143
  Racial Justice Act, 142, 145
  Republican opposition to, 142, 143
  vote on, 142–3
Aid to Families with Dependent
    Children, 18, 19, 22, 113, 158
  benefit value, 113
  cost of program, 113
  length of stay on benefit, 117
  number of recipients, 113, 115,
    117, 170

Baird, Zoe, 138
Barshefsky, Charlene, 65
Begala, Paul, 72
Bentsen, Lloyd, 47, 81, 168
Blair, Tony, 4, 5, 160
Bonior, David, 63, 64, 67, 126
Boren, David, 49, 50, 138
  attack on stimulus package, 72–3
Bowles, Erskine, 163
Bradley, Bill, 39, 54, 108
  campaign 2000, 108, 163–4
Brady Bill, 159
  see also gun control
Breaux, John, 49, 91, 138, 139
Brooks, Jack, 142
Brown, Jerry, 39
Buchanan, Pat, 64, 136
budget

budget of 1993, 47–53, 83, 160
budget battle of 1995, 53–7, 161
balanced budget agreement of
  1997, 58–9, 86, 161
deficit in 1993, 15, 45, 154
deficit reduction, 16, 42, 44, 48, 52,
  69, 70, 154
spending cuts, 16, 48, 52, 57, see
  also specific issue
surplus in 2000, 1, 16, 86
see also Clintonomics; economy;
  taxation
Bush, George H., 2, 6, 8, 10, 37, 69,
  128, 147, 154, 155
  1988 campaign, 30–1, 33, 46, 140,
    159
  1992 campaign, 42, 119, 132, 136,
    137
  and health care reform plan, 96, 97
  and North American Free Trade
    Agreement, 46, 62
Bush, George W., 80, 159

Carter, Jimmy, 2, 10, 16, 24, 38
  'malaise speech', 32
Carville, James, 72
charter schools, 77, see also education
China, see free trade
Clinton, Hillary, 91, 96, 100, 170
Clinton, William J.,
  on abortion, 134
  on accomplishments as President,
    153
  address to Congress on health care,
    88, 100
  appeal to middle-class, 7, 20, 42,
    45, 59
  chair of Democratic Leadership
    Council, 4, 37, 166
  on Children's Health Insurance
    Program, 107
  and death penalty, 132–3
  defence of Medicaid, 53, 104–6, 158